COMMUNITY LIBRARY

3 2301 00194770 8

MOUNTAIN

TRAVEL & RESCUE

D1476313

MOUNTAIN

TRAVEL & RESCUE

NATIONAL SKI PATROL'S MANUAL FOR MOUNTAIN RESCUE

2ND EDITION

THE MOUNTAINEERS BOOKS

THE MOUNTAINEERS BOOKS
is the nonprofit publishing arm of The Mountaineers,
an organization founded in 1906 and dedicated to the exploration,
preservation, and enjoyment of outdoor and wilderness areas.

1001 SW Klickitat Way, Suite 201, Seattle, WA 98134

© 2012 by National Ski Patrol System, Inc.
All rights reserved

First edition 1995. Second edition 2012.

No part of this book may be reproduced in any form, or by any electronic, mechanical, or other means, without permission in writing from the publisher.

Distributed in the United Kingdom by Cordee, www.cordee.co.uk

Manufactured in the United States of America

National Mountain Travel and Rescue Program Director: Rick King
Mountain Travel and Rescue Manual Coordinator: Chuck White
National Ski Patrol Education Director: Darcy Hanley
National Ski Patrol Communications Director: Candace Horgan
Mountain Travel and Rescue Developmental Editor: Carrie Click
Copy Editor: Colin Chisholm
Cover, Book Design, and Layout: Emily Ford
Illustrator: Jennifer Shontz, www.redshoedesign.com
Cover photograph: Anton Art/Alamy

Library of Congress Cataloging-in-Publication Data
National Ski Patrol System (U.S.)
 Mountain travel and rescue : a manual for basic and advanced
mountaineering courses / National Ski Patrol System, Inc. — 2nd ed.
 p. cm.
 Includes bibliographical references and index.
 ISBN 978-1-59485-708-9 (ppb)
 1. Ski patrollers—United States. 2. Skiing accidents—United States. 3.
Skiing injuries—United States. I. Title.
 GV854.N34 2012
 617.1'0276522—dc23
 2012025375

ISBN (paperback): 978-1-59485-708-9
ISBN (e-book): 978-1-59485-709-6

Certified Chain of Custody
SUSTAINABLE Promoting Sustainable Forestry
FORESTRY
INITIATIVE www.sfiprogram.org
SFI-01268

SFI label applies to the text stock

National Ski Patrol System, Inc.
133 South Van Gordon Street, Suite 100
Lakewood, Colorado 80228
303-988-1111
www.nsp.org

National Ski Patrol System, Inc. is a federally chartered educational association serving the ski and outdoor recreation community by providing exceptional education programs.

ACKNOWLEDGMENTS

NATIONAL SKI PATROL CONTRIBUTORS

CENTRAL DIVISION
Chuck White, Mount Holly Ski Patrol, Holly, Michigan

EASTERN DIVISION
Karl Auerbach, Bristol Mountain Ski Patrol, Canandaigua, New York
Mark Connolly, Genesee Valley Nordic Ski Patrol, Rochester, New York
Matt Fulton, Dartmouth Skiway Ski Patrol, Lyme Center, New Hampshire
Matt Speier, Belleayre Ski Patrol, Highmount, New York

FAR WEST DIVISION
Keith Gale, Pinecrest Nordic Ski Patrol, Pinecrest, California

INTERMOUNTAIN DIVISION
Colin Grissom, M.D., Park City Ski Patrol, Park City, Utah
David Sutherland, M.S., EMT-1, Park City Ski Patrol, Park City, Utah

NORTHERN DIVISION
Rusty Wells, Flathead Nordic Ski Patrol, Whitefish, Montana

PACIFIC NORTHWEST DIVISION
Bob Hollingsworth, Mount Baker Ski Patrol, Glacier, Washington
Jeff Leenstra, Mount Baker Ski Patrol, Glacier, Washington
Frank Rossi, Summit East Ski Patrol, Newcastle, Washington

ROCKY MOUNTAIN DIVISION
Myron Allen, Medicine Bow Nordic Ski Patrol, Laramie, Wyoming
Dale Atkins, Loveland Ski Patrol, Clear Creek County, Colorado
Doug Ginley, Loveland Ski Patrol, Clear Creek County, Colorado
Candace Horgan, Arapahoe Basin, Summit County, Colorado

OTHER CONTRIBUTORS

Justin McCarthy, Garmin International, St. Louis, Missouri
Charley Shimanski, American Red Cross, Washington, DC; Mountain Rescue Association, Evergreen, Colorado
Deborah Shulman, Ph.D., BodyScience, Fort Collins, Colorado
J. Michael Wallace, M.D., Division of Emergency Medicine, University of Utah, Salt Lake City, Utah

PHOTOGRAPHERS
Candace Horgan (pages 12 and 78)
Geoffrey Ferguson (page 128)
Jason Saslow (page 180)

THANK YOU
Thank you to National Ski Patrol's Rocky Mountain Division members Ron Splittgerber, Rob Anderson, Aaron Anderson, Hans Roder, Bob Skaggs, Bart Daly, John Kalk, Debbie Miles, Bob Wissing, Jill Yarger, Michael Dento, Jerry Hammon, Ken Cramer, Ranie Lynds, Bill Cotton, Ed Gassman and Ann Gassman; International Mountain Guides Director and Crystal Mountain Ski Patrol Director Paul Baugher; and Mount Baker Ski Area Operations Manager Gwyn Howat for their assistance with this book.

The last edition of the National Ski Patrol's *Mountain Travel & Rescue* manual was published in 1995. Much has changed since then; equipment has improved, procedures have changed, organizations have grown, and world events have caused changes to our daily lives.

In 1995 the use of global positioning systems (GPS) from a civilian standpoint was still in its infancy, and handheld units were heavy, large, and accurate to only about 100 meters. The Incident Command System (ICS) had been around since the 1970s, beginning with wildfire suppression efforts in California. However, the terrorist attacks of September 11, 2001, shook up procedural changes, with the newly created US Department of Homeland Security mandating that all federal, state, and local agencies use ICS methodology of the National Incident Management System (NIMS).

With all these changes taking place post 9/11, ski patrollers needed new sources of information and training to stay current with industry and rescue standards. Ski patrollers could turn to many good publications focused on training tools and mountain rescue and survival skills, but most were designed for general outdoor enthusiasts or climbers. The new *Mountain Travel & Rescue* manual is designed to help ski patrollers train, rescue, and survive in mountain and outdoor environments, at resorts, in the backcountry, and at any time of season.

When building the outline of chapters for this manual, we looked to not only what the NSP's Mountain Travel and Rescue Program currently includes, but what other organizations have for similar training, written documentation, and guidance. We looked to the Mountain Rescue Association (MRA) and National Association for Search and Rescue (NASAR) for additional and updated rescue techniques. To be responsible stewards of the backcountry, we included material from Leave No Trace. We reached out to some of the industry-leading equipment manufacturers such as Petzl and Garmin to help with rope rescue and GPS technology. For our extended backcountry first aid, Wilderness Medical Society took good care of us. Overall our intent is to provide a manual not one sided or limited in scope but collaborative in techniques, training, and procedures. This manual is not a step-by-step guideline, but an educational tool for individuals and training programs alike.

HOW TO READ AND USE THIS MANUAL

The *Mountain Travel & Rescue* manual is organized into five major sections.

Survival. Reviews and reinforces the concepts rescuers need to know when entering an extended period of exposure to conditions in the backcountry.

Travel. Provides information on travel equipment from skis to climbing gear, forms of navigation, and precautionary measures to ensure the safety of the rescuer.

Backcountry Considerations. This group of four chapters is focused on conditions that require staying in the outdoor environment, working with teams in stressful conditions, and caring for a rescued individual or group.

Search and Rescue. Explores two main categories: location of an individual or group using basic search and rescue techniques, with an introduction to the organization of a major rescue effort using the Incident Command System; and the mechanics of rescue techniques for various types of terrain, from setting anchors to rigging rope rescue systems.

Appendix. Provides useful references and resources to help rescuers expand their knowledge and skills on the main topics of the manual.

This publication is intended to educate and to promote travel, safety, and rescue in the outdoor environment. It is in no way intended to cover all details or be the authoritative text of such topics, but rather is a tool to be used in conjunction with training programs. There is no substitute for hands-on training with qualified instructors in a controlled environment.

Lastly, the Mountain Travel and Rescue Program Committee would like to thank all the dedicated contributors who spent hundreds of hours writing, researching, and collaborating on this manual. Without your dedication, this publication would never have been completed.

Rick King
National Mountain Travel and
Rescue Program Director
National Ski Patrol

A NOTE ABOUT SAFETY

Safety is an important concern in all outdoor activities. No book can alert you to every hazard or anticipate the limitations of every reader. The descriptions of techniques and procedures in this book are intended to provide general information. This is not a complete text on mountain travel and rescue techniques. Nothing substitutes for formal instruction, routine practice, and plenty of experience. When you follow any of the procedures described here, you assume responsibility for your own safety. Use this book as a general guide to further information.

—*The Mountaineers Books*

PART ONE

SURVIVAL

CHAPTER 1

BODY TEMPERATURE REGULATION

Doug Ginley, Loveland Ski Patrol, Clear Creek County, Colorado

....

OBJECTIVES:

o List, describe, and give examples of how the body generates heat.

o List, describe, and give examples of how the body loses heat.

o Explain the consequences of heat imbalances.

o Learn methods to control the body's energy balance.

....

It was a cloudless spring day, and the sun shone brightly in a clear blue sky. As we trudged up the trail high above timberline with our skis slung over our shoulders, the snow reflected the heat back to us, making it feel like we were in an oven. Still, the snow off the top promised to give us a great ski run, if a slushy one.

As we crested the ridge, we noticed that Jim was not with us. Usually one of the stronger climbers in the group, he was lagging behind. A few minutes later he made it to the top. He complained of feeling nauseous and having an extreme headache. He looked pale, said he felt dizzy, and wanted nothing more than to sit down in the snow and not move. In short, he was exhibiting the classic signs of heat exhaustion.

What made Jim fall into this state? How do our bodies adjust to changes in climate? What might have been done to prevent Jim's problem?

Understanding how our bodies work and how we can prevent environmental injuries caused by either heat or cold is important to our enjoyment of and our ability to work in the harsh conditions that we experience as members of the National Ski Patrol. Our bodies can function only in a narrow range of temperatures—either too hot or too cold, and our bodies shut down. Severe difficulty or even death may occur. Cold injuries include hypothermia and frostbite; heat

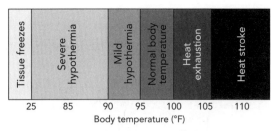

Source: *National Ski Patrol:* "Outdoor Emergency Care," Fifth Edition, 2011

Figure 1-1. *Environmental injury temperatures*

injuries are heat exhaustion and heat stroke (Figure 1-1).

HEAT GAIN

There are three ways the body can gain or produce heat: by the body's metabolism, through muscular activity, or through external heat sources.

METABOLISM

The human body, at quiet rest, requires energy to perform basic body functions. This basic energy level is referred to as the basal metabolic rate, or the heat produced by constant internal metabolic processes (50–60 kcal per square meter of body surface per hour in an average person). The rate varies by the person's sex, size, age, physical makeup, and other physical traits and attributes. Any physical activity will alter the metabolic rate and require additional fuel to match the energy output of the metabolism. A typical adult, at rest, will generate energy at a rate approximately equivalent to lighting a 75-watt bulb.

MUSCULAR ACTIVITY

The human body is capable of converting chemical energy to mechanical energy. Chemical energy is gained by the body's intake of food and liquids. Water is a key component in creating this chemical energy. Water is the principal vehicle for transporting substances within the body, and acts as the medium by which many of the body's chemical reactions occur.

It must be noted, however, that the human body is inefficient at the conversion of chemical energy into mechanical energy. Only about 25 percent of the possible energy available from the intake of food and fluids is actually changed into mechanical energy. The remaining 75 percent is converted into thermal (heat) energy.

Mechanical energy is used to produce motion and perform useful work. Muscular activity is one way of creating heat energy. The harder we use our muscles, the more heat is produced. Involuntary muscular activity, such as shivering, is the body's way of generating heat when its temperature starts to fall. Extended muscular activity requires large amounts of fuel in the form of food and fluids. Even with additional fuel, the muscles will eventually start to fatigue, and rest is necessary. Muscular activity is a very effective means of creating heat within

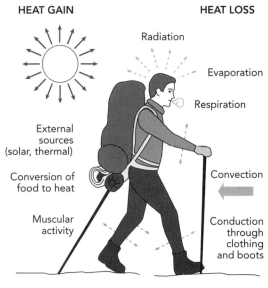

Figure 1-2. *Activity affecting body efficiency*

HEAT GAIN   HEAT LOSS

Radiation

Evaporation

Respiration

External sources (solar, thermal)

Convection

Conversion of food to heat

Muscular activity

Conduction through clothing and boots

the body, but is inefficient in that the body must convert chemical energy into mechanical energy to generate this heat (Figure 1-2).

EXTERNAL HEAT SOURCES

There are essentially two external sources of heat that the human body can use: solar and thermal heat. Solar heat is the warming effect of the sun. The heat from the sun is lessened during the winter due to shortened days, the angle of the sun, cloud cover, and other weather patterns. In snowy conditions, the sun is reflected off the snow, slightly increasing the warming nature of the sun. During outdoor activities, thermal heat is obtained from fires, chemical heat packs, and stoves. Ingesting liquids that are warm can also help maintain or increase the body's temperature. Fires can be a good external heat source, with beneficial psychological effects as well.

HEAT LOSS

The body loses heat in five specific ways:

» Conduction
» Convection
» Evaporation
» Radiation
» Physiological losses

A resting body in still air at 70 degrees F will lose 76 percent of its heat by radiation, conduction, and convection. Twenty-one percent will be lost by evaporation, and only 3 percent through physiological respiration and the elimination of bodily wastes (Figure 1-3).

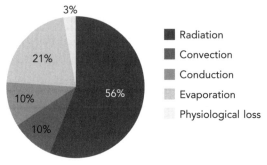

3%

21%

10%

10%

56%

- Radiation
- Convection
- Conduction
- Evaporation
- Physiological loss

Source: *Regulation of Heat Loss from the Human Body*, by James D. Hardy and Eugene F. DuBois © 1937 National Academy of Sciences

Figure 1-3. *Percent heat loss for the human body at rest*

Wind Speed (MPH)	What the thermometer reads (degrees °F)											
	50	40	30	20	10	0	-10	-20	-30	-40	-50	-60
	What it equals in its effect on exposed flesh											
Calm	50	40	30	20	10	0	-10	-20	-30	-40	-50	-60
5	48	37	27	16	6	-5	-15	-26	-36	-47	-57	-68
10	40	28	16	4	-9	-21	-33	-46	-58	-70	-83	-95
15	36	22	9	-5	-18	-36	-45	-58	-72	-85	-99	-112
20	32	18	4	-10	-25	-39	-53	-67	-82	-96	-110	-121
25	30	16	0	-15	-29	-44	-59	-74	-88	-104	-118	-133
30	28	13	-2	-18	-33	-48	-63	-79	-94	-109	-125	-140
35	27	11	-4	-20	-35	-49	-67	-82	-98	-113	-129	-145
40	26	10	-6	-21	-37	-53	-69	-85	-100	-116	-132	-148

Little danger if properly clothed	Danger of freezing exposed flesh	Great danger of freezing exposed flesh

Source: US Army

Table 1-1. *Windchill*

Physical activity will drastically change the way the body loses heat. Wind and cold temperatures will also contribute to heat loss, creating a potentially dangerous situation for the individual.

CONDUCTION

Conduction is the transfer of heat by direct contact of one object to another, when the two objects have different temperatures. In conduction the temperatures of the two objects will always try to seek equilibrium. The rate at which the heat is lost from the warmer object depends on how well the material the object is made of conducts heat and on the temperature differential.

Materials that transfer heat readily, that is, have high thermal conductivity, are known as conductors. Metals are the best conductors. Liquids are also potentially good conductors. Liquid water conducts heat many times faster than dry air.

Materials that do not transfer heat well, those having low thermal conductivity, are known as insulators. Still, dry air is a very good insulator. Insulation is made of materials that conduct heat poorly and trap large amounts of air. Keeping insulation dry is important for it to function at its fullest capacity.

CONVECTION

Convection is the transfer of heat when a different temperature liquid or gas is passed over another material. The rate of heat loss or gain is dependent on the temperature of the liquid or gas and the speed at which it passes over the other material.

TABLE 1-2. SIGNS AND SYMPTOMS OF COMMON HEAT AND COLD INJURIES

Environmental Injury	Signs and Symptoms
HEAT EXHAUSTION	Sweating heavily. Cold, clammy skin with ashen pallor. Dizziness, weakness, or faintness with accompanying nausea or headache. Normal vital signs, although the pulse is often rapid. Slightly elevated body temperature.
HEAT STROKE	Sweating ceases as body temperature rises. Skin is hot, dry, and flushed. Changed behavior (irrational or uncooperative). Patient quickly becomes unresponsive. Pulse is rapid and strong but becomes weak as body temperature rises.
MILD HYPOTHERMIA	Shivering increases and becomes violent. Patient stumbles and exhibits loss of coordination, weakness, difficulty speaking, slow thinking, and mild confusion.
SEVERE HYPOTHERMIA	Shivering stops and patient becomes stiff. Patient is incoherent and is unable to walk. Exposed skin is blue or puffy. Impaired responsiveness. Breathing and pulse slow down.
FROSTBITE	Painfully cold body part suddenly stops hurting when it is not getting warmer. The skin is not pliable. Affected part is cold, solid, and numb and has a pale waxy color.

Source: Data compiled from National Ski Patrol: "Outdoor Emergency Care," Fourth Edition, Ch. 15.

For instance, the rate at which flesh cools depends upon the temperature of the air passing over it and the speed at which the air is moving. This change in actual temperature is called windchill (Table 1-1).

EVAPORATION

Evaporation is the loss of heat when liquids are converted to vapors. It takes a great deal of energy to convert liquid water to vapor (one pound of water requires approximately 240 kcal to be converted to vapor). The human body will naturally try to dry itself by evaporating excess moisture that has collected on the skin. Preventing evaporation by keeping the body dry is very important. This means keeping the body dry from external sources such as rain and snow, and also preventing excessive perspiration.

RADIATION

Radiation is the loss of heat when infrared waves emanate from the body outward. Exposed skin surface removes body heat by emitting these waves. This process can continue past the point where the body is in balance, creating a heat loss condition that must be addressed.

PHYSIOLOGICAL LOSSES

Physiological heat losses occur through respiration and the elimination of bodily wastes. Cold air brought into the lungs is heated by the body before being expelled.

The cold air is heated by its passage through the throat and lungs. The colder the air is and the greater the respiratory rate, the greater the heat loss. Heat loss can be lowered by preheating the air before it enters the body. This is accomplished by wearing some form of face protection such as a balaclava. The elimination of bodily wastes simply removes heat from the body as the waste is expelled.

CONTROL OF BODY TEMPERATURE

Our bodies function within a narrow range of temperatures. That is why it is important to maintain a heat balance for our bodies regardless of the level of activity. An inability to recognize and correct for these imbalances can lead to either hyperthermia or hypothermia (Table 1-2). Both conditions may be life threatening. By being aware of heat loss and heat gain mechanisms, we can control body temperature and enjoy living, working, and playing in the outdoors.

There are many ways to control heat loss. Adding insulating layers may be used to prevent evaporative cooling and convection cooling. Covering exposed skin and finding shelter will also lessen heat loss. Using insulation to put barriers between ourselves and high conduction materials minimizes loss through conduction. Heat may also be generated to offset cooling. Consuming enough water, eating high-energy foods, participating in muscular activities, and finding protected areas with positive heat sources all lead to heat gain.

There are also many ways to control heat gain. Removing yourself from close proximity to a heat source such as a fire, thermal heater, or the sun will slow or lessen heat gain. Removing layers of insulation will let your body use its natural cooling mechanisms to dissipate heat. Drinking water to aid metabolism and prevent dehydration will also help to reduce heat gain.

There are many ways to balance heat loss versus heat gain. The balance is different for each individual and is dependent on both external and internal factors. Is it a warm day? Is the wind blowing? Is there a lot of moisture in the air? Have I eaten correctly for the activity I am going to do? Do I have the proper equipment, food, and water to make my activity safe and enjoyable? These are all questions that should be asked every time we set foot outside the door.

....

SUMMARY

o Enjoyment of and working in the outdoors is dependent on recognizing opportunities for both heat loss and heat gain.
o Having a plan and managing the balance between heat loss and heat gain is essential for survival and the prevention of environmental injuries.
o Manage heat loss and heat gain by
    » wearing appropriate clothing.
    » drinking enough water.
    » eating properly before and during the activity.
    » recognizing potentials for unacceptable heat loss or gain and avoiding them.
o Heat gain comes from metabolism, muscular activity, and external heat sources.
o Heat loss comes from conduction, convection, evaporation, radiation, and physiological losses.

....

CHAPTER 2

WATER AND HYDRATION

Deborah Shulman, Ph.D., BodyScience, Fort Collins, Colorado

....

OBJECTIVES

o List three ways the body loses water.

o Describe symptoms and effects of dehydration and proper hydration.

o Describe hydration needs for different activity levels and climatic conditions.

o Compare and contrast benefits and detriments of fluids other than water.

o Describe safe sources of water and how to obtain it safely.

o Describe how to store and transport water.

o Describe how to purify water.

....

It is easy to forget that you are always losing water to the environment. You lose water in sweat. You lose water in each breath you take. At high altitudes and low ambient pressures, water loss is accelerated. The low humidity of a cold and dry environment increases fluid loss. In a dry climate the water may evaporate so quickly that you are unaware of how much you are sweating. When you lose more than you ingest, you are at risk for dehydration.

Life began in water and our physiology is based on water. The internal environment is a fluid one. Hormones, the immune system, cells, and nutrients that compose the blood are transported in a watery medium. The myriad of chemical reactions of metabolism in each cell require water.

Humans are about 60 percent water by weight. Blood alone is 7 percent of a person's weight. Around 60 percent of the blood is plasma (water). When you are dehydrated your blood becomes thicker. Imagine a boat on a river of flowing water. Now imagine that river as thick and gooey. The flow rate diminishes and the boat moves more slowly and has trouble navigating. This is what happens during dehydration. The blood becomes thicker and transport of oxygen and nutrients to the muscles is reduced. Waste products and toxins are not efficiently removed, and the kidneys work harder and harder to filter the thickened blood.

Dehydration can cause muscle cramping, nausea, headaches, fatigue, and a decrease in exercise capacity. Classic symptoms of a hangover are due to dehydration. Maximal oxygen uptake (VO_2) and endurance is diminished. Dehydration approaching 5 percent of body weight decreases VO_2 max. Blood volume and muscle blood flow is reduced. Cellular dehydration and reduced blood flow to the muscles increases the risk of frostbite. At higher levels of fluid loss, a person can become disoriented. At high altitude, dehydration can cause mental and physical impairment, and may contribute to the development of acute mountain sickness.

Thirst is a delayed indicator of dehydration, since when you are thirsty dehydration has already begun. In cold environments the sensation of thirst is reduced even in a dehydrated state. A better way to monitor hydration status is by observing the color and volume of urine. A low volume of urine is indicative of dehydration. Even though vitamins, foods, and other substances can cause urine color changes, dark urine often signals dehydration. Well-hydrated people will have large volumes of clear or pale urine. A sudden drop in body weight of three or more pounds may also indicate dehydration.

It is advisable to begin any backcountry trip in a well-hydrated state. Drink two to three quarts of fluid daily prior to the trip or during periods of heavy training. However, avoid drinking too much plain water at one time since plain water dilutes sodium and electrolytes in the blood. Doing so can wash these constituents out of the tissues and lead to a dangerous condition called hyponatremia. Those with conditions such as high blood pressure need to avoid chlorides, so salt ingestion should be monitored. For those who can handle sodium, it's a good idea to include some salt, such as soy sauce or salted nuts, as well as electrolytes and foods high in potassium and magnesium in the days before an extended backcountry trip.

FLUID REQUIREMENTS

During a prolonged trip, adequate fluid should be taken at regular intervals and also with meals to maintain adequate hydration. During a vigorous, multiday trip, a person may require a total of approximately five to six quarts of water per day. For a single day trip it is best to carry water with you rather than rely on surface water or snow.

Drink frequently during physical activities. Water needs will depend on environmental temperature, individual sweat rates,

> ### TABLE 2-1. CALCULATING SWEAT RATE
>
> Weigh yourself without clothes prior to and immediately after an exercise session. Drink approximately one quart for every 2.2 pounds lost.
>
> » Calculate your per hour fluid loss to determine your sweat rate.
> » Subtract the weight of any ingested fluid during the exercise session. Sweat rates will vary depending on environmental conditions and how well acclimated you are to those conditions.
> » To plan for your fluid intake during your trip, determine your sweat rate under conditions specific to your activity. If you have been exercising in frigid weather and the day is warmer than you have been accustomed to, you will be losing more fluid.
> » For an accurate assessment, make your calibration based on your hydration levels during various degrees of exercise.

acclimatization, and fitness level. Sweat rates can range from 32 to 64 ounces per hour, in some people even higher (Table 2-1). In very cold climates, sweat rates may be as little as 16 ounces per hour. In general, plan on 20 to 30 ounces of fluid per hour with 24 to 30 ounces per hour in warmer conditions, and 20 to 24 ounces per hour in cold (Table 2-2).

WATER ABSORPTION

Water absorption is enhanced in the presence of electrolytes and glucose. Sports drinks with electrolytes will help maintain adequate hydration. Otherwise, include other sources of electrolytes and sugar during your day. Most sports drinks have a 6 to 8 percent sugar solution, which is the optimal concentration for gastric emptying, that is, the rate at which the stomach empties into the intestine during exercise. Gastric emptying is slowed at higher or lower sugar concentrations in most people.

Be methodical in your hydration. Plan your interval and stick with it. If you are drinking every 30 minutes, drink 12 ounces each time or 6 ounces every 15 minutes, which is the equivalent of 2 quarts in 6 hours, and 3 quarts in 8 hours.

> ### TABLE 2-2. FLUID INTAKE WHILE EXERCISING
>
> Each hour while exercising:
>
> » 20 to 30 ounces of fluid.
> » Drink at fixed intervals every 10–30 minutes.

Be familiar with the appropriate volumes to avoid underhydration. If you are using a hydration pack, test how many sips it will take to deliver the appropriate quantity of fluid.

REHYDRATION

Under warm conditions, you may lose more fluid than you've taken in. It appears that 30 to 32 ounces—just under a quart—per hour is the upper limit of fluid absorption during exercise. If your sweat rate exceeds your absorptive capacity during a long, hard backcountry trip, you may become dehydrated, even with regular fluid intake, so be sure to rehydrate immediately after exertion. Include electrolytes in your drink or food to increase fluid retention. It takes longer to rehydrate with plain water than with a sports drink. This is especially important on multiday backcountry trips, or successive days of long, vigorous training.

WATER SOURCES

On multiday backcountry expeditions, water needs to be obtained from the environment. Snow is often the only available water source; however, it is inadvisable to eat snow. In the frigid cold, eating snow can lower body temperature and increase the risk of hypothermia.

During a warm, sunny ski day, clean snow can be packed into water bottles and placed in the sun to melt. Snow can be melted in a pot on a stove, but this uses fuel. Plan your fuel needs accordingly, and on longer trips carry foods that do not require excessive amounts of water or time to cook. When melting snow on the stove, start with some water in the pot to avoid scorching the pot with dry snow.

Avoid allowing your fluid to freeze by keeping your water bottles inside your pack or next to your body while you sleep. You can use hydration packs with insulated feeding tubes, but on very cold days the fluid will freeze even in a neoprene-covered tube, which may be disastrous if that is your only access to fluid. Keep the tube out of the environment, tucked into your pack, or under your clothing and next to your skin. Some packs have a sleeve for the feeding tube built into the shoulder strap, but this is not guaranteed to prevent freezing. Another technique is to clear the tube of fluid between sips by blowing air into the tube to push the fluid back into the main water bag.

WATER PURIFICATION

Surface water from streams, puddles, ponds, or lakes is desirable because you don't have to melt it, but there is a risk of contamination. Even in remote areas of the high country, water may contain pathogens: bacteria, parasites, and viruses. Mercury can be found in the pristine waters of high mountain lakes. Chemicals and heavy metals can contaminate surface water near mining operations, even long after a mine has been abandoned. It is unknown if these chemicals and metals can be filtered with 100 percent certainty, which is an important consideration when treating water in the backcountry.

Pathogens such as the protozoa *Giardia lamblia* and *Cryptosporidium parvum*, and bacteria such as *Salmonella*, *Campylobacter jejuni*, and *Escherichia coli* are increasingly common in surface water in the United States. These can cause debilitating illness. Bacterial illnesses take anywhere from 12 hours to 5 days to manifest symptoms. Parasites will cause illness anywhere from 2 to 20 days. Viruses and the parasite *Cyclosporum sp.* are less common in North America but are still considerations when choosing purification methods.

BOILING

Boiling is the most reliable method for killing waterborne pathogens. Boiling at a rolling boil for one minute—longer at altitude—should suffice to kill all bacteria, viruses, and parasites. For extra insurance, boil the water up to five minutes. During a long, vigorous backcountry trip this may not be feasible due to

fuel limitations, so other purification methods should be included.

CHEMICALS

The most common chemicals used for disinfection of water supplies are iodine and chlorine dioxide. Both treatments are effective against most bacteria and viruses and are considerably less expensive than ultraviolet treatment or water filters. Be aware that some people are allergic to iodine. A soak period is required for the iodine and chlorine dioxide to penetrate the cyst walls and be effective against *Giardia* and *Cryptosporidium*. Iodine requires a 30-minute wait period, and up to an hour if the water is very cold. Chlorine dioxide requires a three-hour soak, which is a consideration when you should be drinking at more frequent intervals.

One of the drawbacks of iodine treatment is the unpleasant taste, though you can purchase iodine packaged with another chemical that reduces the iodine taste. In addition, running the water through a filter that contains charcoal will remove the taste. Vitamin C can also remove the taste but should be added after the germicidal period has been completed or it will reduce the effectiveness of the treatment.

When you are using chemicals, avoid dipping the water container into the source because this may contaminate the rim, lid, and threads of the bottle. If you do dip the container, be sure to clean areas with the disinfected water.

FILTERS

There are a number of filters on the market. They are effective against most pathogens but do not filter viruses, which are smaller than the pore size of the filter. Some small bacteria may also pass through. Look for a pore size of 0.4 micron or less. For more complete disinfection, pretreat the water with disinfecting chemicals before filtration. Some water filters come with iodine pretreatment chambers.

When purchasing a water filter, consider cost, the speed of filtration, weight, and ease of cleaning and maintenance.

Water filters can also remove debris and some chemicals. When traveling through old mining districts or areas with polluted water, a water filter might be the preferred method of treatment.

ULTRAVIOLET LIGHT

Lasers are fast and highly effective against likely pathogens. The light stick is dipped into the water source and swirled until an indicator light comes on within a minute or two. Newer models are small and light. The disadvantage of ultraviolet treatment is that it requires batteries. Some models come with a solar panel and rechargeable batteries. It can take many hours to recharge batteries, even in full sun.

....

SUMMARY

o   Humans are about 60 percent water by weight, and blood is about 7 percent of a person's weight. Around 60 percent of the blood is plasma (water). During dehydration, blood becomes thicker and transport of oxygen and nutrients to the muscles is reduced.

o   Hydration needs increase during increased activity. During a vigorous, multiday backcountry trip, a person may require a total of approximately five to six quarts of water per day.

o   Drinking too much plain water at one time can dilute electrolytes in the blood. Sports drinks with electrolytes are a good choice to maintain hydration.

o   In the backcountry, water can be purified through boiling, chemicals, filters, or ultraviolet light.

....

CHAPTER 3

NUTRITION

Deborah Shulman, Ph.D., BodyScience, Fort Collins, Colorado

OBJECTIVES

o Describe why, what, and when you eat is as important as how much you eat when exerting energy in the backcountry.

o Describe symptoms of insufficient calorie intake.

o Explain the role of ingesting essential nutrients such as vitamins, minerals, antioxidants, anti-inflammatory substances, and fibers when exerting energy.

o Describe an ideal menu for a multiday backcountry trip.

In the early part of the twentieth century, the world was riveted by stories of men on skis. First it was Arctic exploration and the race to the North Pole. Next was the quest into the wild and unknown Antarctica, and the race to be the first to reach the South Pole.

Antarctica is a desolate, inhospitable place with extreme weather that challenges the very limits of human physiology. Before modern communications, air rescue, reconnaissance, or weather forecasting, men had to rely on their knowledge, preparation, survival skills, and wits.

In extreme conditions like this, nutritional errors could be fatal.

WHAT YOU DON'T EAT CAN KILL YOU

Robert Scott was a British naval officer who led the Discovery Expedition to the Antarctic from 1901 to 1904. Most of the men had never been on skis and were skeptical about using dogs to pull sleds. Despite inexperience in extreme climates and many harrowing, life-threatening events, Scott, along with Ernest Shackleton and Edward

Wilson, managed to come within 530 miles of the South Pole.

Scott returned to Britain a hero and was quickly integrated into the social circles of high British society. Several years later, Scott decided to return to Antarctica during the Terra Nova Expedition, from 1910 to 1913, determined to be the first to the South Pole for Britain. After he arrived in Antarctica, however, Scott learned that a Norwegian, Roald Amundsen, was camped in Antarctica just 200 miles away and had arrived with the same objective. The race was on.

Amundsen had previous experience in the Arctic and had studied Arctic explorations. Stories abounded of both successful and disastrous expeditions. He studied the traditional lore of Norwegian sealers and Viking explorers, and he read about the diet of the native Eskimo people.

Based on these observations, he planned his expedition food assiduously. He knew that the Vikings ate the Arctic cloudberry, a wild shrub with edible orange fruit, to prevent the ravages of scurvy; and he knew that fresh, uncooked seal meat could also prevent scurvy. Vitamin C had not yet been discovered and the word "vitamin" had not even been coined, but Amundsen knew that nutritional mistakes could cause an expedition to fail.

After arriving in Antarctica, he was careful to make sure that his crew was well nourished prior to the 750-mile trek to the South Pole. They ate butter on whole grain bread made with extra wheat germ, whole grain pancakes with preserved cloudberries and whortleberries, and undercooked or uncooked deep frozen seal meat covered with whortleberries. Amundsen strongly believed in the importance of "fresh" food, and he chose foods that supplied nutrients and calories vital to human performance in extreme conditions.

Robert Scott, on the other hand, fed his crew white bread and butter, overcooked seal meat only sporadically, and heavily processed, nutrient-poor canned food. The canning processes of the time destroyed much of a food's nutritional content.

Scott left his base camp on November 1, 1911, with some ponies, one dog team, and four men. When he arrived at the South Pole in the middle of January 1912, after hundreds of miles and 73 days of difficult and dangerous travel, he found Amundsen had beaten him to the South Pole by more than a month. Amundsen had left his base camp on October 20, 1911, with four men, four sleds, and 52 dogs. They traveled fast and strong, arriving at the South Pole on December 15, tackling the 750 miles in 56 days. Amundsen and his crew returned to base camp five weeks later in good health.

The Scott expedition did not fare well on the return trip. Demoralized, emaciated, and depressed, the crew succumbed to exertion and cold. They exhibited classic signs of scurvy: fatigue, depression, pale skin, immobilization, nosebleeds, weakness, frostbite, intermittent paralysis, wounds that refused to heal, bleeding, gangrene, and tissue degeneration. Muddled thinking led to bad decisions and accidents, including falls into crevasses. By March 29, 1912, all five men in Scott's crew were dead.

Daily rations for each expedition consisted of approximately two pounds of food per man. The daily allocation of calories was nearly the same for both expeditions, but the difference was the nutritional quality. Each day, Scott's men had tea, nonfat cocoa, butter, sugar, pemmican—a paste made of lean ground dried meat and melted fat—and one pound of biscuits made from white flour. In contrast, Amundsen fed his crew dried milk, chocolate, whole grain biscuits, and Amundsen's version of pemmican, which consisted of meat, fat, oats, peas, and frozen seal meat from depots that had been stored two and a half months prior. Amundsen's crew ate foods rich in B-vitamins and magnesium, vital for energy generation in the muscles, and other important nutrients for nerve, brain, and muscle function. Even though they were unaware of it at the time, they started the expedition with good stores of vitamin C and ate enough during the trek to prevent the symptoms of scurvy from which Scott's men suffered.

Scurvy is caused by a deficiency of vitamin C, which is an important antioxidant.

However, its most vital role in the body is the synthesis of collagen, which is the basic tissue matrix in the body upon which all structures are built. The calcium phosphate mineral of bone is packed into collagen, and collagen is in cartilage. Muscle fibers, blood vessel walls, skin, and the lining of the intestines are all built within a matrix of collagen.

The amount of time it takes for an individual to develop scurvy is dependent on the body's stores of vitamin C. Those with a diet deficient in vitamin C can develop scurvy in less than a month, while people who preload with a supplement of 70 milligrams a day of vitamin C can take six to eight months to develop the disease. Scurvy can be prevented with as little as 10 milligrams of vitamin C a day. The Eskimo natives, who eat little of the fresh plant foods rich in vitamin C, have been found to derive as much as 70 grams per day from fresh, undercooked, or uncooked seal or whale meat.

Vitamin C also has other important functions. The synthesis of carnitine, the compound that shuttles fat into the mitochondria to be burned for energy, and epinephrine, the hormone that modulates energy available for exercise, are dependent on vitamin C.

Certainly the catastrophic failure of the Scott expedition can be explained, in part, by poor nutrition. While few of us will ever make such an extreme and harrowing journey, it can serve as an illustration of the importance of basic, core nutrition and the quality of food.

WHAT YOU EAT MATTERS

When researchers studied the nutrition of participants in a two-day ski mountaineering race with considerable elevation change, what they found was revealing. The skiers who did not take in sufficient carbohydrates were slower, had poorer performance, higher cell damage, and increased stress markers. Low intake of the minerals potassium, magnesium, calcium, iron, and zinc, as well as a low intake of antioxidants, were correlated with higher stress markers and increased cell damage. B-vitamins such as folate, riboflavin, and thiamin participate in the breakdown of carbohydrates. Inadequate B-vitamins led to fatigue and increased cell damage. The message is simple: What you eat matters.

Backcountry activities place heavy demands on the human body. Endurance, strength, speed, skill, mental clarity, and manual dexterity are all required for successful backcountry travel and search and rescue. All of these attributes are affected by nutritional practices both at home and in the backcountry, whether it is a one-day trip or a multiday expedition. A patroller who is unprepared or cavalier about the importance of informed nutritional

TABLE 3-1. MEET THE CALORIES	
CARBOHYDRATES	4 kcal/g
PROTEIN	4 kcal/g
FAT	9 kcal/g
ALCOHOL	7 kcal/g

practices can quickly turn from an asset to a liability. Improper or inadequate fueling in the backcountry can cause fatigue, injuries, poor judgment, and increased risk of hypothermia and other cold injuries.

A calorie is a unit of energy. Calories are the amount of energy released when food is combusted. In the human diet calories are supplied by carbohydrates, fat, protein, and alcohol. Carbohydrates and protein deliver four calories per gram; fat, nine calories per gram; and alcohol, seven calories per gram (Table 3-1). For the same gram weight, fats supply more than twice the calories of carbohydrates and protein. The concentrated calories of fat make them a good choice on a multiday expedition when you need to limit food weight, but a bad choice if you need to trim calories to lose weight.

Even within each category of calories, the type will make a difference. Saturated fat is different than unsaturated fat and has different functions in the body. Saturated fat is stable and does not go rancid without refrigeration. The body uses short chain saturated fatty acids as an energy source during aerobic exercise. Both of these qualities make saturated fat such as chocolate, butter, and cheese good choices in the backcountry. However, excess saturated fat in your daily diet at home when you are not engaging in heavy exercise will have deleterious health effects.

The quality of protein depends on the amino acid composition. High-quality proteins supply the proper constellation and levels of essential amino acids. The protein in peanut butter is lower quality than the protein from beans, milk, or meat. Different carbohydrates will elicit different hormonal responses.

Essential vitamins, minerals, antioxidants, anti-inflammatory substances, and fibers are packaged within those calories. Purified calories such as table sugar or protein powder are often termed "empty calories" because they do not deliver vital nutrients for body growth and function, and too often they burden the body with excess calories. In your core diet, make sure to choose foods that meet your nutrient needs (Table 3-2).

The main function of carbohydrates is to provide energy as fuel. The ability to sustain prolonged, vigorous exercise is directly related to carbohydrate stores. The brain, nerves, and muscles consume most of the dietary carbohydrate requirement. The brain requires carbohydrates exclusively for

TABLE 3-2. CORE CALORIE NEEDS

Daily core calorie needs for an endurance athlete (grams per kilogram of body weight):

CARBOHYDRATES (g/kg)	3–7
PROTEIN (g/kg)	1.2–1.5
FAT (g/kg)	0.8–1

One kilogram is equal to 2.2 pounds.

its energy source while the muscles oxidize a mix of carbohydrates and fat. Additional dietary carbohydrates are needed for exercise and to replenish carbohydrate stores between exercise sessions. Carbohydrate needs range from 130 grams a day for sedentary individuals to 600 grams daily during a rigorous, high altitude mountaineering trip with large changes in elevation.

Fats, at nine calories per gram, are a concentrated energy source. Fat is the preferred fuel source for cardiac muscle, while skeletal muscle—with its mix of fast and slow twitch muscle fibers—burns a mix of fat and carbohydrates, depending on the intensity of the exercise. Endurance training increases mitochondrial density and the capacity to burn fat as fuel, reducing reliance on carbohydrates. However, even with well-developed fat metabolism, carbohydrates remain the primary energy source for muscle contraction.

Fat oxidation is also increased in the cold and contributes to shivering thermogenesis. Cell membranes are composed of fat, or lipid bilayer. The types of fat in the diet will affect the composition on the cell membrane and membrane function. Hormones such as testosterone, cortisol, and estrogen are synthesized from fat. The nervous system, composed of brain and nerves, is largely composed of fat. Fat should contribute 25 to 30 percent of core calories. It may be beneficial to consume some fat during prolonged ski sessions; however, the capacity to digest fat during exercise is limited.

Many people mistakenly believe that protein is the key to athletic success. Protein is important for growth, maintenance, and repair, and as a source of nitrogen for the body. High-quality protein is necessary for synthesis of muscle, hair, nails, hormones, bone, organs, and enzymes, and for most body functions. That said, protein needs are considerably less than those for carbohydrates or fat. Endurance athletes need more protein than sedentary people but tend to get more than they can utilize. Protein is burned as fuel, primarily in the absence of carbohydrates. Excess protein tends to replace important foods and nutrients, acidifies the blood, increases fluid loss and dehydration, and contributes to osteoporosis and excess body weight.

CORE NUTRITION: QUALITY AND VARIETY

Nutrition is the provision of vital substances, or nutrients, that provide calories, vitamins, minerals, phytochemicals, fibers, and antioxidants to the body for optimal performance, physiological function, maintenance, growth, and repair.

Nutrition remains a science of discovery. The first nutrient identified was vitamin C in the 1930s, though the first phytochemical (phytochemistry is the branch of chemistry concerned with plants and plant products) was not identified until the 1990s.

Core nutrition is your daily nutrition—what you eat in your meals and snacks. In the case of ski mountaineering, sports nutrition involves how you fuel for physical performance in the backcountry. When you eat is as important as what you eat. When planning for a multiday trip, plan primary meals first, followed by your sports nutrition.

Carbohydrates should supply around 50 percent of our daily core calories. Each gram of carbohydrate we absorb provides four calories. Carbohydrates come from plants—fruit, vegetables, tubers (such as potatoes), grains, legumes, and milk. Sugar is purified, concentrated carbohydrate. For meals during a multiday trip, good sources of carbohydrates are dried fruit, dehydrated vegetables and legumes, instant cooked cereal, instant rice granola or muesli, dense breads resistant to crushing, crackers, rice noodles, pasta, brown sugar, honey, syrup, and jam.

Protein should supply 12 to 20 percent of core calories, or 1.2 to 1.5 grams per kilogram a day depending on age, gender, activity level, and type of exercise. A body builder or strength athlete needs more protein than a skier. An average of 1.2 to 1.4 grams per kilogram, or 0.5 to 0.6 gram per pound, are recommended intakes for endurance athletes.

Additional protein is not needed during endurance exercise. Cheese, dried milk, dried meat, sausage, precooked dehydrated beans, tofu, and canned or vacuum-packed fish provide high-quality protein for long-duration ski trips.

Your core nutrition is best met by eating a plant-based diet of unprocessed foods, supplemented by animal proteins from dairy, fish, and meat. Unprocessed foods are largely in their original state. For example, whole grain flour is unprocessed and contains all parts of the grain and delivers important B-vitamins, vitamin E, magnesium, fiber, and phytochemicals. Processed flour has had nutrient-rich bran and germ removed and is composed of nutrient-poor endosperm. Adding synthetic vitamins and minerals does not replace lost nutrients. That's why pretzels are a bad substitute for brown rice or whole grain bread. A meal bar does not replace a sandwich. Protein powders are not a good substitute for nutrient-rich, high-quality protein sources.

EAT BY FOOD GROUP

Although the list of nutrients and their actions can be daunting, the practice of good, core nutrition is simple. Eat by food groups both at home and in the backcountry. Foods can be categorized into groups according to the nutrients they deliver (Table 3-3).

A balanced diet includes foods from each of these food groups daily. Ninety percent of the food that passes your lips should come from these groups. Choose two to three servings in each group. Include three or more food groups at each meal. If you eliminate a group or substitute nutritionally poor foods, such as bagels made with processed flour in lieu of whole grain breads, your nutrition, exercise performance, and health will suffer.

TABLE 3-3. THE FOOD GROUPS

DAIRY	PROTEIN
VEGETABLES	FRUIT
STARCH	FAT

One helpful guideline is to largely stick to foods that existed before 1950. On backcountry trips, substitute dehydrated foods for fresh foods when possible. Think about food group choices and balance each meal with three or more food groups.

DAIRY

The most important nutrient in this group is calcium. Most people need 800 to 1,200 milligrams of calcium daily. Dairy, such as milk, yogurt, cheese, kefir, cottage cheese, and calcium-fortified soy milk, is the richest and most bio-available source of calcium, at 300 milligrams per cup. Three servings are recommended daily, with additional calcium from secondary sources such as white beans, almonds, seaweed, and soy beans. Dairy also delivers eight grams of high quality protein, rich in branch chain amino acids, per serving. One serving is one cup of milk or yogurt, or one ounce of cheese.

PROTEIN

Eat two servings per day from this group. Animal protein includes meat, chicken, turkey, eggs, and fish; vegetable protein includes beans, peas, lentils, tofu, tempeh, and products made with soy protein. Each ounce of meat or fish or half cup of legumes, such as refried beans or lentils, delivers eight grams of protein. A serving size is three to five ounces of animal protein, two eggs, or one cup of legumes. Emphasize lean, lower fat protein sources.

VEGETABLES

Eat three cups a day from this group. Choose fresh or frozen at home, and dehydrated on multiday excursions. Each serving includes one cup of fresh vegetables or a half cup of sauce or salsa.

FRUIT

Eat two to three cups a day from this group, either fresh or frozen. Dried fruit is good for trips but has a higher glycemic content than fresh fruit. Minimize juice consumption due to high sugar and low fiber content.

STARCHES

Eat three servings daily of whole grain breads and cereal, brown rice, potato, pasta, corn, tortillas, and/or quinoa. Eat a serving at each meal.

FAT

Eat two to three servings from this group, emphasizing beneficial fats such as extra virgin olive oil, canola oil, nuts, nut butters, seeds, olives, and avocado. At home, minimize the use of saturated fats such as coconut milk, palm oil, butter, sour cream, and cream cheese.

Ultimately, healthy eating is about the whole foods you eat. Core nutrition, both at home and in the backcountry, is about eating a variety of real, wholesome food. Supplements or protein powder cannot replace the complexity of food or cover the myriad of nutrients required, and may even prove detrimental. Studies about using supplements are generally disappointing, show little or no results, or sometimes even have adverse effects. Vital nutrients and compounds in whole foods are packaged within a complex environment that we do not fully understand. For millions of years our bodies have adapted to extracting and exploiting nutrition from these foods. Humans survived and thrived not because of any specific food or diet but because of our adaptability to available food sources.

CARBOHYDRATES FOR ENDURANCE, STRENGTH, AND SPEED

People often talk about the number of calories they eat every hour during a training session or the calories they are getting in their diets. In order to properly plan your ski mountaineering trip or fuel your training sessions, it is important to distinguish between these forms of energy and how they are used by the body (Table 3-4).

Each type of calorie has specific roles in human metabolism, health, and athletic performance. Carbohydrates are the predominant fuel for endurance exercise.

TABLE 3-4. NUTRITION DURING EXERCISE

Daily calorie distribution for heavy exercise at three-plus hours at 65 percent maximal oxygen uptake (VO_2); core diet plus added carbohydrates during and after exercise:

» 60 to 70 percent carbohydrates
» 25 to 30 percent fat
» 12 to 15 percent protein
» Total calories: 2,500–4,500 per day

During exercise, your muscles burn a mix of carbohydrates and fat. Protein is insignificant relative to the contribution of carbohydrates and fat. The relative contributions of carbohydrates and fat to the fuel mix will depend on the intensity of the exercise, the duration of the session, and the fitness level of the skier. Cold, excessive heat, age, and altitude also impact the rate of carbohydrate oxidation.

As the intensity of exercise and heart rate increases, there is an exponential increase in the amount of carbohydrates burned. Carbohydrates are the predominant fuel for high intensity and strength activities such as sprinting, climbing, and ascending hills. Under anaerobic conditions, energy is generated through the breakdown of glycogen, with the production of lactic acid as a byproduct. Fat, in contrast, requires oxygen for catabolism, or breakdown, inside the mitochondria. This is a consideration for high-altitude travel, with its resultant increase in the reliance on carbohydrates for fuel.

When you are enjoying a respite on the couch, your predominant fuel is fat and your calorie burn is the basal metabolic rate. When you get off the couch to walk your dog, you are at just 25 to 30 percent of your maximum oxygen capacity, so your energy requirements are easily met by fat. During a moderate run your calorie burn increases. Carbohydrates are burned at a higher rate and contribute 50 percent to your energy needs. The rate of carbohydrate oxidation increases with intensity of the exercise performed. During races of less than 30 minutes, sprints, or the explosive movements of climbing and strength training, carbohydrates will contribute 100 percent of energy needs.

CARBOHYDRATES ARE SKI FOOD

We store a limited supply of carbohydrates in the body in the form of glycogen. Each gram of carbohydrate is stored with three grams of water, making it a bulky molecule, thus reducing storage capacity. Glycogen is stored in the muscles, where it is used for local muscular activity and is stored in the liver to maintain plasma glucose levels for the brain. The brain does not store glycogen to a measurable degree and is dependent on the blood glucose for its fuel source.

Endurance training increases glycogen storage capacity. There is enough glycogen stored in the muscles to fuel moderate effort activities at 65 percent maximal oxygen uptake for 90 minutes in a trained individual. Higher intensity work increases the rate of carbohydrate oxidation. Cyclists racing in criterions near the top of their exercise capacity have been shown to deplete leg muscle glycogen in as little as 30 minutes.

When glycogen stores in the muscle and liver become depleted, exercise capacity is reduced to levels compatible with fat metabolism. The familiar term "bonking" is used to describe the fatigue, weakness, and mental confusion that results from carbohydrate depletion. When plasma glucose falls during exercise, the brain will reduce muscle fiber recruitment, with a subsequent loss of strength, endurance, and energy. This can occur even in the presence of adequate muscle glycogen. Symptoms of hypoglycemia (low blood

TABLE 3-5. EASILY DIGESTED CARBOHYDRATES FOR SPORTS	
GELS	SPORTS DRINKS
SPORTS BARS	GUMMY BEARS
DATES	FIGS
BANANA	DEFIZZED COLA
CHOCOLATE	TRAIL MIX

sugar) and inadequate carbohydrate levels are nausea, fuzzy thinking, shakiness, fatigue, irritability, lack of concentration, loss of fine motor skills, and diminished strength. This is an impediment to the mental clarity required in the backcountry, especially in extreme, dangerous conditions or terrain, or during a rescue.

Carbohydrates are important for maintenance of body temperature in the cold and shivering thermogenesis. Low carbohydrate levels impair thermoregulation and increase the risk of hypothermia and cold injury. This underscores the importance of frequent doses of carbohydrates during prolonged exercise sessions. The goal is to eat frequently to avoid dips in blood glucose and take in enough easily digested carbohydrates to minimize muscle glycogen depletion.

There is an upper limit for digestion and absorption of carbohydrates during exercise: 1 to 1.5 grams per minute or 60 to 85 grams of carbohydrates per hour are recommended. The optimal fueling interval is 10 to 15 minutes. However, this

TABLE 3-6. MEAL SUGGESTIONS

BREAKFAST	Quick and easy, warm and nutritious. Instant cooked cereals (oatmeal or cream of wheat) with dried fruit and nuts or cold cereal (granola or muesli), whole meal pancakes with syrup or jam, coffee, tea, cocoa, Instant Breakfast, Tang, or other powdered drinks.
LUNCH	Make it packable. Dense, whole grain bread such as pumpernickel bagels, or whole grain pita bread with butter or peanut butter and jam, hard cheese, meat jerky, salami, fresh carrots, dehydrated fruit.
SNACKS	Chocolate bars, trail mix, energy bars, cookies.
DINNER	Be creative! Delicious meals can be made in camp, such as cheesy tuna pasta, pad thai, chili with beans, mashed potatoes, smoked salmon, and stir-fried vegetables. Avoid foods that require excessive cooking times such as lentils or rice. Choose noodles and pasta that cook quickly or don't require boiling. Dried herbs and spice mixes can add a flavorful punch and boost nutrition. Carry a small container of vegetable oil for cooking and be sure to include recipe cards. Canned or vacuum-packed meats and fish in foil packets are good choices for protein but be sure to carry a can opener if necessary.

may not be practical for backcountry ski travel. Feeds at 30-minute intervals will suffice as long as sufficient carbohydrates are consumed at each feed and the hourly requirement is met.

GUIDELINES FOR FUELING DURING EXERCISE

Start fueling within the first hour of exercise, at a rate of 60 to 85 grams of carbohydrate per hour, every 15 to 30 minutes. Including fat such as chocolate, nuts, or peanut butter may be beneficial in cold conditions or during prolonged, moderate-level exercise lasting more than three hours (Table 3-5).

FOOD FOR MULTIDAY TRIPS

Follow the food group guidelines when planning meals, substituting dried or dehydrated foods for fresh foods. Include easily digested carbohydrates during activity to maintain performance and strength. Plan on two pounds of food and 3,500 to 4,500 calories per person per day, with 65 percent carbohydrate, 10 to 15 percent protein and 25 to 30 percent fat (Table 3-6).

Repackage foods to minimize waste. Package food in clear resealable plastic bags and label them. Include cooking directions or recipes when necessary. Freeze-dried foods are very light and a good option for very long trips but are expensive. You can find many quick cooking, easy-to-prepare items in grocery stores.

Meals should be planned to minimize cooking time and fuel use. Fuel requirements will increase in the cold and at high altitude, so bring enough for melting snow as well as cooking. Plan on 140 to 200 milliliters of white gas per person per day.

SUMMARY
o Explorer Robert Scott's failed expedition to the South Pole in the early twentieth century can be explained, in part, by his crew's poor nutrition options. In the backcountry, making poor nutritional choices can cause fatigue, injuries, poor judgment, and increased risk of hypothermia and other cold injuries.
o What you eat matters, particularly when exerting energy in the backcountry. Core nutrition, both at home and in the backcountry, is about eating a variety of real, wholesome food.
o When planning your backcountry meals, stick to foods that existed before 1950, substituting dehydrated foods for fresh foods when possible. Think about food group choices, and balance each meal with three or more food groups.
o When preparing menus for a multiday trip, plan on two pounds of food and 3,500 to 4,500 calories per person per day, with 65 percent carbohydrate, 10 to 15 percent protein, and 25 to 30 percent fat.

CHAPTER 4

CLOTHING

Rusty Wells, Flathead Nordic Ski Patrol, Whitefish, Montana

OBJECTIVES

o Compare and contrast commonly used materials for various layers of clothing.
o Recognize differences in clothing construction and features.
o Explain the purpose and techniques of layering, venting, and other dressing strategies.
o Explain the basics of proper footwear and foot care.
o Explain how to repair, care for, and maintain personal clothing.
o Discuss additional clothing needs and considerations for multiday trips.

Clothing is the first line of defense for survival in the backcountry, since its purpose is to keep the backcountry recreationist warm and dry while protecting him or her from physical harm. Therefore, when selecting clothing, the traveler must pay attention to the type of materials and the quality of construction, as well as understand the strategies of dressing.

Each person has different needs, and conditions on any given trip are different. Thus, the beginning backcountry recreationist must experiment with different clothing types and dressing strategies to discover what works best. Before any trip, clothing should be tried for comfort and features.

CLOTHING MATERIALS

Clothing helps the traveler stay warm by trapping air against the skin. Once the air is warmed by the body and is not allowed to cool, the body stays warm. Materials with fibers that trap large amounts of air relative to their weight and bulk will be warmest. Clothing must not only create this warm air layer but keep it in place and prevent it from cooling. Both the type of material and the way the clothing is constructed play important roles.

FIBERS AND FABRICS

One way air is cooled is through humidity, either from the environment or from perspiration. Water conducts warmth away from the body quickly, and humid air is slower to warm than dry air. Therefore, fabric must be made of fibers that either resist water absorption or that pass water quickly by way of wicking or hydrophobic qualities (Table 4-1).

Most synthetic fibers, such as polypropylene, Capilene, fiberfill, etc., do not absorb water and are suitable for the winter environment. Some natural fibers are suitable, too. Down, if kept dry, provides an exceptional amount of air space relative to its weight. Wool has the ability to stay warm even when wet because the fibers are hollow, and new wool fiber technology has made wearing wool next to the skin quite comfortable. Silk has many of the characteristics of synthetics, and silk garments today are much more durable than previous generations. Cotton, however, absorbs water like a sponge and holds it next to the skin. Cotton, either pure or mixed with other fibers, should be avoided in mountain environments.

Some clothing is constructed of a mix of materials to take advantage of characteristics from each of the fibers and/or to enhance durability. While some blends like wool, nylon, Lycra, and various synthetics work well, other mixes such as wool and polypropylene are only a compromise and may be difficult to care for. The fiber content label, as well as the care instructions should be checked. Not only should unsuitable fibers be avoided, but the type of care must also match the wearer's lifestyle, abilities, and resources.

Fibers are woven or knitted into a variety of fabrics. Knitted fabrics usually fit closely and are soft. Fleece, also a soft material, is produced much like felt, where fibers are woven or knitted and then matted or brushed together into a fabric. Both fleece and knitted fabrics snag easily and are not wind- or waterproof, although many modern fleece garments now have a layer of Gore-Tex added to provide wind and water protection while also maintaining breathability. Such fabrics are often best used as undergarments or an insulating layer.

Woven fibers can either be made into soft fabrics for shirts and pants or into a smooth, tough fabric suitable for outerwear. Outerwear fabrics may have coatings applied to the inside to render them water-repellent or waterproof. Additional coatings, usually applied as a spray on the outside, can enhance the water repellency of the fabric. Some coatings on water repellent fabrics have micropores that allow water vapor to pass through them but not water droplets. If conditions allow, moisture that builds up

TABLE 4-1. FIBER COMPARISON CHART

Fiber	Layer	Insulation Dry/Wet	Compressibility	Durability	Comments
Natural fibers					
DOWN	insulation	high/low	high	low	insulation value varies with moisture, quality, and aging
WOOL	all	high/medium	medium	medium	best all around
SILK	under	medium/low	low	low	expensive
Synthetic fibers					
POLYESTER SOLID	wicking	medium	medium	medium	
POLYESTER HOLLOW	insulating and wicking	medium/high/low	medium	medium/high	
POLYPROPYLENE	wicking	medium/medium	medium	low	holds body odor/ shrinks in dryers
NYLON	outer	low/low	low	high	needs treatment for waterproofing

from perspiration on the inside can pass through to the outside.

These fabrics are termed "breathable." In conditions of high air humidity, however, the fabric may not breathe very well. Totally waterproof fabrics prevent water from penetrating from the outside, but often create sauna-like conditions on the inside.

Another way for the body to lose the warming air layer created by clothing is through convection from the wind. Because of this, at least one of your layering garments needs to be windproof, even though a windproof garment is not necessarily water-repellent. Check the label or ask the salesperson to make sure it's made of Gore-Tex or another waterproof/breathable material.

CONSTRUCTION AND FEATURES

Besides suitable fibers, clothing materials for the backcountry need to be durable and of high quality. For a major purchase, such as a parka, sleeping bag, or boots, articles in current magazines that test and rate clothing may be helpful. When purchasing items, a well-informed salesperson can be the biggest help. Each garment should also be carefully inspected for defects. Make certain the merchant or catalog has an acceptable return policy.

For outerwear, extra reinforced and waterproof areas on the knees, seat, elbows, and shoulders are keys to garment durability. If possible, seams should be taped to enhance waterproofing.

Zippers should be heavy duty (size eight-plus), two-way, and covered with outside protective flaps, which keep the zipper from freezing and reduce air infiltration. Flaps should seal over the zipper with Velcro tabs and be difficult to snag in the zipper.

Pull strings attached to zipper tabs make them easier to use, especially when wearing gloves. Pockets should have flap covers and good closures (zipper or Velcro). The garment should be equipped with drawstrings, Velcro closures, or elastic around all openings to provide a good weather seal without restricting blood circulation.

FIT

Clothing should be purchased for comfort in the intended activity without compromise to function. Loose fit provides comfort, but too much bagginess could increase heat loss and restrict movement, while tight clothing restricts both circulation and movement. For inner clothing, a snug but not tight fit is best.

Outer layers can be looser. All layers should nestle together, feel comfortable, and be functional. Clothing should be easy to put on and take off, or at least to open and close up in order to regulate body warmth.

COLOR AND FASHION

Clothing colors seem to change with fashion's whims. Dark-colored clothing absorbs the sun's radiant heat and is good in winter; light clothing reflects the sun's heat and is beneficial in summer. Orange and other bright colors are great for visibility, which is helpful in search-and-rescue activities. Subdued, natural colors are available for those seeking to blend in to the natural world. The clothing industry now provides many options for fashion alongside function.

COST

Cost is often a major constraint on purchases. However, once the principles of clothing materials, construction, and dressing strategies are understood, suitable clothing can be purchased from a variety of sources.

Surplus, discount, and used clothing stores are good sources of inexpensive clothing. Minor alterations may turn an ordinary item into a serviceable winter travel garment. Kits also are available for those with good sewing skills and can save a good deal of money. Look for off-season sales during the year to add to your winter wardrobe.

DRESSING STRATEGIES

Clothing needs to be worn correctly if it is to function properly. Several strategies can help produce the best results in the backcountry.

LAYERING

Most novices underestimate the amount of heat and sweat produced by the active body. If not kept in balance, the traveler can overheat during activity, only to be dangerously chilled during rest periods.

Appropriate layering and venting provide the best method for the winter traveler to balance heat loss and gain. Constant monitoring and adjustment of clothing is necessary if the traveler is to maintain a

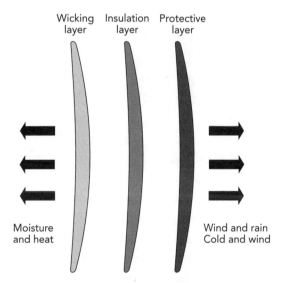

Wicking layer: Wicks moisture away from skin to the outside of the garment where it can evaporate (synthetic long underwear, thermal tops, etc.)

Insulation layer: The mid-layer provides insulation while transporting moisture to the outside (fleece, down-filled garments, etc.)

Protective layer: The outer layer protects inner layers from outside elements (shell pants, shell jackets, etc.)

Figure 4-1. *The layering system*

steady body temperature and to stay comfortable and safe.

The layering concept is a modular approach to dressing, wherein several thinner layers of clothing are used. These layers are added or removed in response to varying activity levels and environmental conditions.

Three different functional layers are recognized: wicking layer, insulation layer(s), and protective layer (Figure 4-1).

Wicking layer

The underwear layer, worn next to the skin, is responsible for keeping the skin dry. This layer must be able to wick the water vapor caused by perspiration away from space around the body, thereby reducing heat loss by conduction and evaporation. Generally, synthetic fibers such as polypropylene and Capilene are favored, because they do not absorb moisture and readily wick body moisture into the outer layers. Silk also has these properties and is smooth and lightweight. Both silk and polypropylene dry quickly. It cannot be stressed enough that cotton must not be worn in the mountain environment, especially during the cool season.

Insulation layer

Following the wicking layer, insulation is then provided by one or more layers of clothing. The clothing is usually made of the same fabrics as underwear (except silk) but is of heavier weight. The most common synthetic insulating materials are pile, fleece, and bunting. Additional layers (sweaters, jackets, vests, etc.) are added during periods of inactivity. Heavier synthetic fiber and wool garments, as well as down-filled garments, are suitable.

Clothing layers must be easily added and removed. It should be possible to open or to easily remove the garments in areas where perspiration is the highest, such as at the neck, head, hands, torso, underarms, and along the sides of the legs.

Protective layer

The ideal material allows perspiration to escape while keeping outside water droplets from entering. This seemingly impossible task is achieved by a membrane of waterproof and breathable materials. This membrane is made with microscopic holes small enough to keep water from entering, but large enough to allow water vapor to pass through.

Gore-Tex was the first material boasting this property. Now there are a number of manufacturers that process materials with similar abilities.

The outer layer provides protection from the environment, so this layer must be windproof, rainproof, and snowproof. It should seal tightly around all openings when necessary. It also protects the insulating layers from sharp and abrasive objects such as branches and rocks.

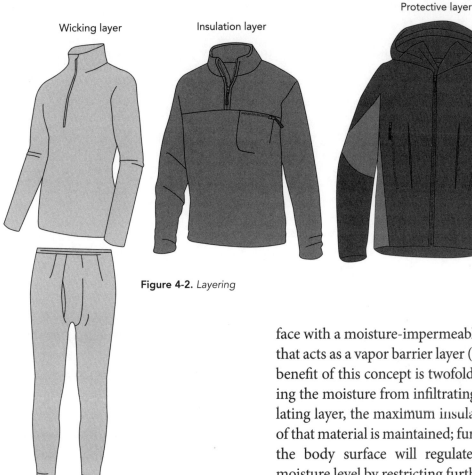

Wicking layer Insulation layer Protective layer

Figure 4-2. *Layering*

Zippers in key areas of a garment allow both venting and efficient dressing. The outer layer should have pockets that are easily accessed even when wearing a pack (Figure 4-2).

Vapor barrier layer

An alternative to wicking the moisture away from the body is to surround the body surface with a moisture-impermeable material that acts as a vapor barrier layer (VBL). The benefit of this concept is twofold: By keeping the moisture from infiltrating the insulating layer, the maximum insulating value of that material is maintained; furthermore, the body surface will regulate the skin moisture level by restricting further perspiration, thereby conserving body water and minimizing dehydration.

This concept works well for the feet, where it is difficult to keep adding insulation but where dryness is important. Additionally, wicking does not work well with waterproof boots. The obvious downside is that socks get wet, so be sure to have extra dry socks if using VBLs.

Another application for a vapor barrier is inside a down sleeping bag when

TABLE 4-2. C.O.L.D.

The following cold guidelines used by the military summarize the principles of proper dressing.

C = CLEAN	Clean clothing is much more efficient than soiled clothing.
O = OPEN	The ability to open clothing at the neck and cuffs prevents overheating and moisture due to sweating.
L = LOOSE, LAYERS	Multiple layers with air spaces between allow more insulation and air flow, allowing easier adjustability and prevention of moisture problems.
D = DRY	Dry clothing will prevent excess heat loss due to evaporation and conduction.

maximum insulation is required. Especially on extended trips, it is difficult to dry a bag from respiration, perspiration, and water melt. It is possible to obtain an improvement of around 10 degrees F by using a VBL system. Some people find this system too uncomfortable for practical use, while others utilize it with great success.

DRESSING APPROPRIATELY

As a rule of thumb, the ratio of layers is three to two (3:2), that is, three layers on the torso area for every two layers on the extremities. Remember, it is important to dress appropriately for the level of activity and expected weather changes (Table 4-2). The key is anticipation. It is best to start an activity slightly underdressed, because the activity will quickly supply the extra warmth.

The traveler should be able to make minor adjustments in temperature on the trail by opening up and closing the venting areas. Many novices do not want to stop, and they end up overheating, getting wet, then chilled and uncomfortable. This can lead to hypothermia.

Conversely, layers should be added as soon as the traveler stops so that precious heat is not lost. Every effort must be made to avoid getting wet from the weather or from snow.

Try on all layers together. Each subsequent layer will need to be slightly larger to accommodate the layers beneath. When shopping for clothes, take the layers you plan to wear with you to ensure proper fit.

If layering and venting strategies do not seem to work adequately, then the VBL system should be considered.

SPECIAL CLOTHING NEEDS

Clothing is specially designed for the body part it protects. Following are special features to look for when dressing each specific body part.

THE HEAD

The head area is the body's best thermal regulator. With a good insulating hat, around 30 percent of the body's heat can be conserved. Temperature regulation can be achieved by removing or putting on a hat.

A hat should fit snugly without being uncomfortable and without restricting visibility. An under-the-chin tie-down will keep it from getting lost or blown off and will also provide a snugger fit. Peruvian-design hats with ear flaps provide good ear and neck protection without compromising vision.

A balaclava made of silk, polypropylene, wool, or light pile is an excellent means to insulate the neck, head, face, and ears. This type of head cover will not slide off easily and rolls down to cover the face and neck.

For extremely cold days, adding a face mask, neck gaiter, or scarf provides additional protection for the nose, mouth, and neck area. Hats with sun visors or wide brims provide some protection from direct sun.

The layering concept can be applied to headwear. A thin silk or polypropylene hat or balaclava can be worn under a heavier, insulating hat, with a parka hood providing the protective layer. The hood, therefore, is an important feature to consider when selecting a parka. It should be easy to pull up and close tightly, and it should not restrict vision.

THE EYES

The sun's ultraviolet rays, especially the ultraviolet beta (UVB) rays, are the most dangerous to the eyes and are intensified at higher altitudes and by the snow. It is important that goggles and sunglasses pass no more than 1 percent of UVB rays and have equal screening of ultraviolet alpha (UVA) and visible light. Glasses that have good optical clarity and do not distort the view are ideal. Plastic lenses should have a scratch-resistant coating and be stored and handled carefully. Lens color is a matter of personal preference. The neutral gray or green lenses provide the least color distortion. Yellow and rose colored lenses work well in low light.

Goggles offer good protection against wind, blowing snow, and sun and are needed when the weather deteriorates. On bright, sunny days, sunglasses might be preferred. Plastic-covered wire-wrap temples or restraining devices will hold glasses on securely while a retainer strap around the neck provides backup. Avoid metal-frame glasses that could freeze to the skin. Side shields protect eyes from wind and side glare from the snow, and can be purchased separately and added to glasses, but they work best attached directly to the frames. When traveling through forested areas, the traveler should wear either sunglasses or goggles as protection from twigs and branches.

THE HANDS

The layering concept can be applied to keep hands warm while still allowing for finger dexterity. Generally, fingered gloves are less warm than mittens. To maximize warmth, a combination of both should be worn. An inner, fingered liner of silk, wool, or polypropylene will allow both dexterity and a little protection from the elements. A mitten worn over the liner will protect the hand from colder temperatures.

Mittens are available that allow for the portion over the fingers to be pulled back as needed. A pair of water-repellent or waterproof overmitts can be worn as an outer protective shell. Overmitts with a rubber-type grip surface on the palm and thumb are best. Overmitts should have a long cuff with a closure capability at the wrist. A nose-wipe cloth on the back of the glove is a luxury that can be added later.

Avoid leather gloves because leather absorbs moisture and takes a long time to dry. Since gloves are likely to become wet on a trip, always bring extra pairs. Extra neoprene gloves are handy when working in cold, wet conditions, such as when building snow caves or during rescue work. Since neoprene gloves are totally waterproof, a poly or fleece liner is necessary or the hands will sweat and actually get colder.

THE TORSO

The torso is the most vital part of the body for temperature regulation. Since much perspiration is emitted from the torso area, it is critical to have a good wicking and venting system.

Before the advent of soft wool synthetic products, few people felt comfortable wearing wool next to their skin. More and more, these products are becoming the norm for base layers, as well as other synthetics or silk. The wicking layer is usually a thin, snugly fitting pullover style with either a crew neck or a turtleneck. While the turtleneck style will be warmer, it vents poorly. Therefore, a front zipper that opens the turtleneck is desirable. Mesh in the underarm areas will enhance venting, too.

Depending on the temperature and activity, one to two medium-weight layers of wool or any of the synthetics can be added over the underwear for additional insulation. A combination of long-sleeved and vest-type garments provides a good mix for achieving adequate insulation while still maintaining mobility of the arms. Since venting is a major concern, garments with neck zippers (especially on turtlenecks) or full-length front zippers are the most versatile. A pullover sweater may work for one layer, but be aware of its limitations for easy venting.

The outer protective shell is usually some type of hooded parka. Since the traveler still may be working hard and producing much heat and perspiration, the shell must allow venting but still protect against the direct blast of the wind. Underarm zippers are most effective for providing good torso venting without having to leave the front of a jacket wide open. An added benefit of underarm zippers is the option of putting someone else's cold feet into armpits for rewarming without removing the outer layer. Finally, the hood should have a drawstring that allows for good closure around the head without blocking vision or limiting head movement.

THE LEGS

The layers covering the legs are similar to the torso's layers in thickness and materials. The wicking layer is often long underwear. The insulating layers are a matter of preference based on temperature and weather conditions and the activities being pursued. Some people prefer light- or medium-weight long underwear paired with fleece pants, topped with shell pants. Others forego the insulating layer and pair

medium-weight long underwear with soft shell or Gore-Tex pants, with either full length, half, or quarter side zippers.

An important consideration in pant selection is body excretion. When it is sub-zero, skin freezes very quickly. Pant design should accommodate bodily needs and minimize total exposure. On expedition-type trips, bibs are commonly used and quite effective. Other alternatives, such as ski pants with full length zippers can accommodate the needs of most patrollers.

Finally, all layers must be compatible. Having pit zippers or side zippers on only one layer will not do much good if the layers underneath do not have them as well.

THE FEET

A major clothing purchase should be a good pair of boots. Proper fit, durability, and waterproof construction are the primary criteria.

Socks should be selected first and worn while fitting boots. A wicking sock with a heavier insulating sock is recommended. The inner socks should not wrinkle, because wrinkles cause blisters.

The outer layer should not be too bulky as it will restrict circulation. Many socks are a blend of fibers to achieve insulation, durability, and a snug fit. The use of wool, silk, and synthetics applies here, as does the avoidance of cotton. The vapor barrier system also may work well to keep feet warm and socks dry. A thin plastic bag can be used, especially when first experimenting with this system. Placing the bag over a light layer of socks will feel most comfortable on the feet. Use of the VBL bag during the day will maximize insulation, although the feet will perspire and be wet. At night the VBL is removed and the feet and the inner socks are thoroughly dried. An extra pair of dry socks should be used for sleeping to prevent problems with immersion foot (also called trench foot), which is caused by prolonged exposure to damp, cold conditions.

Boots are designed according to the intended activity and must be compatible with the type of travel equipment being used. Plastic and leather boots are often used for mountaineering and cold-weather conditions, while lighter-weight canvas or fabric-top boots may be acceptable for summer hiking but generally are not waterproof or warm enough for mountain conditions during winter. If leather boots are purchased, the manufacturer's recommendations for care and maintenance must be followed. Frequent applications of the recommended waterproofing compound, especially around the welt and stitched seams, will help keep leather boots dry.

Some boots are made with soles and uppers that are molded together. This approach is less expensive to make and initially more waterproof than a stitched seam. Unfortunately, when this molded seam fails, as it eventually will, resoling is impossible.

The type of boot and its construction will determine the amount of insulation value. If boots are large enough, a foam foot pad can be inserted for additional insulation.

Fit is most important for proper function and comfort. The heel should be snug and allow no slippage. The toes should have ample wiggle room and not bang into the front of the boot when walking down a steep slope. When fitting, kick the toe of the boot into the floor to check for toe/boot clearance.

Above-the-ankle boots are necessary for ankle support on uneven surfaces, especially when wearing a heavy pack. Although most ski pants have gaiters built in, the use of independent gaiters in the backcountry prevents excessive snow from wetting pant legs, socks, and feet.

Gaiters, worn over the boot and lower leg, are made from nylon or pack cloth and are often reinforced with extra material on the inside ankle area, which is subject to cuts and rubbing from such things as ski edges, crampons, and snow surfaces. Gaiters made with waterproof material on the bottom half and breathable material on the upper half perform better overall. Gaiters with full-length heavy duty zippers or snaps are among the easiest to put on and the most durable. Velcro zipper flaps are a must to keep zippers from freezing and also provide a backup if zippers fail.

Insulated overboots that cover the complete boot are available to provide additional insulation for cold feet.

Extra footwear for camp may be taken on overnight trips. These can be pack boots or down, neoprene, or fleece booties inside waterproof outer shells. The boots worn during the day can be set out to dry or put in a nylon stuff sack inside a sleeping bag to keep warm for the morning. If using plastic boots, only the liner needs to go inside the bag (although it is important to make sure the outers are left wide open in case any moisture is present that can cause them to freeze shut). Bring extra socks, which may also be used as emergency hand protection.

CLOTHING REPAIR, CARE, AND MAINTENANCE

Regardless of cost, if a product does not work when needed, it is of no value. Because things do break and accidents can happen, the best defense is to carry a basic repair kit and to know how to repair clothing and equipment in the field. Duct tape, dental floss, pre-threaded, heavy sewing needles, and large safety pins will work for most clothing repairs.

It is important to check all clothing before and after each trip. The ends of zippers should be examined for wear and tears. Loose stitching or pulled threads should be resewn. If fabric is worn thin in an area, a patch of more durable material should be sewn on.

Clothes should be washed after each trip to maintain the full performance of the fabric. Synthetic-filled materials break down rapidly with repeated washings, so in some instances, if no serious soiling is present, leaving them in the sun will let UV rays clean them. All manufacturers' labels should be checked for cleaning care recommendations. When in doubt, hand wash garments with a detergent designed for hand washables. Most wools and silks must be hand washed or machine washed in the gentle cycle. For some wools, only dry cleaning is appropriate.

Polyester and polypropylene also benefit from regular washing. Line drying is recommended to prevent shrinkage. Special soaps are available to remove body odors that build up in polypropylene. Breathable fabrics should be washed regularly with plain detergent and line dried.

Down will lose its loft as it becomes dirty. However, too frequent washing is not recommended as it removes the natural oils. Hand wash down with mild, liquid soap (never use detergent) in a tub, or in a front-loading washer since the wet down gets very heavy and can tear the internal baffles if agitated too vigorously. Down products should be rinsed several times to remove all soap, then carefully squeezed to remove as much water as possible.

The wet down material should be placed over a large surface for air drying. It may take several days for the down to dry. The sun works best. When nearly dry, the down will still be lumpy. The down item can then be machine-dried on low heat. Clean tennis shoes or tennis balls placed in the tumble dryer with the down item will help break up the clumps of down. Alternately, some commercial cleaning businesses are experienced in washing down products.

All garments, as well as sleeping bags, should be stored unstuffed in a cool, dry, well-ventilated area. Be aware that the waterproof coating on fabrics used in tents, bivouac bags, etc. can be attacked by mold that partially dissolves the coating.

PACKING FOR MULTIDAY TRIPS

Even on day trips, bring some extra clothing. Extra insulating layers are needed during rest stops, and extra gloves, mittens, and a hat are important, as these are most likely to get wet. However, on multiday trips, what and how much to take becomes as much a packing problem as one of need. Most clothes do not compress well. The extra clothes plus all the camping paraphernalia must fit into a pack and still be light enough to carry. The traveler must carefully consider each item and the likelihood that it will be needed.

Generally, the amount of extra clothing taken on a multiday trip will be dictated by the local climate, the current weather in the area, and by the type of activity. In a rainy, warmer climate the chance of getting wet is greater than in a dry, cold climate. In wetter climates, the temperature extremes are less severe than at high altitudes or in dry climates. In drier climates, wet clothing can usually be dried more easily.

Snow caving requires additional discussion regarding clothing. The amount of energy required to build a snow cave or other winter shelter combined with the prolonged contact with the snow usually leaves the traveler very wet. Bring extra clothing for this endeavor, and a waterproof outer layer. Extra waterproof or neoprene mittens or gloves are helpful as well. Before starting, strip down to a level compatible with an active body. Make camp early because extra time will be needed to dry out clothing after snow cave building.

DRYING CLOTHING IN THE FIELD

The first rule in winter is to keep clothing dry. There will be fewer wet clothes to contend with if proper venting and layering techniques are used. If the weather turns foul, consider making camp rather than continuing to travel and arriving at the next camp totally soaked. Returning home is always an option. However, weather, mishaps, and normal body perspiration make it likely that some damp or wet clothing will need drying. Even in the wettest climates, it is possible to dry out clothing.

The sun is an efficient drying machine. On very long trips it may be necessary to devote a sunny afternoon or a complete day to thoroughly drying as many items as possible, especially sleeping bags.

Avoid exposing clothing to direct heat from cook stoves or fire, since most synthetics will melt if overheated and holes are easily burned into clothing and bags from sparks. Leather as well as plastic boots are quickly ruined if exposed too long to high temperatures.

Heat generated by the body is one of the most effective means of drying damp clothes. More heat is generated when moving than when inert at night, so putting wet items on thighs or belly when skiing during the day can be quite effective for drying them out. If something is really wet, all the free water should be wrung out. Swinging the garment can expel additional water by centrifugal force, but care must be taken with delicate items.

The laws of physics dictate that heat flows from warm to cold and moisture from wet to dry, so wicking materials such as polypropylene are effective for drying. Small items can be placed between two insulating layers in the torso area, though adequate venting must be provided for the water vapor to escape. At night, damp items can be put into sleeping bags, though this will only work efficiently with synthetic fill bags, since down will absorb the moisture. Very wet items should first be wrung out and then placed between the sleeping bag and the sleeping mat to start the drying process. Synthetic fills have the ability to sublimate water, moving it from a solid to a gaseous state without going through a liquid stage, so simply hanging a sleeping bag wet with moisture from clothing will cause the moisture to freeze, then dry, through the sublimation process. The greater the temperature variation, the quicker this occurs.

SUMMARY
o Clothing is important to survival.
o Proper clothing, properly worn and cared for, will make the difference between a comfortable and safe trip and a miserable, hazardous one.
o Garments made of cotton should be avoided when dressing for mountain environments.
o When dressing for the backcountry, travelers should employ the layering system: the wicking layer that keeps the skin dry; the insulation layer; and the protective layer, a shell that allows perspiration to escape while keeping moisture from entering.
o People think and function more effectively when warm and dry.

CHAPTER 5

SLEEPING SYSTEMS

Keith Gale, Pinecrest Nordic Ski Patrol, Pinecrest, California

OBJECTIVES

o Describe the importance of a comfortable, efficient sleeping system in the backcountry.

o Compare and contrast sleeping bag materials and construction.

o Explain the importance of understanding temperature variables when choosing a sleeping system for backcountry use.

Sleeping is an important part of your outdoor adventure. The basics of your sleeping system are similar in concept to the layering and materials you consider when choosing clothing (Figure 5-1).

A well-designed sleeping system consists of the following:

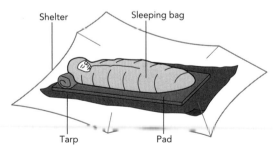

Figure 5-1. *The sleeping system*

» Sleeping bag
» Ground insulation (pad)
» Moisture protection (tarp)
» Sleeping bag liner (optional)
» Shelter

SLEEPING BAG

A good sleeping bag will keep you comfortable and help you sleep well. Sleeping bag design includes several important factors:

» Insulating materials
» Comfort rating
» Shell material

» Weight of bag
» Gender of user
» Shape, length, and fit
» Baffle construction
» Durability
» Compressible size

INSULATING MATERIALS

One of the most important considerations in a sleeping bag is its insulating material because it traps warm air and keeps it close to the body. The more insulation there is in the sleeping bag, the taller the bag will be when it is laid out flat. This is what is referred to as "loft." More loft usually indicates a lower temperature rating and a warmer bag. The higher the quality of the insulating material, the more efficient it is at trapping air.

The goal is to have a bag that is warm, light, and compressible. Sleeping bags are insulated with both natural down and synthetic materials. A high-quality insulating material makes a sleeping bag lighter and more compressible for a given temperature rating.

Down

High-quality down bags are generally more compressible and lighter than synthetic bags. As a rule, down also has a greater warmth-to-weight ratio than synthetic insulating material. However, in order for down insulation to be effective, it must be kept dry. Wet down loses its loft and ability to insulate. Fortunately, improvements in sleeping bag shell material mean that less moisture is able to permeate either a down or synthetic bag.

When the term "down" is used in the context of sleeping bags, the most dominant material is goose down. Down quality is dependent upon the age and maturity of the bird and the processing of the down. The best down comes from larger, more mature birds. Goose down is generally better than duck down although slightly less water resistant when age and maturity of the birds are equal. More mature goose down has larger filament clusters than that of younger birds. These clusters, when grouped, provide many more trapped air pockets and therefore provide better insulation and loft.

To maximize the effectiveness of down clusters, the proper processing of the down (sorting, washing, and drying) is required to open them up. Higher fill power means higher loft, better insulation, lighter weight, and greater durability. Allergies to down are most often attributed not to the down itself but to poor quality down contaminated with dust, irritants, and mites.

Synthetics

Synthetic bags, such as those made with Thinsulate, tend to be a little heavier and less compressible than down bags.

However, synthetic insulation does retain some insulating value when wet. Synthetic bags may not last as long as down bags but they are easier to launder.

Synthetics achieve their loft performance through two design considerations:

» Material thermal properties—manufacturing techniques consisting of crimping (increasing the dead air spaces)
» Filament thickness

By varying the fiber characteristics manufacturers can produce different comfort effects and improve the thermal efficiency of the fill or batting. Manufacturers can vary the fiber diameter and length, the shape of the fiber cross-section, the fiber crimp, and the size and shape of the hollows inside of the fiber. The batting producers will even vary the thickness, weight, and density of the bats, or fiber mats.

Continuous filament insulation material is common and commercially available in the marketplace under many trade names. This type of material is inexpensive and has good mechanical performance, but the thermal performance is significantly poorer than higher quality synthetic and down insulation. A significant advantage of a continuous filament construction is that the resulting web of filaments has a high degree of mechanical integrity, which facilitates ease of handling in any subsequent

manufacturing process and improves the insulation's durability. In assembling sleeping bags and insulating clothing, shingle construction techniques minimize cold spots that usually exist at quilting lines. Cut pieces or sheets of fill are stitched to the shell and lining. They overlap like shingles. Any one point of the sleeping bag has several layers to reduce heat loss.

The insulating properties of fibrous materials improve with reduced diameter of the fibers until an optimum fiber diameter is reached; thereafter further reduction in the diameter of the fibers results in a decrease in the thermal performance of the material. For polyester material a diameter of approximately six microns is the optimum for maximum insulating properties. At any fiber diameter greater than this the thermal insulation properties decrease with increasing fiber diameter. At diameters that are more than three times this minimum the thermal performance of fibrous insulation material starts to deteriorate significantly.

One of the problems with high loft continuous filament insulators is they are generally composed of microfibers of the order of 23-micron diameter. This means they are less efficient as insulators and are much stiffer in compression than high end synthetic fibers or natural down. This compressional stiffness is a distinct disadvantage since sleeping bags containing commercial, high loft insulators cannot be packed into as small a volume as similarly rated down bags.

Down consists of fibers having a range of diameters; these can be classified as hollow microfibers contributing the principal insulation efficiency, and larger hollow fibers providing desirable compressional and lofting characteristics. It is the interaction of the two that provides the unique properties of natural down. Synthetic material achieves its thermal performance by the use of small diameter fibers with the addition of small fractions of larger diameter fibers and/or bonding agents to enhance the mechanical behavior in an attempt to mimic the warmth and compressibility of down. The types and forms of synthetic fibers will vary greatly in both diameter and length. Most are hollow to help them better trap air and fibers, while some are treated with silicone to improve loft.

COMFORT RATING

There are many comfort ratings available for the consumer. Typically these ratings range from 45 to –40 degrees F. The European Norm has four ratings for each temperature: Upper Limit, Comfort, Low Comfort, and Extreme:

Upper Limit. The temperature at which a typical person can sleep without excessive perspiration. It is established with the hood and zippers open and with the arms outside of the bag.

Comfort. The temperature at which a typical person can expect to sleep comfortably in a relaxed position.

Low Comfort. The temperature at which a typical person can sleep for eight hours in a curled position without waking.

Extreme. The minimum temperature at which a typical person can remain for six hours without risk of death from hypothermia (though frostbite is still possible).

SHELL MATERIAL

The sleeping bag shell consists of the outer and inner shell layers. Sometimes these differ to provide more comfort.

The outer shell of a sleeping bag is typically made of nylon, polyester, or other synthetic materials such as Gore-Tex in order to be both tough and light weight. Ultralight sleeping bags use very thin fabric to decrease weight; therefore, the material is more easily damaged and requires careful handling. Trading weight for durability requires being conscientious about protecting and caring for your equipment.

Many bags feature a shell fabric treated with a durable water repellent (DWR) finish, a treatment that allows water to bead up rather than soak through fabric. Water resistance is a valuable characteristic. It keeps the bag from becoming wet and losing its insulating ability. However, the shell should not be waterproof because water vapor from your body needs to pass through easily enough to prevent saturation from inside the bag. Wet insulation loses its ability to retain heat.

Sleeping bag linings should promote the transfer of body moisture, so DWR is not used here. The liner can also be thinner and lighter than the outer shell due to the decreased likelihood of damage from rough handling.

WEIGHT

Weight is a critical consideration and is determined by the insulation, shell material, and temperature rating. There are other design considerations that contribute to weight, including the following:

Zipper

The length and width of a zipper contribute to a sleeping bag's weight. Although zipless bags exist, virtually all sleeping bags have zippers of varying lengths because they make entering and exiting sleeping bags easier. Zippers also help regulate body temperature in warmer conditions by allowing the bag to be opened from the top or bottom.

The length of a zipper thus becomes a balance between weight and versatility. A full-length zipper means a sleeping bag can be opened flat out. A half-length zipper allows only partial venting and is slightly harder to get in and out of. A zip-less design means that the bag will have to be worn like an outer clothing layer without a way to adjust for temperature. Getting into a zipless bag is much like sliding on an oversized sock, and it is not recommended if you are claustrophobic. The benefit of zipless bags is that they are lightweight and compact. A design such as the elephant foot bag is a particularly good choice for emergency shelter situations.

Stuff sack

Stuff sacks can add from one to ten ounces to the bag's weight. Its only functions are to protect the bag during transport and to keep the bag in an easy-to-handle package. Other factors to consider are the sack's water repellency, lightness, and durability. Most sleeping bags come with their own appropriately sized stuff sack, adequate for most circumstances. The stuff sack is not an appropriate container for long-term storage of the sleeping bag because it compresses the insulation and over time may be detrimental to your bag's temperature rating. A storage sack at least three times the stuffed volume should be used; most high quality bags are sold with a storage sack as well as a stuff sack.

GENDER

Because of the physiological differences between males and females, the industry is creating unique designs for women. These design considerations include narrower shoulders, wider hips, and more insulation in the foot box and the core. Women tend to sleep 8 percent cooler than men; thus they need to consider warmer bags for the same environment than do men. Conditions requiring a 20 degree F bag for a man may require a 15 degree F bag for a woman. Having a properly fitted bag decreases the dead air space in the bag and keeps the occupant warmer.

SHAPE, LENGTH, AND FIT

Before purchasing a sleeping bag, you should "try it on." You wouldn't purchase a piece of clothing without checking the fit, so why should a sleeping bag be any different?

There are two common bag shapes: mummy shaped and rectangular/comfort shaped. Because the mummy shape more closely represents the human body, it has better performance characteristics. The lower amount of dead space requires less heat generation and reduces heat loss. The most dominant detriments to sleep cycles are bursts of cold air as a person moves about in the sleeping bag. The mummy bag reduces the size of these bursts and thus provides better conditions for deeper sleep. Mummy bags typically come with a hood, which add tremendous warmth when tightened about the head and face. Some bags also come with a neck collar, which reduces air exchange around the neck and shoulders.

There are typically two lengths for each design: regular and long. Regular typically fits individuals six feet tall or less, and long fits people six feet, six inches or less. There are a few designers that address female-specific bags in shorter sizes. A good fit is important, but it's also important to consider using the sleeping bag as a warmer and dryer for your damp clothes in cold and wet weather applications. If you are less than six feet tall, it may be worth considering a "long" and using the extra space (with its requisite additional weight of about five ounces) for this purpose. Be sure to shake off all excess snow and moisture prior to bringing garments inside your bag. Differential cut is a manufacturing technique in which the outer surface of the top side of the sleeping bag is wider than the lower, inside surface, which helps the fill to expand outward from the centrally located body position, thus facilitating optimum lofting.

Differential fill means that the quantity of insulation in the base is less than the quantity in the top of the sleeping bag. Many manufacturers use a fill ratio of 3:2 (discounting the hood, neck, and zipper baffles). Hence the base has 40 percent of the total insulation instead of the 50 percent it would have if there were no differential fill. The compaction of the base restricts loft and reduces its insulation value so the difference in warmth is insignificant.

On the other hand, having 60 percent in the top adds a significant warmth benefit compared with 50 percent, since no compaction means that the extra fill traps a fully proportionate extra quantity of air, and loft is increased by a fifth. The downside is that although the warmth is optimally distributed when you are lying on your back, to roll on your side you have to roll inside the bag. This means that the hood of the bag is sideways and you are breathing into your bag, allowing moisture to collect there. The other option is to roll the bag with you but this exposes the less insulated side of the bag.

BAFFLE CONSTRUCTION

Baffle describes the space between the outer shell and the inner lining. These chambers are used to hold the insulating material uniformly throughout the volume of the sleeping bag and to prevent the insulation from clumping together in one area. The more aggressive the baffle construction, the less down shifting will occur, the better air will be trapped, and the warmer the bag will be.

The baffle types listed below start with the most basic stitch-through type, increasing in thermal efficiency up to the uncompromising build quality of offset double box wall, or brick baffles.

Stitch-through

The simplest form of baffles is the stitch-through method, wherein the shell and lining are stitched together to create the chambers into which the down is inserted. This system is used on very lightweight products as it allows a limited volume for the down to loft in. This method also allows heat to leak through the corners around the seams where down cannot fill.

Advanced baffle construction techniques

To create a suitable chamber that allows the down to loft and to minimize heat loss, it's necessary to have sidewalls that are between the sleeping bag shell and lining. The generic method is called the box wall construction, which forms the basis of the five major kinds of baffles found in sleeping bags, listed below in order of increasing thermal efficiency.

Box wall. The simplest of the box wall variations, the basic box wall has vertical sidewalls to keep the insulation in place and has no "lines of cold." A uniform thickness of insulation is present throughout the sleeping bag, greatly improving performance compared to stitch-through construction.

Slant box wall. A slanted wall construction creates a more difficult path for heat to escape along the relatively low-density insulation area against the sidewall. This improves the thermal efficiency of the bag even more than box wall construction.

Trapezoidal box wall. This is a popular design for high-quality sleeping bags, as it provides a good compromise between warmth and weight—warmer than box wall, yet lighter than V-tube construction.

V-tube. Here, each baffle sidewall is inclined at an angle and joins its neighbor to form a series of V baffles. For a given size of bag and for a constant width of baffle, the greatest number of baffles is obtained using the V design. V-tubes give twice as many baffles as box wall construction, given equal measurements. For a fixed quantity of down, the more baffles there are, the less chance of the down being displaced. Hence, V-tube construction is better than box wall in regards to warmth. Its disadvantages are weight and cost since it requires twice the number of baffles and additional sidewall fabric.

Offset double box wall. The two box wall layers, one on top of the other, have their baffle walls offset relative to each other, which creates an appearance similar to that of a brick wall. Brick construction is used in sleeping bags that contain a large amount of insulation material.

Perpendicular double box wall. Taking the double box wall one step further, this baffle configuration uses an outer layer of horizontal baffles and an inner layer of vertical baffles to minimize down shifting when rolling from side to side.

Side baffles. Sleeping bags basically have two halves—the top, above the sleeper, and the bottom, below (and compressed by) the sleeper. The top and bottom halves are normally separated by the zipper on one side and a side baffle on the other. Some sleeping bags do not have a side baffle deliberately, so the fill can be shifted from the top to the bottom and vice versa.

The side baffle can be a source of heat loss because down does not always sit in this area well. Consequently, in warmer and more sophisticated designs, an actual chamber (V-tube side baffle) is used for the full length of the bag.

Zipper baffles. Obviously, the most efficient and lightest sleeping bag design would have no zippers. Zippers are heavy, and they're also a source of heat loss. To minimize heat loss, zipper baffles have to be added, thus increasing weight. In cold conditions a lot of body warmth is lost through zippers. Baffles insulate the zipper area and reduce drafts. In lighter weight bags, single baffles are the norm. For extremely cold climates, two overlapping baffles are more effective.

HOOD DESIGN AND NECK COLLARS

The greatest area of heat loss is the head. In cold conditions, closing the hood around the head is critical. This is accomplished with a simple adjustable draw cord. Sleeping bags designed for cold areas usually have more sophisticated, ergonomic hood designs to efficiently envelope the head.

Similarly it is possible for a lot of body warmth to escape from the inside of the bag up past the neck and shoulders. Many cold weather sleeping bags have a neck/shoulder collar, again with an adjustable draw cord. In some bags this collar is removable.

OPTIONAL EQUIPMENT

When purchasing a sleeping bag it is worth considering the following additional items.

GROUND INSULATION
A pad between the sleeping and the ground is a crucial component of a sleeping system. Three main material choices exist:

» Open cell foam
» Closed cell foam
» Inflatable

Of these three choices, closed cell foam and inflatable pads are preferable and may sometimes be used in combination. Open cell pads are easily compressed, creating thin spots at the hips and shoulders and providing a path for heat to escape. Open cell pads can also absorb moisture, becoming heavy and losing much of their insulating value. Open cell pads are not recommended.

The closed cell pad provides a superior thermal barrier. It tends to compress less, reducing cold spots, and doesn't absorb moisture. Closed cell pads are also extremely tough. Even if the pad has holes or is torn, it can still provide effective insulation.

Inflatable pads are more compact, but they tend to be the heaviest choice. Lighter inflatable pads exist with no foam interior. These pads pack smaller but take more time to inflate. They can provide good insulation, prevent cold spots if fully inflated, and be quite comfortable. The downside is that they are not as damage-tolerant as closed cell pads and may leak air if punctured. This can be a serious problem, especially in cold conditions. Therefore, they are often used in combination with a closed cell pad. One excellent cold-weather system is a full-length closed cell pad for insulation and a three-quarter length inflatable for weight savings and comfort. The insulating sleeping pad should be full length to provide adequate insulation for your feet. Make sure the pad fits in your tent. The difference in weight between full and three-quarter length pads (about two to six ounces) is not a worthwhile trade-off for cold weather and snow performance.

MOISTURE PROTECTION
Keeping your sleeping bag protected from the shelter floor is the best way to keep it dry. Some sleeping bags have a slot in which to insert the sleeping pad. To ensure

that moisture does not compromise the sleeping bag in a snow shelter, lay a ground sheet below the pad. The ground sheet needs to have a larger footprint than the sleeping pad. Your winter parka or outer shell can be zipped up and worn over the outside of the foot of the sleeping bag to prevent contact with the side of a snow cave and to prevent getting the foot of the bag wet. A bivy sack may also be useful in a snow shelter. For tent camping, the footprint of the tent provides the necessary moisture protection.

SLEEPING BAG LINERS

To add some warmth to your sleeping system, a sleeping bag liner may be used. A liner provides a layer of protection to the inner shell material, thus reducing washing cycles, which negatively impact durability.

Three sleeping bag liner materials:

» Silk
» Synthetic
» Cotton

Similar to their sleeping bag brethren, sleeping bag liners come in both mummy and rectangular design. It is optimal to match the liner shape to the bag shape but it's not essential. Silk and synthetic tend to cling tightly to your body, so micro bursts of cold air are mitigated. Cotton tends to absorb moisture, leaving you chilled. It also tends to be heavier. Using silk or synthetic, the maximum temperature increase is about 10 degrees F; cotton adds approximately 5 degrees F.

OTHER SLEEPING SYSTEM CONSIDERATIONS

Your sleeping comfort is affected by many factors. Some you may control, others you may not.

All temperature comfort ratings presume that you are well fed, well hydrated, and wearing an upper and lower body base layer and socks. Ideally these base layers are clean and dry. Remove day-worn underwear and dedicate a clean, dry set just for sleeping. You can increase heating efficiency simply by adding a layer to your head, where almost 60 percent of body heat is lost.

Proper hydration (to insure the heat is distributed throughout the body) and food consumption (the fuel for the heat) is paramount to a proper night's sleep. Do not consume alcohol; it can help with falling asleep but interferes with later stages of sleep. Avoid caffeine prior to bedtime. Restrict nicotine.

Slight activity before bedtime increases blood circulation and thus warmth. Do not exert to the point of perspiration. Exhaustion reduces the body's ability to maintain temperature regulation.

Urine bottles for both men and women (female adapters are available) can come in handy, reducing the need to exit the shelter and expose your body to the elements.

Urine bottles should be clearly marked, have a wide mouth and tight sealing lid, and hold at least one quart. Waiting to urinate only deprives you of sleep. If you awaken needing to relieve yourself, do so immediately.

Sleeping with your head inside the bag is ill advised because it builds up harmful moisture inside the bag and restricts the exchange of oxygen. It is possible to increase carbon dioxide concentrations to levels that can awaken a sleeper. Keep your face outside the bag.

There are also some important personal considerations to keep in mind:

» Age: More mature individuals do not require as much sleep as younger, active members. Older people feel the cold more than young adults. Also, young children cannot self-regulate their temperature very well.

» Body build: A slim man at five feet, six inches fits a sleeping bag differently than a large six-foot man, so both men may find that the same bag feels warmer or cooler.

» Body weight: A light layer of body fat insulates you against cold, but the larger the surface area of the body, the easier it is to lose heat.

» General health: Medical conditions may make one person more susceptible to cold or heat than another. Circulatory problems can affect the tolerance of cold and resistance to frostbite. Additionally, medications may have an effect on a person's ability to withstand cold or heat.

SUMMARY
o A backcountry sleeping system consists of a sleeping bag, ground insulation, moisture protection, and a shelter.
o Sleeping bags generally come in two shapes (mummy and rectangular), range from simple to more complex baffle construction, and are filled with materials ranging from goose down to synthetic fibers.
o Factors affecting sleep include age, body build, weight, circulation issues, medications, comfort level, hydration, and nutrition.

CHAPTER 6

EMERGENCY SHELTERS

Bob Hollingsworth, Mount Baker Ski Patrol, Glacier, Washington
Jason Kammerer, Mount Baker Ski Patrol, Glacier, Washington
Jeff Leenstra, Mount Baker Ski Patrol, Glacier, Washington

OBJECTIVES

o Describe the purpose of emergency shelters and the features that distinguish them from camping shelters.

o Identify types of shelters that are appropriate in emergency situations.

o Explain the techniques necessary in constructing emergency shelters.

In the event of an emergency, backcountry recreationists—even those who are venturing out just for the day—need to be prepared to spend a night outside. Furthermore, it is imperative that ski patrollers and search-and-rescue (SAR) personnel who may be called on to operate outside of serviced ski areas be properly outfitted in order to be part of the solution rather than part of the problem.

From a shelter perspective, the ski patroller must be equipped with a sturdy shovel, avalanche transceiver, probe, and a tarpaulin, bivy sack, or poncho. Raingear and extra dry clothing are advised if

digging a cave is a possibility. Also, in compactable snow areas such as the Pacific Northwest, a snow saw is a valuable tool for shelter construction. The more equipped a recreationist is, the smoother an emergency situation can go.

Whether a person is forced into an emergency bivouac or simply chooses to sleep outdoors, many of the same general principles apply regardless of the season. The backcountry recreationist should use knowledge and experience to locate a campsite respecting the local ecology, the safety of group members, protection from the elements, and convenience to the objective. As with most endeavors, the proper equipment and experience make for a backcountry operation that is both safe and productive.

Many factors influence a person's decision to construct a shelter. The primary reason is the need to protect oneself—and/or an injured person—from the weather. Two basic requirements for doing this successfully are an insulating layer underneath and a waterproof and windproof layer over the top of the occupants.

The amount of available time to construct the shelter and the anticipated length of stay influences what type and where the shelter is constructed. Safety and accessibility need to be considered, as well as the shelter inhabitants' physical conditions. How long the shelter is expected to be used not only influences decisions about the type of shelter to be constructed but also where to construct it.

Immediate safety concerns in all seasons—such as inclement weather, rockfall potential, creek beds, and widow-maker trees—should be evaluated no matter what type of shelter is constructed. In winter, factors such as avalanche zones, hanging seracs, and additional snow on existing snowpack—particularly if the stay may extend through weather changes—need to be considered.

Although emergency shelters can help a person retain body temperature, humans also need external heat sources. If a fire is needed it should be made as efficiently as possible with additional structures to aid in reflecting and retaining heat, optimally guiding it into the structure. In a more sophisticated structure, such as a snow cave, burning a few candles inside can easily raise the temperature at least 10 degrees F, although the shelter must be adequately vented. Sometimes, however, all that is needed is a hot cup of cocoa from a backpacking stove.

TYPES OF SHELTERS

The following are different types of emergency shelters, progressing from the most simple to the more complex. When preparing an emergency shelter, keep in mind

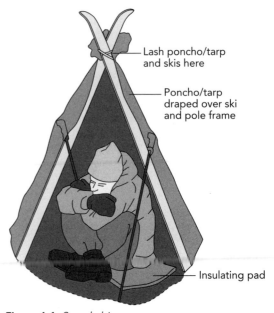

Lash poncho/tarp and skis here

Poncho/tarp draped over ski and pole frame

Insulating pad

Figure 6-1. *Sample bivouac*

the importance of quickly and efficiently constructing an enclosure with materials immediately available.

BIVOUAC

This most fundamental shelter, an improvised bivouac, or bivy, consists of a ground insulating layer and a waterproof, windproof layer over the top of the occupants. It may be as simple as a space blanket to wrap around a person and a foam pad large enough to sit on inside the space blanket.

An effective bivouac can be quickly constructed with skis, poles, and a lightweight tarp (Figure 6-1). It is most effective on the lee side of some natural obstacle. While not luxurious, its purpose is to allow the body a few hours rest until daybreak.

Some bivouacs are more sophisticated, with a lightweight, waterproof, and windproof outer layer and an insulated sleeping bag combined with a sleeping pad. Compact, lightweight sleeping bags, such as elephant foot bags, are excellent choices in emergency situations. This type of bag, which comes to the armpits, can be combined with a warm jacket to keep a person warm during an emergency.

HASTY SHELTERS

Shelters that have to be made with little or no snow must utilize existing structures such as rocks and trees, either exclusively or in conjunction with snow and/or tarps (Figure 6-2).

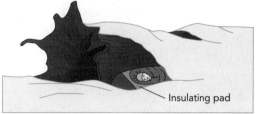

Natural opening in drift

Insulating pad

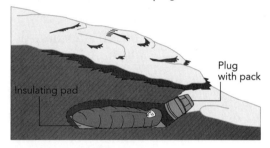

Natural cave beneath buried sapling

Insulating pad

Plug with pack

Natural hollow in snow at tree base

Skis covered with plastic tarp for wind protection

Pad on ground for insulation and dryness

Snow block anchors

Figure 6-2. *Using large natural objects*

Since the patroller or recreationist is constructing something around pre-existing objects, imagination is required since no two shelters are the same. Common useful items to look for are large rocks with noticeable overhangs and downed trees. Tree wells can also be used. However, in deep snow it is advisable to avoid trees with branches low on the trunk, such as fir and spruce, since time can easily be wasted fighting these buried branches. Also be aware that tree wells in deep snow can become traps for the unwary.

Tarps are quick to set up and may be the only alternative in an emergency, but they offer limited protection from weather, rodents, and insects. Tarp corners need to be anchored to trees, or tied to rocks or sticks, which are then buried. A cozy shelter can be constructed in minutes by throwing a tarp over a horizontal tree, burying the edges of the tarp, and using snow blocks or branches to close the ends.

The advantage of building shelters in winter is that snow may often be used for fast and easy construction. Backcountry ski patrollers need to carry shovels in order to construct shelters and perform avalanche rescues. There are an infinite number of ways to construct a snow shelter, but hasty shelters are useful for immediate need. Following is one example.

Snow Trench

A snow trench (Figure 6-3) is a simple shelter, constructed by digging a trench large enough to lie in, typically 3½ feet wide, 2½ feet deep, and 7 feet long. Pile the excavated snow on both sides of the trench; this reduces the depth required. To finish it, some sort of roof needs to be constructed over the trench. If the snow is consolidated it can be cut in blocks and leaned against other blocks to make an A-frame over a trench. A tarp with buried corners can also serve as a roof.

A few easy modifications include undercutting the sides so the floor is wider than the opening at the top, digging the trench a foot wider (4½ feet total), then using the additional space to dig a foot-wide trench below the sleeping platform for a cold sink. The term "cold sink" arises from simple physics. Hot air rises and cold air sinks, especially in areas with limited air movement such as igloos and snow caves. Thus

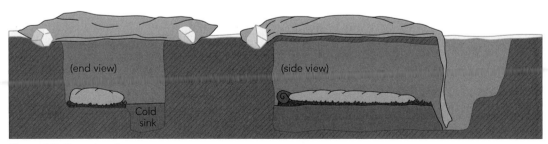

Figure 6-3. *Snow trench*

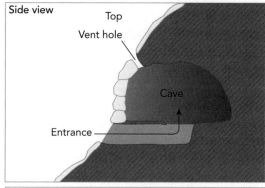

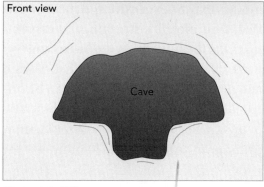

Figure 6-4. *"T" type snow cave*

cold air tends to settle at floor level where the inhabitants are. The secret for comfort is to dig a pit, a cold sink, where the cold air will settle, leaving the floor level somewhat warmer. You may dig it several feet longer for a fire pit, though the roof should not cover the area over the fire.

Some additional pointers:

» A plastic roof should slope slightly so condensation runs down the sheet and does not drip on the inhabitants.

» If using a brush roof, three to five inches of snow may be put on top of the roof for insulation and to serve as a windbreak.

» For an open-front lean-to, a good supply of wood is needed for a fire in front, or snow blocks should be made for sealing the entry.

» If the snowpack is marginal, boot pack an area the size of the trench then allow a half hour to an hour to elapse for the snow to harden. Then cut the snow into blocks and use them to build the perimeter of the trench in order to get enough depth. It may be necessary to boot pack another area to harvest additional blocks, depending on the snow depth.

SNOW CAVES

Snow caves take more time to build than hasty shelters. They are constructed either into the side of a hill or on flat terrain, and because of the need to work inside the cave the builder will likely get wet. Snow caves require more planning than hasty shelters.

The minimum additional equipment necessary to build a snow cave includes an extra pair of gloves and a full change of clothes. The advantage of a cave is that it provides longer-term protection if help is not anticipated for some time, or if the location is to be revisited. Caves are also much quieter in windy conditions and much warmer than a tent (Figure 6-4).

Some basic components of cave construction include

» an elevated sleeping platform to capture warmer air.

» a smooth, convex roof inside the cave, which prevents snow from dripping as it melts.

» a ski pole pushed through the roof to provide ventilation.

» enough structural roof strength to hold additional weight from snowfall. Usually a thickness of at least 12 inches of reasonably consolidated snow is adequate, though some sagging may occur if the snow is soft. Excessive snow accumulation on the roof and/or too large an unsupportive span inside the cave may result in a collapse, which can be dangerous.

One technique for building a cave is to dig a T horizontally into the side of a hill. The two arms become the sleeping platforms. Additional fingers will accommodate more personnel. After excavating, the top of the T slot is closed off with snow blocks, making the lower portion of the center trench the entrance. Always cordon off the surface area above the cave with flagging and ski poles to prevent people from walking over the top of the cave and causing a collapse. When making a snow shelter, another person should be standing by with a shovel in case a collapse occurs with someone inside.

TENTS

Tents provide a mobile shelter from sun, precipitation, and wind. Although some models may be expensive and must be carried, their mobility, strength, and easy setup make them useful in the backcountry.

Tents can be quite noisy in heavy wind and need to be anchored. They can be oriented to face the morning sun for warmth, or positioned on the lee side of rocks, snow drifts, or in groves of trees to minimize the wind.

In some SAR missions, an injured recreationist may not be prepared with a tent and a sleeping bag. Therefore it's a good idea for rescuers to carry extras for the lost/injured party. Ultimately patrollers need to plan ahead in order to provide proper overnight shelters in the backcountry for themselves and those they rescue.

SUMMARY

o Ski patrollers and emergency responders called on to operate in backcountry rescues must be properly outfitted with emergency shelter materials to protect themselves and their patients from weather and elements. The more prepared backcountry recreationists are with emergency shelter materials, the better the outcome usually is.

o When constructing an emergency shelter on a SAR mission, two basic requirements are an insulating layer underneath and a waterproof and windproof layer over the top of the patroller and/or his or her patient.

o Emergency shelters include improvised bivouacs, hasty shelters, snow caves, and tents; they are selected depending on available materials and time constraints.

CHAPTER 7

ESSENTIAL AND GROUP EQUIPMENT

Chuck White, Mountain Travel & Rescue Manual Coordinator,
Mount Holly Ski Patrol, Holly, Michigan

OBJECTIVES

o Identify and explain the purpose of including the 10 essential categories of equipment for both individuals and to groups in backcountry settings.
o Explain the importance and methods of selecting and checking equipment prior to a trip.
o Describe techniques of organizing personal and group equipment.

Mountain travel for either a recreational tour or a search-and-rescue (SAR) mission requires considerable equipment in addition to the necessary clothing, food, and water that must be transported by the individual or group. During the 1930s The Mountaineers—a hiking and climbing organization and the parent organization of The Mountaineers Books—developed a list of 10 items to always bring into the backcountry (Table 7-1). This list has evolved through the years from 10 individual items to a systems approach that reflects new technologies. However, the Ten Essentials' purpose remains the same: to give backcountry

TABLE 7-1. THE TEN ESSENTIALS

1. Navigation (map and compass)
2. Sun protection (sunglasses and sunscreen)
3. Insulation (extra clothing)
4. Illumination (headlamp or flashlight)
5. First-aid supplies
6. Fire (firestarter and matches/lighter)
7. Repair kit and tools (including knife)
8. Nutrition (extra food)
9. Hydration (extra water)
10. Emergency shelter

—The Mountaineers

travelers the ability to respond positively to an accident or emergency and to include the equipment necessary to spend a night or more in the outdoors.

How you carry these essentials—either in a pouch or in your pack—is up to you. And how you as a ski patroller, rescuer, or backcountry recreationist modify this list to reflect your patrol division's unique preferences, your circumstances, or the terrain and climate you travel through is a group or individual's call (Table 7-2).

THE TEN ESSENTIALS

The Mountaineers recommends that all who venture into the backcountry carry these Ten Essentials with them on all trips. The first five are the most critical, though each item is important. The Ten Essentials allow the backcountry traveler to respond positively to an accident or emergency, and to spend a night or more out if necessary.

1. NAVIGATION

Topographic maps and compasses are standard gear. Global positioning satellite (GPS) devices and cell phones can be helpful but are useful only with charged batteries and strong satellite signals.

2. SUN PROTECTION

Sunglasses, sunscreen, lip salve, and sun-shielding clothing constructed with ultraviolet protection factor (UPF) all

---

TABLE 7-2. SUGGESTIONS FOR A PERSONAL SURVIVAL KIT, EXCLUDING CLOTHES

» A zippered pouch large enough to carry the following gear
» A sharp knife of appropriate size; Swiss army or lock back
» Personal meds, toilet paper
» Two types of firestarter (matches, striker and flint, butane lighter)
» Small flashlight or headlamp with extra batteries
» 50 feet of light cord
» Signaling devices; mirror and whistle
» Space blanket
» Heavy plastic garbage bags
» Sunscreen
» First-aid supplies (bare minimum: alcohol swabs, Band-Aids, moleskin)
» Folding water bottle, Ziploc bags or other water storage devices, plus purification tablets

---

provide protection against sun and wind. Make sure that the protection is adequate for the sensitivity of your own skin. Zinc oxide gives maximum protection and should be applied to sensitive areas such as the nose and ears. Unless materials are treated with UPF, hats and caps do not offer complete protection because the sun's rays reflected from the snow can cause severe sunburn. Be sure to apply sunscreen under the chin and around the nose and ears. Reapply sunscreen frequently.

3. INSULATION

Bringing gear for the unexpected is always in order. Lightweight, wicking, windproof, and waterproof are key characteristics for backcountry clothing.

4. ILLUMINATION

A flashlight or headlamp is an essential item for any backcountry travel. Headlamps are preferable as they leave both hands free to perform chores. For SAR missions, larger, more powerful lamps are often included in the group equipment. Regardless of what type of lamp is used, carry spare batteries and bulbs. Sometimes it is wise to carry a low-amp bulb or LED lights to conserve batteries. These bulbs do not provide the intense light of high-amp bulbs, but they provide sufficient light for camp chores. Use the highest quality batteries available. Some newer equipment uses flat disc batteries rather than the conventional AA or AAA and can be difficult to obtain.

5. FIRST-AID SUPPLIES

Each person should carry an individual first-aid kit to deal with headaches and muscle tenderness, and minor problems such as blisters, small cuts, and insect bites. A group first-aid kit should contain the supplies needed for dealing with a major mishap and needs to include rubber gloves, a pocket mask, and general first-aid supplies. SAR groups naturally carry more extensive first-aid and rescue kits.

6. FIRE

Your life might depend on a good supply of waterproof matches in a waterproof container. Waterproof matches can be purchased or can be made by dipping strike-anywhere kitchen matches in paraffin. Small wide-mouth plastic food containers provide good waterproof protection. To ensure a dry place to strike your matches, glue a piece of fine sandpaper inside the match-container lid.

Alternatives to matches include a welder's flint attached to a screw. Steel wool can be used to start a fire if dry tinder is not available. The lower branches of a pine tree offer a good source of dry pine needle tinder. A butane lighter may be difficult to use in very cold conditions.

In an emergency it may be necessary to build a fire for warmth or for drying wet clothing and/or equipment. When winter camping, a fire can be a source of warmth, comfort, and a beacon for rescue activities. Because it is difficult to find dry fire-building materials in winter, it is sometimes necessary to use commercial firestarters or candles to provide the initial heat to get the fire started. Fire tabs, fire gel, fire ribbon, and chemical powders are available commercially and provide enough heat to dry most tinder. Some people prefer candles as they can be used both to start fires and to provide light and warmth in shelters. When using candles for illumination in tents, it's best to enclose them in commercial candle lanterns.

7. REPAIR KIT AND TOOLS

A pocket knife is an invaluable tool and should be carried where it is easily reached. A knife's most important feature is its sharpness, so it should be kept sharp and in good condition. Consider both functionality and weight. Many people prefer various combination knives that provide other items useful for repairs and other camp chores. Attach the knife with a lanyard or cord to a belt loop or a small carabiner.

Carry a lightweight shovel as individual equipment; it's essential when constructing emergency shelters and when traveling in avalanche terrain. Many small shovels are constructed of plastic or metal, and are strong enough for the rigors of shelter construction or digging in avalanche debris. The scoop of the shovel should be big enough to move snow efficiently. If you choose a metal shovel try to get one that is coated to prevent snow from sticking. A removable handle is helpful for stowing and transporting.

It is a good idea to include signaling devices in your tool kit. Sometimes it is necessary to signal your position to aircraft, to other members of your group, or to SAR members. This can be accomplished with flashlights, signal mirrors, and strobe lights. Besides being useful for emergency shelters, a brightly colored tarp or piece of clothing can serve as a signaling device or landing marker for helicopters in SAR missions. A space blanket's shiny side can also be used as a reflecting device. Flashlights work best in good visibility, low-light conditions. The contrast is what attracts attention.

In addition, a non-breakable plastic whistle should be carried for signaling and communication. Many backpacks include whistles on sternum straps. Another option is to tie one on a lanyard so it can be worn around the neck and inside clothing so it doesn't freeze. Metal whistles are not recommended because they can freeze to your mouth in extreme cold.

Fifty feet or more of light nylon cord is useful for shelter construction, as part of a repair kit, for emergency toboggan construction, and many other uses.

8. NUTRITION

High energy snacks provide quick energy and many have a long shelf life. (See Chapter 3, Nutrition, for more information on selecting the best foods for refueling.)

9. HYDRATION

A means of carrying and purifying water is essential. Wide-mouth bottles, collapsible hydration bags, purification tablets, handheld water purifiers, and compact water filters are available at outdoor retailers. (See Chapter 2, Water and Hydration, regarding the importance of proper hydration.)

10. EMERGENCY SHELTER

Portable shelter materials such as heavy-gauge garbage bags, plastic sheeting, or rain ponchos are lightweight and can be multifunctional. A nylon tarp or space blanket provides protection from wind and wetness. Make sure the tarp or blanket has plenty of grommets for tying. (See Chapter 6, Emergency Shelters, for descriptions of the various types of shelters.)

GROUP GEAR

In addition to the individual's Ten Essentials, backcountry groups as well as SAR teams should always be equipped with the following items. This equipment can often mean the difference between an unsuccessful trip or rescue, and one that ends with a safe and healthy outcome.

THERMOMETER

A thermometer should be included in the group's equipment. Many individuals carry a thermometer to determine the proper ski wax to use, for forecasting the weather, determining clothing and shelter needs, and for snow pit analysis.

STROBE LIGHT

For all light and visibility conditions, a high-intensity, omni-directional, stroboscopic lamp or strobe lamp is best. High intensity means that it's extremely bright, making it visible in all light conditions and poor visibility. Omni-directional means it is visible from all directions and does not need to be aimed at the receiver. Stroboscopic means that it flashes on and off, attracting attention better than a steady beam. Because the light is intermittent it uses less power so the batteries last much longer.

Strobe lights can be used for position markers to guide helicopters in rescue operations and for signaling and communication. A strobe light can be used to mark the position of your campsite or snow shelter, which allows you to find your camp with minimal difficulty when returning from a night operation or night skiing. Strobe lamps are sold by many rescue and recreational equipment suppliers and are generally reasonably priced.

Signal mirrors with mesh screen around the sighting hole are excellent for attracting a helicopter on a sunny day.

AVALANCHE TRANSCEIVERS

Everyone who travels with others in avalanche terrain should wear an avalanche transceiver. Backcountry recreationists and SAR members should be well practiced in transceiver use, and groups should formulate rescue plans before any trip. Transceiver batteries should be tested or recharged before each trip, and it's advisable to carry extra batteries. Manufacturers recommend using only alkaline batteries. A transceiver test should be conducted before setting off to ensure that all units are working and on compatible frequencies.

Only 457 KHz avalanche transceivers are sold today. No one should be using the 2275 Hz low-frequency beacons as they are not compatible with any modern beacon. Old dual frequency beacons should be replaced. Most users will find the modern three-antenna digital beacon superior to the old one-antenna analog beacon.

PROBE POLES

Probe poles come in three basic varieties. The first are ski poles that convert to avalanche probe poles. Some come with a ball or cutting disk near the pointed end of the probe. This makes it easier to push the wedged pole into the snow. Ski pole probes allow a user to eliminate carrying a separate probe; however they can be problematic to assemble in cold conditions and under time constraints.

Collapsible probe poles are preferred for backcountry travel because they are easy to assemble and use. Also, having a separate probe allows a rescuer to still have use of his ski poles while searching on variable terrain. Larger diameter probes are deflected less than narrow probes.

The third type of probe is the standard non-collapsible probe poles used at ski areas and by rescue groups. These are not practical to carry on recreational trips.

SNOW SAW

While not necessary on all trips, a snow saw can be used to speed up the construction of snow shelters by cutting blocks of snow. A saw is also useful for isolating columns of snow for shovel shear and column loading tests during avalanche danger assessment. Saws can also be used for constructing Rutschblock tests, which help determine snow stability. Several kinds of snow saws are available, such as folding saws and saws that fit on ski poles.

EQUIPMENT POINTERS

From the moment you step into the backcountry, you are dealing with a new set of rules and considerations. That's why the care and handling of your equipment is vital, not only for your survival, but for that of those around you. These are some important points to keep in mind:

» Your safety and comfort depend on good equipment. Well-constructed equipment will last for many years.

» Learn to care for your equipment. Make certain that it is functioning properly before and after each use. Take necessary supplies and tools for repair in the field. Replace badly worn or damaged equipment.

» Reverse the polarity of half of the batteries in lamps and other battery powered equipment stored in your pack. This will prevent them from being discharged in the event the switch is accidentally turned on. Replace batteries before they become completely discharged. When traveling in freezing temperatures, keep batteries inside your clothing to keep them warm. Keep a spare bulb inside the flashlight.

» Do not become separated from your gear. Many people have gotten in serious trouble by leaving their gear before being caught in severe weather. Never put your pack down without securing it. Your personal survival pack should always remain in your possession. Mittens, hats, and other loose equipment should also be secured to your pack, in a pocket, or inside your parka when not in use.

» Try to make all equipment serve more than one purpose, for example, ski poles that convert to probe poles, etc. Avoid gimmick items, however; stay with proven, reliable equipment.

» Carry a notepad and pencil. Consider write-when-wet pens and waterproof paper. Keep notes on equipment that you might want to add or delete from your pack. Make recommendations for group equipment that would be useful on future trips.

» Get information from manufacturers on the general and specific use of your equipment. Know the limits of the equipment.

» Be inventive. Design and build lightweight equipment such as pack cloth windscreens for your stove, splints for broken ski poles, sleds for travel, etc.

SUMMARY

o Members of backcountry trips—both recreationists and rescuers—should remember to include the Ten Essentials. In addition to extra water, food, sun protection, and clothing, bring firestarter, emergency shelter, navigation, flashlights, first-aid supplies, and a tool kit.

o Group equipment should include a thermometer, strobe lights, avalanche transceivers, probe poles, and snow saws. Make sure trip members coordinate supplies so all items are included.

o Keep notes about what items were useful, and what you would add or delete on future backcountry trips.

PART TWO

TRAVEL

CHAPTER 8

TRAVEL EQUIPMENT

Candace Horgan, National Ski Patrol Communications Director, Lakewood, Colorado;
   Arapahoe Basin Ski Patrol, Summit County, Colorado

OBJECTIVES

o   Study the benefits and drawbacks of various types of equipment used in backcountry travel.

o   Learn about different equipment styles.

o   Learn about waxes and climbing skins used for ski mountaineering.

o   Examine various accessories useful for backcountry travel.

When it comes to backcountry travel, having the right equipment can mean the difference between an enjoyable day outside and a day of misery leading to calling for rescue. Taking the time to properly plan and select your gear is an important part of going into the mountains. In winter, with the added difficulties of less daylight, extreme cold, and changing snow conditions, your gear can literally save your life.

When selecting equipment for backcountry travel, many factors need to be considered, including skill level, pack weight, trip goals, terrain difficulty, and the region in which you are traveling. For instance, you may need different equipment for the

dry, light snow of the Rocky Mountains than for the heavy, wet snowpack of the Pacific Northwest.

Regardless of what type of gear you eventually choose, you should be familiar with all its inner workings and practice with it on short day trips before embarking on a long multiday trip. Make sure you carry a repair kit and that you know how to use it, so that if something breaks 20 miles from the trailhead you have the ability to fix it. A well-stocked repair kit should have replacement parts, some extra screws and bolts, and the ubiquitous roll of duct tape, which can fix a surprising number of breakages.

SNOWSHOES, SKIS, AND SNOW-BOARDS

Depending on the season and trip goals, the backcountry offers a variety of ways to travel. Many people enjoy backcountry travel on foot, which requires adequate footwear in order to keep feet dry and warm and to maintain stability and balance on slippery and uneven surfaces.

During winter, while packed-down snow can be hiked with boots and crampons, travel in the backcountry on unconsolidated snow usually requires either snowshoes or skis. Both have their advantages and disadvantages.

Snowshoes are easy for the novice to use and require little more than a slight modification of the standard walking gait. Snowshoes are light and compact, so if you are venturing into steeper terrain that requires step-kicking, it is easier to climb with snowshoes attached to your pack than skis. Even for experienced skiers, snowshoes are easier to use than skis on slopes steeper than 30 degrees. Snowshoes can also be easier to use in tight trees and on exposed, rocky terrain.

Skis offer several advantages over snowshoes in varied, mountainous terrain. For one, their greater surface area keeps the skier closer to the surface of the snow, meaning less work for breaking trail. Skis also allow for glide, while snowshoes do not glide at all; this

Figure 8-1. *Snowshoe*

makes skis significantly faster, especially on downhills. This can be a great boon when trying to get out of the backcountry ahead of an approaching storm. For experienced skiers, the downhill ski out of the backcountry is one of the best parts of the day.

Snowboards can provide the same benefits as skis on the downhill, but can be cumbersome to carry into the backcountry. Splitboards, a subset of traditional snowboards, offer the advantages of skis and snowboards. They come apart and function like skis while climbing, then can be hooked back together for the downhill.

SNOWSHOEING

While it is still possible to find old-style wood snowshoes, you might as well look for a Model T to drive you to the slopes. Modern snowshoes have little in common with the vintage variety, though still share the same purpose: to travel on snow (Figure 8-1).

Snowshoes

Modern snowshoes are made with lightweight aluminum frames, space-age decking fabrics, and efficient bindings. Modern snowshoes need little, if any, maintenance.

Snowshoes come in several different types, including those for mountaineering, running, and recreational. Running/aerobic snowshoes are lighter and have a modified tail shape that helps lighten the shoe. The bindings for running snowshoes are not hinged, so the snowshoe lifts up with each stride. This allows you to move quickly with a natural running stride, but it also reduces flotation.

Mountaineering and recreational snowshoes typically have a bear paw, or teardrop, shape, and a hinged binding that leaves the snowshoe on the snow when the foot lifts up. Mountaineering snowshoes are also typically bigger, to provide more flotation in deep snow.

Almost all snowshoes have some sort of crampon underfoot, but snowshoes designed for mountaineering have a more aggressive, heavier-duty crampon that can provide more bite on steep, icy slopes.

Snowshoe size is largely dictated by the user's weight. However, you also need to account for the weight you will be carrying on your back, as well as factoring in the type of terrain you will be on. For instance, in the dry, light powder of the Rocky Mountains, a larger snowshoe will be needed than one used in the heavy snow of New England. Most manufacturers have a suggested weight range they publish for each model; look carefully at the number, then add 50 to 60 pounds or so to your body weight to see where it falls in the range. Look for the smallest snowshoe that will support your weight as a smaller shoe will be more maneuverable.

Snowshoe boots

Many types of boots, including ski boots, can be used with snowshoes. For general walking and recreational use, a backpacking boot is sufficient. Many boot manufacturers offer insulated versions of popular hiking boots that are suitable for trail use and light climbing. For mountaineering and for steep, cold-weather hikes and climbs, look to the wide variety of winter climbing boots on the market.

Cold-weather climbing boots have evolved in the last 30 years. Up until the late 1970s most winter mountain enthusiasts used some sort of heavy, leather double boot, which consisted of a removable inner boot and an outer boot of heavy leather that was typically treated with a water-repellent product. The sole was attached with a Norwegian welt. These boots provided the needed support for kicking steps in snow and for crampon technique, but they were heavy.

As ice climbing grew in popularity, manufacturers began incorporating plastic into the outer shell of double boots, which made them more waterproof. Additionally the plastic did not stiffen when camping overnight to the degree that double leather boots did. However, plastic mountaineering boots, while good for front-pointing up steep ice fields, were a hindrance in hard mixed climbing, because the climber lost the sense of feel for the rock. In the early 1990s many top climbers such as Jeff Lowe went back to leather boots. To make the boots suitable for winter use, manufacturers melded the leather to lightweight synthetic insulating fabrics, and added Gore-Tex inner boots to the leather to make them waterproof.

The next evolution was the incorporation of lightweight synthetic fabrics instead of leather into the uppers of the boot, making boots lighter and more maneuverable. These all-synthetic boots have up to nine layers of thin insulation to provide warmth at the highest altitudes and coldest climates. They also usually incorporate a gaiter into the boot.

Using snowshoes

Snowshoes are easy to put on. Most modern snowshoe bindings have one-pull straps over the forefoot and another strap that goes around the heel. Loosen the straps and slide the foot into the snowshoe binding until the ball of the forefoot is over the pivot point of the binding. Cinch the straps snugly over the forefoot, then cinch the heel strap in place. Test that the binding is attached securely by lifting your foot up to your knee.

Snowshoeing itself is relatively simple. A slightly wider gait than a normal walking stance is required; shoulder width is about right. Conserve energy by lifting the snowshoe just high enough above the snow so that you can move it forward. Do not try to lift the shoe up to your knee.

A variety of techniques can be employed if the terrain is too steep to walk up with a normal stride. A herringbone pattern, with the heels close together and toes splayed out, can be used to ascend moderate inclines. On steeper pitches it is best to traverse back and forth across the slope. If the snow is soft enough it may be possible to kick steps directly up the slope.

ALPINE TOURING AND TELEMARKING

Since the publication of the last *Mountain Travel & Rescue* manual in 1995, the entire subculture of backcountry skiing has undergone a paradigm shift. It used to be that skiers used either telemark equipment, which left the heel free and employed lighter boots (usually leather) and narrower skis, or they used alpine skis mounted with alpine touring equipment (or randonée), which offered performance advantages on the downhill by enabling a locked heel but severe handicaps on the uphill due to the weight.

Today, skis are available in a dizzying array of styles and designs. Modern backcountry skiers are often pursuing ski lines even more extreme than the steepest, double-black diamond runs at ski resorts. More and more skiers are choosing the same skis for both lift-served skiing and backcountry skiing to get the best performance on steep terrain.

Choosing skis

Aside from weight there is little to differentiate skis designed for lift-served skiing from skis designed for backcountry use. Many backcountry skiers simply mount resort skis with a pair of alpine touring or telemark bindings and call it good. A beefier ski will handle a wide variety of conditions better, but a lighter ski will allow you to move faster on the ascents.

Shape. Ski design has changed drastically in the last 20 years, especially with the advent of shaped skis, which increases the ski's sidecut (the difference between the width of the shovel, or tip, the middle, and the tail of the ski). Skis with more sidecut resemble an hourglass and are easier to turn.

The sidecut of the ski also creates a turning radius, or the size of a circle that a ski would make if it was placed on edge and allowed to turn a full circle. Skis with shorter turning radiuses are more maneuverable and are excellent for skiing in tight trees and steep chutes. Skis with longer turning radiuses are favored for faster skiing and long, giant-slalom-type turns.

Many skiers who pursue extreme ski mountaineering on high peaks prefer straighter skis with a longer turning radius. A straighter ski has more edge in contact with the snow and thus provides greater edge control on steep, icy terrain where one slip can have deadly consequences.

Camber. Another increasingly popular design change involves the ski's camber, which measures how much of the middle of the ski is in contact with the snow surface if it is laid flat (Figure 8-2). Skis can be single, or traditional, camber (downhill skis) or double camber (cross-country skis). Single camber skis have a pocket underfoot that is not in contact with the snow. Double camber skis are stiffer and have a larger pocket underfoot that does not contact the snow.

Reverse camber skis, often called rocker skis, resemble a banana, with the tip and the tail raised higher than the middle of the

Camber

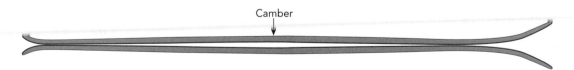

Figure 8-2. *Camber*

ski. Reverse camber skis float more easily in deep powder, an excellent advantage in the backcountry; they are a good choice if no hard snow or ski mountaineering will be encountered. Reverse camber skis are also relatively easy to turn; however, they do tend to be wider and heavier.

While reverse camber skis are gaining in popularity, traditional cambered skis that have early tip rise offer the best of both worlds. These skis have some rocker shape at the tip, which helps the ski float in powder and blast through crud and difficult snow, while the traditional camber underfoot helps the skier carve on hard snow.

Length and width. A ski's length and width are also key considerations, and the two work together to create the ski's surface area. This area affects the ability of the ski to keep the skier on top of the snow surface.

Skis have gotten wider in recent years, with some now resembling water skis. While wider skis provide better flotation in powder, they are more sluggish in edge-to-edge transitions. The wider a ski is, the shorter it can be while still providing the same amount of surface area. Longer skis are more stable at speed while shorter skis are more maneuverable and lighter, making them less fatiguing during uphill travel.

Choosing skis for backcountry use demands careful consideration and may depend on the geographic region where you are skiing. Those venturing into back-

country areas with deep powder in the West and Alaska will prefer a ski that is 100 millimeters (mm) to 120 mm underfoot. These skis can either be reverse camber, which float better in powder, or single camber. For skiing in the East, where the snow is often harder and not as deep, a skier may find a narrower ski adequate.

Weight. Weight is an important factor to consider when selecting skis for backcountry travel. An old credo says that a pound on the feet is equivalent to five pounds on the back. The lighter the ski, the less fatiguing it will be to use. However, lighter skis are more likely to be thrown around in difficult snow conditions like crud and heavy spring corn, so many hard-charging backcountry skiers sacrifice ease of uphill travel for a heavier ski that has better downhill performance.

Alpine touring and telemark bindings
Backcountry skiers need a binding that will allow the heel to remain free for hiking uphill. It used to be that backcountry skiers had the choice between lighter telemark cable bindings and heavier alpine touring bindings that gave skiers downhill performance and release capability. However, binding technology has changed dramatically and the lines have blurred.

Alpine touring bindings have become very light. They enable a skier to free the heel for hiking uphill, then lock the heel down for power and control during descents. Alpine touring bindings usually have DIN-certified ("Deutsche Indust-rie Norm" German industrial standards) release settings so that during a hard crash the skier releases from the binding and ski.

For those not wedded to the telemark turn, modern alpine touring bindings have several benefits. For one, those that employ tech fittings are the lightest bindings on the market, weighing as little as 11 ounces per pair while still offering a release function. Tech fittings create a seamless interface between the boot, which has metal inserts at the toe designed to fit with the toe piece of the binding, and the binding.

Other popular alpine touring bindings typically have a plate system and resort-type toe piece, providing a better release system in multiple directions. These bind-ings weigh three to five pounds on average.

Telemark bindings have also evolved and are now similar to alpine touring bind-ings, providing better climbing efficiency. Cable bindings work better for downhill performance when they are stiffer and keep the heel closer to the ski. This hin-ders the skier on the upward track, so binding makers created a free-pivot tour-ing mode that can be activated by switch-ing a small lever at the binding toe. While the free pivot is heavier than a non-free-pivot binding, it is much more efficient for uphill travel.

Most telemark bindings do not release, which exposes the skier to greater danger in avalanche-prone areas. Some telemark bindings, however, such as the New Tele-mark Norm (NTN) system, do incorporate release. It is also possible to mount a stan-dard telemark binding on a release plate, though this makes the binding nearly as heavy as an alpine binding.

Alpine touring and telemark boots

As skiers started pursuing bigger and steeper lines in the backcountry, the equip-ment, especially the boots, had to evolve. While a couple of manufacturers still offer leather telemark boots, most telemark ski-ers use plastic boots. Modern telemark boots are often just as heavy as their alpine counterparts, and they enable free-heel ski-ers to drive heavier, wider skis in all kinds of snow.

While telemark boots have gotten heavier, alpine touring (AT) boots have gotten lighter. Alpine touring boots are a downhill ski boot with three or four buck-les and a lugged sole for hiking in moun-tainous terrain. The evolution of tech fit-tings—two round metal holes at the toe of the boot that line up with inserts on the toe of certain bindings, such as Dynafit—has made alpine touring gear lighter than most telemark gear while providing addi-tional security features, such as releasable bindings and more power to drive the skis when traveling downhill.

When choosing a boot it is important to consider both weight and performance. Stiffer boots with a higher cuff and four buckles will perform better on the downhill. Three-buckle boots are lighter and more appropriate for less aggressive skiing. Boots with a walk mode are more comfortable for skiing uphill. These boots have a lever at the heel of the boot that can be flipped up to make the boot flexible and easier to hike in; this lever can then be locked when skiing down.

Alpine touring boots look like a cross between mountaineering boots and ski boots. They typically have four buckles, a stiff plastic shell, a removable inner boot, and a lugged sole. Some models have a removable lug sole that is attached via screws; by removing the sole the boot becomes compatible with traditional downhill resort bindings. If you are looking at getting tech-fitting type bindings, make sure that your boots have the proper inserts at the toe.

One of the more recent developments in boot technology has been the advent of carbon fiber boot construction. Carbon fiber boots are amazingly lightweight and also offer excellent downhill performance. While just a few years ago carbon fiber boots were used mainly by elite racers, they are increasingly employed by Average Joe skiers looking to maximize uphill benefit but not sacrificing downhill performance. While still very expensive, carbon fiber boots are now relatively affordable for the average backcountry skier.

Traditional telemark boots have a duckbill shape at the toe that measures 75 mm across, which slots into the binding's toe piece. Compatibility with crampons is dependent on the shape of the crampon toe piece, so if you need crampons make sure to test the crampon on the boot first.

NTN boots lack a duckbill, and have a toe shaped much like a downhill boot. Some NTN boots also have tech fittings so that they can be used in either an NTN free-heel binding or in an alpine touring binding. Because the toe of the boot is traditionally shaped, most models of crampons fit on NTN boots.

Regardless of which binding you choose, check the binding components and make sure that the binding is working properly before venturing into the backcountry.

SNOWBOARDING
When snowboarders first began venturing into the backcountry they were limited to using snowshoes and carrying their boards on their backs. Snowboarders now have backcountry travel options, such as splitboards.

Splitboards
Snowboards were originally intended to be used in powder snow to approximate surfing, and early snowboarders were hiking for their turns. This was in an age when

many ski resorts would not even allow snowboarders on the slopes. Gradually this bias was overcome and snowboarding rapidly became popular at ski resorts. The invention of the splitboard has made it easier for snowboarders to get back to their backcountry roots. Splitboards are snowboards that are split down the middle. The two sides are held together by metal hardware, which can be unlocked to allow the two halves to be used like skis for the ascent.

For backcountry trips, look for a splitboard that is slightly longer than your ski resort snowboard, as it will provide more flotation when traveling in deep powder with a heavy pack. The width should be wide enough to accommodate your boots without "booting out" on a turn.

Splitboard bindings

Any traditional strap or plate binding can be used on a splitboard. Some companies now make bindings that have a splitboard-specific highback, a wider lean adjustment, and a built-in touring bracket so that you do not need a separate slider plate to use your existing bindings in tour mode. These splitboard-specific bindings are lighter than the traditional slider plate and standard binding.

Splitboard boots

Any standard snowboard boot can be used on a splitboard. Some backcountry snowboarders prefer to use AT ski boots or mountaineering boots, which make climbing on snow and ice easier and also accommodate crampons.

NORDIC SKIING

The oldest form of winter snow skiing, Nordic skiing developed thousands of years ago as a practical form of transportation on snow. Snowshoes evolved into skis to meet the needs of people to go farther and faster.

Nordic skis

Nordic skis are lighter and narrower than skis designed for downhill skiing. They typically are no wider than 65 mm, and they are often as narrow as 50 mm underfoot, with little sidecut because they are not used in terrain that demands a lot of turning. Some Nordic skis, designed for skate skiing, have a reverse sidecut. Nordic skis are designed to be used either at Nordic touring centers or for backcountry tours on low-angle, rolling terrain.

Many Nordic skis have no metal edges, which makes them lighter. Others are built with partial metal edges along the middle of the ski. Some have full metal edges, which allows for touring on slightly steeper and more challenging terrain.

Nordic skis have either a waxless pattern or a wax pocket under the foot (also called a "kicker") where wax is applied to provide grip for the classic Nordic stride. Waxless skis have the advantage of requiring little maintenance for general touring purposes, but waxable skis outperform waxless skis for both uphill and downhill travel. Waxable skis use two types of wax: a kick wax for the uphill and a glide wax for the downhill.

Nordic bindings

There are three types of bindings for Nordic skis, three-pin, New Nordic Norm (NNN), and Salomon Nordic System (SNS). The 75 mm three-pin binding is the original; although still relevant it is less efficient than the NNN and SNS bindings. The three-pin binding has three metal pins rising out of the base plate, which insert into three holes in the sole of the boot's duckbill toe. The skier aligns the metal pins with the boot holes, steps down, then flips a gate closed on the top of the boot sole. With the toe secured the skier can kick and glide with the heel free.

Three-pin bindings have largely been supplanted by NNN and SNS bindings, both of which have a step-in feature. Boots are equipped with a bar at the toe that slides into the binding. The use of a bar allows full free-pivot range of motion. Both NNN and SNS have sturdier backcountry versions.

NNN and SNS boots are not compatible with each other, so you have to choose a system and stick with it. If you have boots already and are purchasing bindings, make sure they are compatible.

Nordic boots

Be sure to select a boot appropriate for your activity. Many Nordic boots are low cut, lightweight, and designed for speed and efficiency on flat to low-angle terrain. They are not appropriate for backcountry use.

Some NNN and SNS boots are built for lightweight backcountry travel. These boots have a higher cut and are stiffer. They are often reinforced with plastic for more stability. They are appropriate for lower-angle tours but not for aggressive backcountry travel.

ADDITIONAL EQUIPMENT

The type of backcountry trip or rescue a group is embarking on determines the supplemental gear that needs to be included on the packing list

Poles

Ski poles are constructed of a variety of materials, including fiberglass, carbon fiber, aluminum, or steel. Carbon fiber poles blend the best of durability with lightness. Fiberglass poles, while light, are less durable.

Choosing the proper-length pole depends on the type of activity. Nordic poles are generally sized longer, with the hand grips at armpit to nose level. For recreational cross-country skiing the armpit length is sufficient. For skate skiing choose a pole that reaches to the tip of your nose. For downhill skiing, flip the pole upside down and grasp it with your hand under the basket; your elbow should be bent at a 90-degree angle when the pole grip touches the floor.

For backcountry skiing, adjustable poles offer several advantages. They can be lengthened when skiing over flatter terrain or traversing slopes, and then shortened for skiing downhill. Adjustable poles typically have two sections that can be lengthened or shortened. Some models can be turned into an avalanche probe pole.

The basket of the pole is an important consideration. Baskets for ski poles used at ski resorts are typically small, as the pole is usually used on groomed terrain or shallower snow. In the backcountry a bigger powder basket helps prevent the pole from sinking too deep into the snow and provides more surface area from which to push.

Those traveling in steep terrain should consider a self-arrest pole. This is a traditional ski pole that has an ice ax pick attached to the top. The most commonly used in North America is the Whippet, by Black Diamond Equipment. While it is not a replacement for an ice ax when traveling in the mountains, the pole can work for emergency self arrests when skiing steep couloirs or climbing steep terrain with skis on your pack.

Wax

Waxing a ski improves its performance. To understand the need for wax you need to understand how a ski moves over snow. Much like an ice skate, the pressure of the ski on snow crystals creates a thin film of water that the ski slides on. The warmer the snow, the more water is created, and the more critical it is to use a wax that moves that water out of the way of the ski.

A glide wax should be applied to the ski base to make it slide over the snow more efficiently and turn quicker. With alpine skis and snowboards, apply glide wax to the entire base. With Nordic skis, apply glide wax only to the tip and tail.

Glide waxes are engineered for temperature performance; that is, the temperature of the snow. These waxes are usually color coded. If you are unsure of what the snow temperature will be, err on choosing a colder wax. Applying a warmer wax for travel on cold snow severely diminishes the performance of the ski.

Waxes come in a variety of compositions. Less expensive waxes are made of hydrocarbon. Ultra-high performance waxes favored by racers are made with fluorocarbon. These waxes push the water out of the way more efficiently but are expensive.

In addition to the temperature component, waxes come in either hot wax or rub-on styles. Rub-on waxes are inexpensive, and keeping one or two in your pack for emergency application in the backcountry is a good idea. Hot waxes perform better.

To apply hot wax you need a waxing iron that maintains a constant temperature output. Avoid using standard household irons because their temperature often fluctuates.

Hold the wax against the iron and drizzle a layer on the ski base, then use the iron to evenly distribute the wax on the base. Alternatively, you can rub the wax onto the ski base, then iron it into a smooth layer.

After letting the wax dry (or rubbing it on), scrape most of the wax off so only a fine layer is left. Use a plastic scraper and, holding it at a 45-degree angle to the ski base, remove the excess wax by scraping from tip to tail. When finished, a thin, barely-visible layer of wax should be left. Finally, buff out the wax with a nylon hairbrush or buffing pad.

For waxable Nordic skis, a kick wax must also be applied to the wax pocket, located underfoot of the binding on the ski. The length of the wax pocket varies depending on snow conditions and temperature. A kick wax provides traction for the kick and glide technique, as well as for uphill travel. While waxless skis, which have a fish-scale pattern under foot, are increasingly popular, waxable skis outperform them if they are waxed properly. Keep in mind that waxing Nordic skis is part science, part art form, so it may take you a while to become proficient at it.

Similar to glide waxes, kick waxes are designed to work according to snow temperature. Kick waxes, however, are rub-on or spray-on waxes, and very easy to apply in the field. To apply a kick wax, rub the wax back and forth over the base in the kick zone. Begin with a small kick zone, perhaps only twelve inches; test the glide to see how the wax is working, and if necessary you can lengthen the kick zone to create a less "slippery" glide. Use a cork to buff out the layer of kick wax, then apply another layer and buff it out. With a spray-on wax, you simply spray it on (no cork needed).

You will know immediately if the wax is working properly. If your skis are slipping, you need a softer wax or a longer kick zone, whereas if the snow feels sticky, you may need a harder wax or a shorter kick zone.

Climbing skins

Backcountry skiers use climbing skins to travel uphill. Kick waxes are not designed to be used on single camber or reverse camber skis favored by downhill skiers, so climbing skins are the best way to provide traction.

Climbing skins were traditionally made of animal fur, but today they are typically made of either nylon or mohair, which is a silk-like fabric made from the hair of angora goats. The nylon or mohair "hairs" are aligned in a single direction so that when you move forward, they slide, while backwards movement is restricted. While mohair skins tend to glide better than nylon skins, mohair wears out faster. The current trend in manufacturing is to combine nylon and mohair to create a durable skin that also glides well.

Purchasing skins that can be fitted exactly to your skis will provide much better traction for uphill travel, but the skins will require trimming. You can also buy straight skins that are the same width as the waist of the ski.

While standard climbing skins can be trimmed to fit each half of a splitboard, the attachment mechanism isn't always as secure. Some companies make climbing skins specifically for splitboards, and these are a better choice.

To get the best coverage, buy a climbing skin that is approximately 10 mm thinner than the width of your ski tip. Most skins come with a trimming tool and a template to trim the skin for the attachment mechanism (usually clips). It is easier to trim the skin if you have a workbench with ski vise clamps to hold the ski in place while trimming the skin (vise clamps are also useful for waxing).

Most skins come with an adhesive that sticks to the ski base to hold it in place, along with a loop for the ski tip and a clip for the ski tail. This adhesive does not stick to your ski base when the skin is removed, so it will not impede downhill performance. Skins that lack adhesive have largely fallen out of favor due to performance problems.

Safety leashes

Safety leashes are usually required of telemark skiers at ski resorts to prevent runaway skis. If you don't have ski brakes, you may want to consider leashes, but with a caveat: In an avalanche you do not want to remain attached to your skis because they will serve as an anchor. Leashes, therefore, are not recommended for backcountry travel in avalanche terrain. On the other hand, if you pop out of your binding while skiing, a leash will prevent the ski from disappearing.

Crampons

Ski crampons attach to the ski underfoot for uphill travel on steeper terrain. Many skiers traveling on very steep terrain simply remove their skis and attach them to their packs, then put regular crampons on their ski boots. However, on lower angle but hard-packed snow and ice, ski crampons can make it easier to move quickly with security. These crampons typically slide right over the ski underfoot, but many require some sort of binding compatibility.

Repair kit

A repair kit should be considered mandatory for backcountry travel. It should have binding parts (including cables and heel throws for telemark bindings), duct tape, a ski pole basket, rub-on ski wax, a diamond stone (for quick touch-ups of damaged edges), and spare parts for climbing skins. A multitool is also critical, as well as a small screwdriver to tighten binding screws. Extra binding screws are a good idea as well.

PACKS

When traveling in the backcountry, a pack that can hold extra clothing, food, water, avalanche equipment, and your skis is mandatory. There are many options available on the market (Figure 8-3).

PACK TYPES

Roughly speaking, day packs have an internal volume of 1,500 to 3,000 cubic inches. Packs for multiday trips generally are sized up to 4,500 cubic inches, while expedition packs are usually 5,500 cubic inches or more.

Packs typically have some sort of frame to help manage the load. While it is still possible to buy external frame packs popular in the 1970s, these packs have largely been supplanted by internal frame packs, which have two aluminum stays that can be bent to the shape of the shoulder blades. Sometimes these stays are part of a plastic frame sheet that provides more support. Internal frame packs are designed so the load is carried close to the back, which reduces the chance of sudden weight shifts throwing a hiker or skier off balance. Many day packs do not have any frame. Careful packing can help improve the carrying comfort, but these packs are not designed for heavier loads.

PACK CONSTRUCTION

Packs should be built from some form of durable nylon, with reinforcements in key areas. Lash straps on the outside enable ski carrying, while ice ax tool loops make it easier to carry axes when not using them. A spindrift collar is a large, extendable collar near the top that

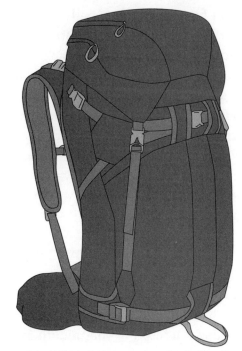

Figure 8-3. *Multiday ski mountaineering backpack*

helps minimize the chances of snow getting into the pack.

A zipper near the bottom third of the pack makes it easier to pack gear, especially infrequently used items like a sleeping bag. An external pocket that can hold an avalanche probe and shovel is a useful feature. Skis can be carried either A-frame style, with the skis lashed to the side of the pack and tied together at the tips, or diagonally across the back of the pack, depending on the ski-carry system.

Daisy chains on the outside of the pack make it easy to clip gear or climbing equipment to the pack with carabiners.

The top closure can either be a zipper or a drawstring with a top pocket, which is useful for carrying frequently used items such as a compass, headlamp, and trail food. With a top pocket, the pack can also be overfilled when necessary by extending the spindrift collar.

The carry system of the pack should include a comfortable, padded hip belt, padded shoulder straps, load lifter straps on the shoulder straps, anti-sway straps on the hip belt, and a sternum strap to keep the load close to the body.

SPECIAL PACK CONSIDERATIONS

Skiers can also choose special packs with avalanche safety equipment. An AvaLung pack has a built-in AvaLung and a breathing tube you insert in your mouth in case of an avalanche burial. When you exhale, carbon dioxide is expelled to the side, where it can't cause an ice pocket to form around your limited air supply.

A less common pack for avalanche safety is the airbag pack, which has an airbag built into it that inflates automatically when a cord in the shoulder strap is pulled. During an avalanche an airbag helps to prevent burial and protects the skier's head, neck, and upper body from trauma.

Some packs are also expandable. These packs can carry expedition-sized loads, but through a combination of zippers can be shrunk down to a day pack size for summit attempts. These packs eliminate the need to carry a separate day pack, but they do not always fit well.

Some packs also have a removable foam pad and extendable sleeve that can turn the pack into a half-bivy sack for unplanned overnights. While not an excuse to go unprepared, it is a nice survival tool.

Packs with a hydration bladder make it easy to stay hydrated while on the move. These packs have a sleeve in the main compartment where the hydration bladder is placed, and a sleeve on one of the shoulder straps through which you extend the drinking tube. Though these tubes are often insulated, in very cold weather they are prone to freezing.

FITTING THE PACK

A properly fitted pack can seem like an extension of your body and make carrying even heavy loads bearable. Conversely, an improperly fitted pack can make even light loads seem like torture.

Several important considerations factor into fitting a pack. Check your torso length in relation to the pack. The waist belt should wrap all the way around your hip bones, and the shoulder straps, when pulled snug, should wrap around your shoulders and be closer to the hip belt than your armpits. There should be no gaps between the shoulder straps and your shoulder and upper back.

It is best to load a pack in the store and walk around with it to see how comfortable it is before buying it.

PACKING

With an internal frame pack, packing is critical to getting it to carry the load efficiently. Pack the heaviest items close to your back, centered between your shoulder blades. For off-trail travel, put those heavy items lower in the main compartment to increase stability on uneven terrain. For well-built trails, place heavy items higher in the pack. This places more of the load on your hips. The lighter items should be placed near the bottom of the pack, with the rest of the load packed around the heavy items. For instance, with an overnight pack, place the sleeping bag at the bottom of the compartment, the tent in between your shoulder blades, and the stove, fuel, and food around it.

To get a fully loaded pack seated properly on your back, loosen all the straps and place your arms through the shoulder straps. Buckle the hip belt so that the belt is wrapped around your iliac crest and pull it snug. Next, pull the anti-sway straps on the hip belt snug. Now pull the shoulder straps snug, and make sure they are properly fitted to your back. Pull the load lifter straps, usually located near the top of the pack, so that the pack is seated close to your body. Lastly, buckle the sternum strap. Rotate your upper body back and forth and check to make sure the pack does not throw you off balance.

SLEDS

For overnights and expeditions, a sled can be an additional means of carrying gear; in an emergency it can also double as a means of extracting an injured person. Sleds vary in effectiveness and attachment systems. Climbers on mountains like Denali have used all kinds of sleds, from basic saucers to full-blown expedition sleds. The better sleds have metal poles and a waist harness.

Before setting off with a sled, make sure it is securely attached to your body. A backup rope anchor between the sled and skier is a good idea. When traveling with a sled, it is important to always move up or down the fall line; otherwise, the load can pull you off balance.

SUMMARY

o Planning for backcountry travel requires balancing many competing needs and considerations.

o Selecting the right gear is only part of the equation for a successful trip; it also important to maintain the gear in proper working order, to know how to use it, and to check its operation before any trip.

o Carry parts for repair or tune-ups in the backcountry.

CHAPTER 9

NAVIGATION

Rick King, National Ski Patrol Mountain Travel & Rescue Program Director
Justin McCarthy, Garmin International, Kansas City, Missouri
National Ski Patrol Mountain Travel & Rescue Instructors

OBJECTIVES

o Explain the types of maps available.

o Estimate elevation on a contour map.

o Explain some of the difficulties of using a contour map.

o Explain the proper use and care of a compass.

o Use a map and compass to determine a direction of travel between two points.

o Adjust and read an altimeter and explain its uses.

o Describe the advantages and drawbacks of using a global positioning system unit.

It takes a variety of skills to use maps, compasses, altimeters, and global positioning system (GPS) units to navigate in the backcountry. These skills take a lot of time and practice to master, and they must be refreshed often.

MAPS

A map is a scaled representation of Earth's surface. It is a useful tool in planning a trip or locating a position on the ground.

Many different types of maps are available, and choosing the appropriate map is important.

Planimetric maps show general horizontal features such as roads, creeks, trails, and ridge tops. Elevation and terrain can only be inferred from these features. Examples of such maps are US Forest Service trail or fire maps, General Land Office maps, and some hiking maps. It is advisable to use one that shows legal subdivisions, and/or latitude and longitude.

CALCULATING DISTANCES WITH THE SCALE RATIO

Depending on the ground units being used, the scale ratio must first be adjusted.

Metric units: The map is measured in centimeters (cm); the ground is measured in meters (m) or kilometers (km).

1:12000 = > 12,000 cm/100 cm per m = 120 m

120 m/1,000 m per km = 0.12 km

The underlined factors figured above multiplied by the distance in centimeters measured on the map equals the ground distance.

Example: 1:12000 map scale
4.5 cm on map
4.5 X 120 = 540 m on ground
4.5 X 0.12 = 0.54 ground km

English units: The map is measured in inches (in); the ground is measured in feet (ft) or miles (mi).

1:12000 = > 12,000 in /12 in per ft = 1,000 ft

1,000 ft /5,280 ft per mi = 0.2 mi

To calculate ground distance, map inches are multiplied by the factors as calculated above.

Example: 1:12000 map scale
3.5 in on map
3.5 x 1,000 = 3,500 ft on ground
3.5 x 0.2 = 0.7 mi on ground

Topographic maps show the shape of the land using contour lines that follow specific elevations above mean sea level, as well as geographic and manmade features. These maps are best suited to mountain travel.

The US Geological Survey (USGS) publishes topographic maps, which are available from the USGS and can be downloaded through online map services, such as the National Digital Cartographic Data Base. Contour maps are also available at many outdoor sports stores.

MAP SCALE

Earth is roughly spherical and maps are flat. Converting three-dimensional features to two dimensions is accomplished through any one of a number of projection systems. No system is perfect and some distortion always occurs, particularly near Earth's poles. In a small area these distortions are not usually noticed by the map user, but they are noticeable over long distances.

All maps show distances at a certain scale. At the bottom of a USGS map is the scale ratio and lines (scale bar) showing the scale equivalents for feet, miles, kilometers, etc. The scale ratio indicates how many ground units are represented by one map unit. For example, 1:12000 means one map unit (inches, centimeters) represents 1,200 of the same units on the ground.

The USGS maps that a backcountry traveler most commonly uses are in scales of 1:24000 (7.5-minute quadrangles), 1:25000 (7.5-minute and 15 x 7.5-minute quadrangles), or 1:62500—1:63360 in Alaska—(15-minute quadrangles). The smaller the number, the larger the scale and the more detail. (The term "minutes" refers to the minutes of longitude or latitude represented on each side of the map.)

To estimate travel distance, the scale ratio must be calculated or measured using the scale bar on the map.

USING THE SCALE BAR

Another method of determining distance is to use the scale bar found below the map scale ratio at the bottom of the map. This bar usually includes both metric and English units. To determine distance, measure the distance equivalent on the bar, then apply the same measurement to the area on the map you are trying to measure. The ground distance will be determined by how many times the distance equivalent measurement fits into the area on the map you are measuring.

Topographic maps often have grid lines that correspond to a coordinate system. On maps using the Universal Transverse Mercator (UTM) grid system, the grid lines are one kilometer apart. For those maps gridded with the US Public Land System, the lines represent one mile of distance. Counting how many boxes up and over between points is another good estimate of distance.

The distance used on maps is horizontal distance (as the crow flies). The travel distance on the slope is longer. The steeper the slope, the longer the ground distance to be traveled is, compared to the map. For example, a 15 degree slope is 3.5 percent longer than would be measured on the map.

CONTOUR MAPS

USGS contour maps are called quadrangle maps ("quads" for short) because they cover four-sided areas bounded by meridians of longitude (north-south lines) and parallels of latitude (east-west lines). Each corner of the map shows the latitude and longitude. The quadrangle size is given as the number of minutes of latitude and longitude it covers. The usual dimensions of quadrangles are as follows:

1. 7.5 minutes by 7.5 minutes (1:24000 or 1:25000 scale)
2. 15 minutes by 15 minutes (1:62500 scale)—1:63360 scale in Alaska—(15 by 15 are no longer available, but many old ones are still in use)
3. 15 minutes by 7.5 minutes (1:25000 scale—used in only a few areas of the United States)

Although some maps were published with elevations in metric units, the USGS's attempts to go metric have been officially abandoned. All currently published USGS quadrangle maps are in English units. The only metric maps are at the 1:100000 scale. However, 1:25000 maps still in circulation are metric. Topographic maps from other countries are all metric.

Each map is given a name, which can be found at both the upper and lower right-hand corners. The names of adjoining maps are given at each corner, at the top, the bottom, and the sides. Index maps that show the area each quadrangle map covers by state are available from the USGS so that the backcountry recreationist can determine what maps are needed. The map's publication date is printed below the map name. In many areas these maps have been periodically updated. It is advisable to use the most recently published map available and to replace old maps with updated ones as they are published. Beware that many maps are seriously outdated and may be incorrect.

USGS maps use a variety of colors and symbols to represent the terrain and features found on the ground. On updated maps, new information is printed in purple. The brown squiggly lines represent lines of equal elevation. Contour lines are blue over glaciers and perennial snowfields. Every fifth line is darker and has the elevation labeled. These index lines were drawn directly from aerial photographs taken to prepare these maps. The lighter lines are secondary lines interpolated between the index lines by the cartographer.

At the bottom of the map the contour interval is given. The contour interval is the number of units of elevation change between individual contour lines. On maps with steep terrain, contour intervals are typically 40 feet but can be 80 feet. Maps with rolling terrain usually have a 20-foot contour interval and maps showing mostly flat terrain are made with 10-foot contour intervals.

The contour lines show the shape of the land. Contours (ridges) point downhill and are usually rounded. For draws and creek bottoms the contour lines point uphill and come to a sharper point. A full circle shows the tops of hills, while saddles or passes are located where two contours of the same elevation curve away from each other. Contour lines are closer together on steep ground and farther apart on flat ground. The fall line of a slope, as well as the flow of creeks and rivers, is perpendicular to the contours. The aspect of a slope is the compass direction it faces.

Determining elevations from contour maps

The elevations of specific points are shown in different ways:

1. Monuments: ☐ 6935
2. Benchmarks: BM X 7308
3. Single, unmonumented points: X 5720
4. Road intersections: ⊹ 4302

To find the elevation of other points, the backcountry recreationist must first find the two index lines between where the point lies. Determine which way is uphill, then count the number of lighter contour lines from the index to the point. The number of contours is then multiplied by the contour interval (Figure 9-1). The map reader must determine whether to add or subtract this product from the index elevation.

Difficulties with contours

Contour maps are not completely accurate, so the backcountry recreationist must be cautious. The lighter contour lines are drawn evenly between the index lines but the shape of the ground is not always even. Many features such as dips and small cliffs are lost between contours. The recreationist must remember that 39-foot cliffs can hide between 40-foot contours. As a result, flatter ground often loses more features on a map than steeper ground.

In addition, all measurements have some error. National Map Accuracy Standards allow up to $\frac{1}{30}$ of an inch error in 10 percent of tested points on maps with a scale greater than 1:20000. For a 1:24000 scale map, this means a point might be misplaced by 67 feet. The vertical error may not be more than one-half the contour interval for 10 percent of the tested points.

GRID SYSTEMS

Of primary importance to search and rescue (SAR) is the ability to determine a victim's absolute position in order to direct rescue crews, vehicles, and/or air support to the rescue site. A variety of grid methods are used, though only three of the most common methods are outlined here. Other systems, such as State Plane Coordinate system and the Universal Map Grid system, may be in common use in some areas and should be learned as well.

Mercator grid system

The most universal method is the Mercator grid system, which grids Earth into meridians of longitude and parallels of latitude. Meridians of longitude run north-south from pole to pole, and divide up Earth like orange segments. The zero longitude

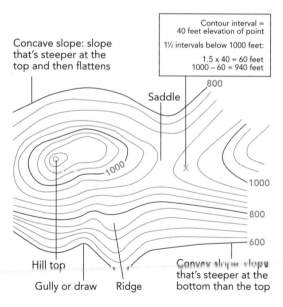

Concave slope: slope that's steeper at the top and then flattens

Contour interval = 40 feet elevation of point
1½ intervals below 1000 feet:
1.5 x 40 = 60 feet
1000 – 60 = 940 feet

800

Saddle

1000

1000

800

600

Hill top

Gully or draw   Ridge

Convex slope: slope that's steeper at the bottom than the top

Figure 9-1. *Contour map*

is the Greenwich Meridian. Meridians are described by the number of degrees, minutes, and seconds west of this starting line. Sixty seconds equal one minute, 60 minutes equal one degree, and 360 degrees complete a circle. Parallel lines cutting east-west slices of Earth are called latitude. The equator is the zero latitude, and parallels are measured in degrees, minutes, and seconds north or south of the equator.

At each corner of a quadrangle map the latitude and longitude are labeled in degrees, minutes, and seconds. At intervals along each side the minutes and seconds are also labeled. From these a backcountry traveler can roughly determine his or her position. However, measurements and calculations are needed to describe the position more precisely.

The distance between degrees of latitude is nearly constant. One minute of latitude equals one nautical mile, or 6,076 feet. However, the distance between degrees of longitude becomes less nearer the poles. Therefore, the minutes per inch should be calculated for the map being used. The length along the bottom, or south edge, of the quadrangle is measured. The number of minutes the quadrangle covers is then divided by this measurement and recorded on the map for future reference. The same process is repeated along one of the sides of the map. This factor should be kept simple so that the navigator can calculate the position in the field easily.

Once the navigator has determined his position on a map, he measures the distance east or west and the distance north or south from the closest map corner. Each measurement is multiplied by the corresponding factor previously calculated. The measurements are added or subtracted to the corner latitude and longitude appropriately to find the absolute position. Keep in mind that in the Northern Hemisphere, degrees of latitude increase as one travels north and degrees of longitude increase as one travels west. Accuracy to one-half minute should be adequate for a person to be located on the ground by other crews.

Universal Transverse Mercator Grid

Another common grid system that may be used to describe a position is the Universal Transverse Mercator Grid (UTM). It is designed for global use between 80 degrees south latitude and 84 degrees north latitude and is used on all military maps of the United States and of NATO countries.

The initial part of the system occurs at a scale larger than the average backcountry traveler needs. It grids Earth into 100,000-meter squares that each have a two-letter designation.

The next part of the UTM system is at the quadrangle scale. Within one of the 100,000-meter squares, a position is described as the number of meters right (easting) and meters up (northing) from the southwest (SW) corner of such a square. Along the sides of the contour map are blue ticks with numbers such as 271 and 3948. The first, small, superscript number can be ignored for a given quad map, but the recreationist must indicate by its name the quad map being used.

These numbers increase west to east and south to north. When these blue ticks are connected, a grid of square kilometers results. On maps for areas not using the legal description system, this metric grid may be drawn in. The backcountry traveler locates the square his position is in, then measures from its SW corner the number of millimeters or inches to the right and up to his position. These measurements are converted to hundreds of meters. (On a 1:24000 scale map, about 4 mm or 0.2 inch equals 100 meters.) The result is appended to the end of the border numbers. For example, a UTM coordinate of 713466 means 300 meters west and 600 meters north of the SW corner of grid square 71E and 46N.

When using this system, a clear plastic overlay gridded into 100-square meters at the map scale is a handy tool to have; make sure the most southwestern box on the template is numbered zero since it is less than 100 meters from the corner.

US Public Land System

All states west and north of the Mississippi and Ohio rivers, as well as Alabama, Florida, and Mississippi, are subdivided into a grid system known as the US Public Land System. Although designed to describe land area, it is also commonly used to describe position to the nearest 10 acres. USGS quad maps as well as many planimetric maps show the Public Land grid if it is used in that area. Where it is in use, local people are often more familiar with it than with other reference systems.

At intervals (because of Earth's curvature) a north-south meridian and an east-west baseline are located. Six-mile square tracts, called townships, are blocked out. A township (T) describes these tracts as so many townships north or south and so many ranges (R) east or west of the center of the reference axes.

Each township is divided into square-mile blocks, known as sections, that cover 640 acres. The sections are numbered 1 to 36, starting from the northeast corner of the township and counting west six blocks, then east and so on. Each section can be quartered by dividing each side in half. Each quarter is defined as northeast (NE), northwest (NW), southeast (SE), and southwest (SW). A quarter covers 160 acres. A quarter can be quartered (40 acres), and those quarters can be quartered (10 acres).

In professional land work for deeds, plats, etc., it is usual to start with the smallest quarter and work outward to the township and range. However, in a SAR situation it is easier to communicate the position over the radio or phone by giving the description from large to small (from the outside edges of the map in to the position). In addition, by counting the number of sections between two points, a quick estimate of mileage can be made.

The various reference meridians for this system are not regularly placed. The reference meridian used often changes across state lines. For example, Washington State is referenced to the Willamette Meridian while Idaho is referenced to the Boise Meridian. Care must be taken when using maps that cover such transition zones in order to determine the correct township and range.

THE COMPASS

Compasses are protractors that measure the amount of angle in degrees one turns from north clockwise around to look at a target point. For reference to north, the compass uses a magnetized needle that lines up with Earth's magnetic field.

There are numerous types of compasses, including digital versions. For the type of orienteering backcountry recreationists most often use, the best compass is the liquid-filled style mounted on a see-through base inscribed with reference lines. This style has a movable dial and the direction is read at the front of the compass. The liquid dampens the movement of the needle quickly and it is easily held

steady. It is advisable to buy one with a settable declination. Compasses with mirrors allow more precise fieldwork and have the added advantage that the mirror can be used for signaling. If money is no object, buying a more expensive model may be worth its weight in gold because it will be more accurate, reliable, and durable.

There are two types of compass scales: quadrant and azimuth. The quadrant scale reads bearings as the number of degrees (up to 90) east and west of north or south. Examples of such readings are N40E, S25E, S60W, and N30W.

The azimuth compass (Figure 9-2) measures the angle from north clockwise around: 90 degrees is east; 180 degrees south; 270 degrees west; and 360 degrees or 0 degrees north. This style is more commonly used and will be the only style discussed here.

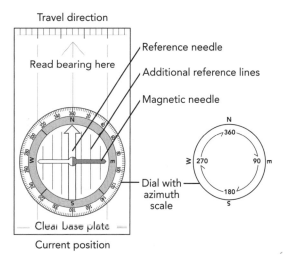

Figure 9-2. *Azimuth compass*

COMPASS CARE

A compass contains a magnet that is attracted to any metal and to other magnets. Metal should not be held near a compass in use. Wire-rimmed glasses, zippers, watches, keys, and mechanical pencils are items that are often overlooked. Metal fences, electrical towers—but not alternating current (AC) lines—vehicles, and certain rock types (basalt, for example) can also cause local attraction. The use of foresights and backsights—readings taken in front of or behind the direction of travel—is the best way to catch these problems. Note, too, that liquid-filled compasses can freeze in severe cold, and even those filled with nonfreezing fluid can contract and create bubbles. Rough treatment may cause the seals to break and the fluid to leak. Therefore, it is best to hang the compass around the neck or to put it in an inside coat pocket. Regardless of price, a compass is an instrument that deserves care if it is to function reliably.

MAGNETIC DECLINATION

All maps have a reference to north. On USGS maps the north reference is at the bottom of the map and north is always the top of the paper. Other maps do not always conform to these conventions, so the navigator first needs to determine which way is north on any map. This north is the geographic north pole, a relatively stable point, which is also called true north. Readings that use true north as the starting point

are true azimuths. When using a compass in the field, the user will line up with the magnetic needle pointing to north. Such a reading is a magnetic azimuth.

Magnetic north is one endpoint of Earth's magnetic field, currently somewhere under Hudson Bay. The difference between true north and magnetic north is called the magnetic declination. For someone standing roughly in a line south of Chicago, the declination is nearly zero (the agonic line). For a person standing east of this area, the declination is west. West of the agonic line the declination is east.

To make matters more complicated, declination drifts with time, which is called secular variation. Therefore, the declination in an area should be updated at least every five to ten years. Isogonic maps, which are available from the USGS and are produced every five years, allow determination of the local declination and of the amount of yearly change.

A USGS quad map shows the declination current for the year the map was made. The date is shown under the quadrangle name in the lower right corner. The map's declination is only usable if the map has been published within the last five to ten years.

Determining the local declination can also be done in the field. Two points are located on a map that are true north-south of each other. Roads are ideal features. The recreationist goes to this feature and takes a reading with an unadjusted compass. The difference between the compass reading and the actual direction is a good estimate of the declination. Wherever zero is located on the compass is the declination direction. For example, in the field, if a compass reading results in 10 degrees, the declination is 10 degrees west. (The zero is counterclockwise, or west, of the magnetic reading.) If the field reading of a true north-south line is 345 degrees, then the declination is around 15 degrees east. (The zero is clockwise, or east, of the magnetic reading.)

Adjusting for magnetic declination

If a reading is measured using true north-south lines on a map, that reading is true. If the reading is being set on a compass without a declination setting, that reading will be magnetic. In order for the compass and the map to agree, one or the other reading will need to be adjusted.

Not adjusting for declination results in an error in direction. For every degree off, there is an error of 92 feet per mile of travel. For general orienteering, a certain amount of error may be acceptable. When traveling in an area with less than four or five degrees of declination, adjusting for declination may, therefore, be optional. In dangerous terrain, where careful compass work is necessary, the direction should certainly be adjusted for declination.

The best way to deal with declination is to buy an adjustable compass. The reference arrow in the base plate should be set to the local declination. For the map and compass to agree, the correct number of degrees must be set, as well as east or west. In the field, during low visibility and in stressful situations, not having to worry about declination is worth the extra cost of the compass. In groups, everyone's compass should be set to the same, correct, and current declination.

When traveling outside of the local area more than about 50 miles, the declination needs to be adjusted. The declination should be corrected at least every five years.

It is valuable to know how to correct a nonadjustable compass. Two methods are visual, and the third is to compute the needed reading. Pick the method that works best for you.

Adjustment by calculation

For west declination the true reading is smaller than magnetic readings. To follow a compass after determining a direction from a map, the declination is added. If plotting out a line on a map after taking a compass sighting, the declination is first subtracted (Figure 9-3).

On the map the direction of travel is 234. Set the compass to 239 to actually get there. Sight on an object with the compass and read 59 degrees. To see where that object is on the map, use 54 degrees.

For east declination the true reading is larger than the magnetic reading. The map direction must have the declination

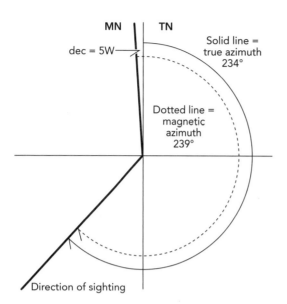

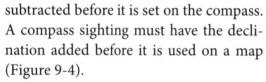

Figure 9-3. *Declination 5 degrees west*

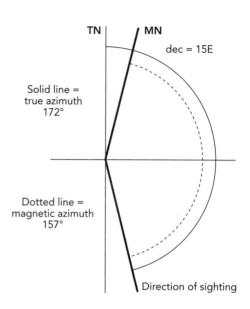

Figure 9-4. *Declination 15 degrees east*

subtracted before it is set on the compass. A compass sighting must have the declination added before it is used on a map (Figure 9-4).

On the map the direction between two points is 172 degrees. Set 157 degrees on the compass to reach that position in the field. A compass sighting on an object is 337 degrees. To find the object on the map the direction used should be 352. If your result is larger than 360, subtract the extra 360. If the result is negative, add 360 to your answer. It is possible to be northwest of one kind of north and northeast of the other.

Marking the compass

Adjusting for declination can also be done visually. To prepare the compass the dial is set to zero degrees. With a marker or with a thin strip of tape, mark the base plate at the amount and direction of declination. This should not be permanently marked because declination changes with place and time.

To convert a true reading to magnetic, turn the true reading at the top of the compass to the mark. The reading at the top is the magnetic azimuth. If the reading at the top is magnetic, the reading at the mark is true. If you need to work with the true azimuth you may dial the reading at the mark to the top.

For very small declinations and on cheap compasses, this method is less precise. It is still necessary to remember which way to turn the dial.

Marking the map

On the map, parallel lines should be drawn, oriented to the declination (referred to as magnetic lines here). When using one of the map techniques described in the following sections, the base plate reference lines should be oriented to these magnetic lines rather than to true north. In this case you are always working with magnetic readings. It is necessary to buy a new map every few years and draw in new declination lines, since declination changes with time.

Regardless of which system you choose, practice it until it can always be done correctly, no matter how tired you are or how inclement the weather.

ORIENTING A MAP IN THE FIELD

Orienting a map in the field combines map reading and compass skills. First, locate your current position on the map. Using the compass, face true north. Hold the map with true north away from your body. Locate major features, either manmade or natural, in the field and match them with their drawn representation on the map. It is best to look all around, not just north.

Once major features are identified, note the finer details. Doing this will give you a feel for the area and a sense of scale. Repeat this process regularly to keep yourself located on the map and on the correct route. With practice and experience it is not necessary to orient the map to north; you can hold the map so it lines up with major terrain features.

Finding the direction of travel

In order to travel from a present-known location to a destination that is known on the map, determine the compass direction first from the map, then adjust the compass. The compass is used as a protractor to determine the angle between the map's true north and the line connecting the starting and ending points of travel (Figure 9-5).

Using one of the side edges of the compass like a ruler, place the back end of the compass (where the neck string is located) over the starting point and the front end of the compass over the destination. Ignore the compass needle. Turn the compass dial until the outline arrow in the base plate points to the map's north. Use the parallel lines in the base plate to fine-tune the direction by placing them parallel with any one of the grid lines (such as UTM or section lines) found on the map.

The true azimuth is read at the top of the dial. If the compass has been set for declination, no further adjustment is needed. If not, then this reading must be adjusted to magnetic before following the direction in the field.

If magnetic lines have been drawn on the map, the lines in the base plate of the compass should be aligned to these lines, instead of to the map's true north. The reading on the dial will be magnetic.

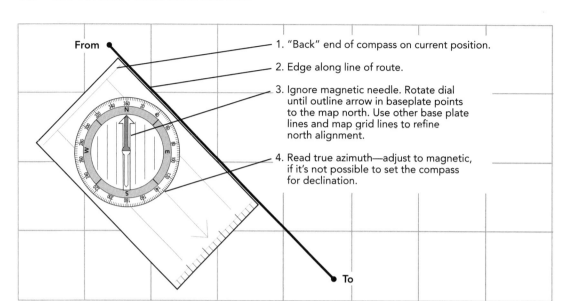

1. "Back" end of compass on current position.

2. Edge along line of route.

3. Ignore magnetic needle. Rotate dial until outline arrow in baseplate points to the map north. Use other base plate lines and map grid lines to refine north alignment.

4. Read true azimuth—adjust to magnetic, if it's not possible to set the compass for declination.

Figure 9-5. *Determining a direction to follow*

It is important to care for the map since it has little value if it is destroyed. The map can be stored in a clear Ziploc bag or a map case. If possible purchase plastic coated maps. The map should be stored in an accessible location.

USING A COMPASS IN THE FIELD

Becoming comfortable with compass use in a variety of settings is key to determining where you are and where you need to go in the backcountry. Practicing these skills until they become rote will give you that much more confidence when involved in backcountry travel or on a SAR mission.

Setting and following a reading

After setting the correct reading on the compass, hold the compass flat in front of you so that you can see the dial. Turn yourself with the compass until the north end of the magnetic needle is directly over the outline north arrow in the compass base plate. Pick an object that is not too far away, walk to that point, and repeat the sighting process. Stay aware of the surroundings and of the distance as you walk. The terrain being traveled must match what the map indicates. If traveling in a party, the first and last person should have compasses. The last person can double-check the direction taken by the leader.

Taking a direction to a point in the field

Aim the compass at the point to which you want to determine a direction. The compass must be kept aimed and as flat as possible.

Rotate the compass dial until the outline arrow in the base plate is directly under the magnetic needle. If the declination is set, the reading just taken is true. If declination has not been (or cannot be) set, the reading is magnetic.

Foresights and backsights

A reading taken in the direction of travel is called a foresight. Looking back from where one came is a backsight. Foresights and backsights should differ 180 degrees from each other. If they don't, there may be several reasons. Often it is local magnetic attraction, such as objects carried close to the compass. If the attraction is caused by manmade objects, such as barbed wire fences, a line should be run about 50 feet away and parallel to the desired route. Nothing much can be done about natural attraction sources. A close watch should be kept on the contour map while traversing through such areas.

Backsights also catch mistakes in navigation. The backsight can be set on the compass to determine if it points to the previous position. The position can be adjusted if it does not line up correctly.

Transferring a line of travel to a map

To transfer a line of field travel to the map, sight the compass on a point that can be located in the field and on the map. Sight on that point with the compass and then determine its direction from your location.

Using true azimuths

If you are using a compass with adjustable declination, no further adjustments are needed. However, with a nonadjustable compass one of the methods discussed previously must be used to determine and set the true azimuth.

Place the front end of the compass over the point that you sighted on. Ignore the compass needle and do not change the setting. Rotate the entire compass until the arrow outline of the base plate points to the map's north. The reference is used to align the compass as finely as possible.

Use a pencil to draw along the compass edge. This is the direct line between your current position and the sighted point; it is called the line of position.

Using magnetic azimuths

When you have no declination setting and have drawn magnetic lines on the map, use the same procedure described above; however, the lines on the base plate will be aligned with the magnetic lines. The outline arrow must point toward the magnetic north of the map.

Resectioning

If you have good visibility and are not sure of your location, taking two readings and drawing intersecting lines of position on the map can help determine your position. This technique is called resection (often incorrectly called triangulation). Locate two points that are fairly far apart, then draw a line of position on the map from each point as described in the previous section. The intersection of these lines is your approximate location.

If two points cannot be identified, then other lines of position, such as the fall line and aspect (which compass direction it faces) of a slope, an elevation contour, a creek drainage, a ridge line, a road, etc., can be used. Using the topographic information provided on the contour map, you can then determine your current field position more precisely.

THE ALTIMETER

Earth's atmosphere is a thick blanket of gases that has a measurable weight. In a standard barometer this weight is measured by the height that mercury will rise up a tube—hence, inches of mercury. Other styles of barometers use finely set springs, but the measurement is still either in inches or in millimeters.

At sea level the average air pressure is about 29.92 inches. As elevation is gained, air pressure becomes proportionately less. An altimeter measures air pressure and this pressure is converted to elevation.

Although mechanical altimeters still exist, most altimeters are digitized. Models come in both handheld and wrist-mounted versions and can incorporate features other than elevation readings, such as thermometers and travel rates.

Air pressure changes with time because air circulation, temperature changes, and passing weather systems change the air density and thus the weight. Before setting out on a trip, you should start at a point of known elevation and set the altimeter to that elevation. It is wise to figure out in advance the elevation of various staging points, so that search parties can set and verify their altimeter readings before leaving.

The group should plan a route that passes through points that have the elevation labeled on the contour map. The altimeter should be reset to the correct elevation as these points are reached. It should be reset at least every two hours. On overnight trips it is not unusual for readings to rise or fall several hundred feet at a campsite because of temperature and weather changes. The altimeter should be reset before setting out the next day.

APPLICATIONS OF THE ALTIMETER

Since the altimeter is a barometer, it can be used to anticipate dramatic weather changes to determine whether to descend to safer terrain or to abandon a high elevation goal before a storm strikes. When navigating in featureless terrain (such as on glaciers), at night, or in the fog, the altimeter can be used to stay on course.

POOR VISIBILITY AND NAVIGATION TECHNIQUES

A number of tricks help a party stay on course when visibility is limited. Although cell phones and GPS units can provide backup navigation aid, an understanding of actual hands-on applications such as the following is indispensible:

» Preparation: Before setting out, study the map and proposed route. Get a feel for the terrain and any possible areas of confusion or danger. At least two group members should carry a map, compass, wands, flagging, and an altimeter and GPS unit if the terrain and conditions warrant them.
» Backmarker: The last person in a larger party can double-check the leader's course.
» Handrail: A handrail is a prominent feature easily followed in good and bad weather, for example, ridges, gullies, and rivers.
» Aiming off: Aiming off means to deliberately aim for one side of a long feature, such as a stream, to reach a particular destination. When the feature is reached the individual can then take the proper direction to reach the destination.
» Catchline: Also referred to as baselines, catchlines are easily identified features such as rivers and trails that lie parallel and are as long as the intended travel area. The catchline can be used as an escape route if necessary.
» Timing and pacing: Positive Azimuth Uniform Layout (PAUL) is a timing and pacing system developed by Sergeant Don Paul during the Vietnam War. Using PAUL, experienced backcountry recreationists and rescuers can gauge the distance traveled by timing and pacing their travel. Time varies by season, mode of travel, obstacles, and individual fitness levels, so groups should take some field time to gauge their rate of travel.
» Concentration: Stay on top of where the party has been to determine their current location. All party members should be actively involved in this process. What one overlooks, another might notice.
» Safety: In low-visibility conditions and on dangerous terrain, it may be wise to rope up or wait out a momentary loss of visibility. Be willing to return over your route to the last known position. Setting sticks, wands, or flagging may make backtracking easier.

OTHER HINTS

At night and during inclement weather, backcountry travelers can implement these additional navigation tips:

» During nighttime or low visibility, headlamps may be used as points on which to take compass readings. The lead and end team members can sight on each other's headlamps to check foresights and backsights.

» Special transparent map holders allow the map to be used without exposing it to the elements. Special wax pencils are available that write on clear plastic.

GLOBAL POSITIONING SYSTEMS

Global positioning system (GPS) technology is changing the way we work and play everywhere, including in the backcountry. Originally developed for the military, GPS is a satellite-based navigation system that sends and receives radio signals. A handheld GPS receiver acquires these signals and transmits information never before available in a backcountry setting.

With that in mind, it is important to know that at times and places a GPS unit does not work well. Satellite signals can be obstructed by forest canopy, high valley walls, and other features. A position cannot be determined if there are not at least three satellites above the visibility horizon with unobstructed sky. Powered by four to six AA batteries, a basic receiver is capable of operating continuously for a full 24-hour period, and less if the unit has elaborate, battery-draining features, such as the ability to download maps. Despite these drawbacks a receiver can be a valuable aid to navigation, especially in poor visibility and confusing terrain.

At least 24 GPS satellites orbit Earth twice a day in a specific pattern. They travel at approximately 7,000 miles per hour about 12,000 miles above Earth's surface. These satellites are spaced so that a GPS receiver can receive signals from at least four satellites. From these signals the instrument computes its position on the ground, usually as either latitude and longitude or as UTM coordinates. Because of this the user must be very practiced at translating GPS output to a map. Best results are obtained by taking several minutes' worth of readings and averaging them.

Solar energy powers GPS satellites. If solar energy is unavailable, for example, when a satellite is in Earth's shadow, the satellites use backup batteries to continue operating. Each GPS satellite is built to last about 10 years. The US Department of Defense monitors and replaces the satellites to ensure that GPS technology continues to run.

When using a GPS unit, follow the manufacturer's direction. Using a contour map and a compass, and having knowledge of manual navigation, is a good, safe practice. A GPS receiver is a complement to navigation and should not be the only navigational tool you use.

SUMMARY

o The purpose of navigation is to find and follow a planned route of travel. As rescuers or backcountry recreationists progress through a series of anticipated features, they need to keep track of their progress.

o Techniques such as aiming off, using catchlines, and timing and pacing can help keep a group on course. Know and understand these strategies to ensure a safe trip in the backcountry.

o With proper physical and mental preparation, no one should ever feel intimidated by the current situation. A traveler is never lost, only temporarily misplaced.

CHAPTER 10

BACKCOUNTRY HAZARDS

Myron Allen, Medicine Bow Nordic Ski Patrol, Laramie, Wyoming

OBJECTIVES

o Review general classifications of mountain hazards.

o Identify the differences between objective and subjective risks.

o Review risk management techniques for some of the most commonly encountered hazards.

o Discuss how to cultivate good judgment in the alpine setting.

A hazard is something that can cause harm. The high mountain environment bristles with them. Rockfall, lightning, slips on ice, and acute mountain sickness are just a few of the more commonly encountered hazards. Indeed, people's attraction to mountains stems largely from the rigorous and inhospitable elements that make the alpine environment so wild, scenic, and potentially dangerous.

Risk is the probability that a hazard will result in harm. The distinction between hazards and risks helps backcountry recreationists and rescuers maintain an analytical frame of mind when dealing with the complex environmental and human factors that can threaten a group's success.

Ski patrollers are far from casual visitors to the backcountry. They patrol in it, conduct search-and-rescue (SAR) operations, and often serve as leaders and educators for less mountain-savvy groups. In these roles, rescuers and backcountry recreationists must understand and recognize mountain hazards and know how to manage the risks associated with them.

GENERAL CLASSIFICATION OF HAZARDS

Backcountry recreationists and rescuers often divide hazards into two categories: objective hazards and subjective hazards. Objective hazards are those that are independent of the group's decisions: rockfall, avalanches, slick footing, lightning, bad weather, and so forth. A group traveling in the mountains has little control over these hazards; they are part of the environment. Subjective hazards are those over which the group has direct control, such as not wearing helmets, ascending unstable slopes, not wearing crampons, traversing an exposed ridge when thunder clouds threaten, and starting a trip when a storm is brewing. A group traveling in the mountains can control the probability of harm from subjective hazards through the decisions it makes.

Regardless of the type of hazard, much of the mental work of mountain travel consists of recognizing hazards and managing risk. However, no chapter in any book is a substitute for on-the-ground training under the guidance of a knowledgeable and experienced person. Mountaineering is no abstract exercise; it is a craft learned in context, through a combination of expert mentoring, systematic study, and focused practice with the appropriate equipment. The fact that highly accomplished alpinists die in the mountains each year suggests the apprenticeship never ends. Instead, the most effective pathway to a long, successful career in the mountains is the habit of tailoring one's adventures so that they remain solidly within the bounds of one's training and capabilities.

SPECIFIC HAZARDS AND THEIR MANAGEMENT

At every turn, it's possible to confront a wide range of hazards in the backcountry. Some are avoidable, some are less so, but one factor is clear: knowledge can help the traveler navigate more safely through dangerous terrain.

ROCKFALL

Falling rock constitutes one of the most common and least appreciated mountain hazards. Rockfall may be either natural or human induced. Natural rockfall normally occurs on slopes at or exceeding the angle of repose, which depends on boulder size, boulder-size distribution, rock type (which affects boulder shapes), and moisture content. Typical angles of repose for talus slopes range from 33 to 37 degrees.

On slopes this steep or steeper, rockfall can result from a variety of triggers:

» Thawing of previously frozen, loose material as sunlight warms it.
» Increased lubrication from precipitation or snowmelt runoff.
» Movement of other climbers or animals.
» Random shedding of rock fragments from the mountain as a result of mass wasting.

In particular, a slope that is solid early in the day may begin to shed rocks spontaneously as the day wears on. Human-induced rockfall is often a greater hazard, especially when the climbing party includes novices or is downslope from novices.

Several safety measures can help manage the risks posed by rockfall. First, in any mountainous terrain exceeding 30 degrees, it is wise to wear helmets. Second, pay attention to the terrain above. If it appears capable of shedding rocks, give it as wide a berth as possible and spend as little time as possible underneath it. The mountain gods' shooting gallery is no place to take a break. Third, when party-induced rockfall is likely, travel in small groups, with group members bunched together to minimize the time available for dislodged rocks to gather velocity. Fourth, urge party members to move quickly through rockfall zones, from one point of relative shelter to another if possible. Finding sheltered stances is especially important for party members who are belaying from below or waiting while people above descend.

WEATHER

Weather represents a constellation of overlapping hazards.

Lightning

Lightning tends to be more prevalent on summer afternoons, after the warming effects of sunlight cause thermal convections and the resulting vertical development of cumulus clouds. However, anyone who has spent enough time in lightning-prone mountain ranges has heard thunderbolts early in the morning and during the winter. For this reason it is imperative that backcountry groups recognize and seek shelter in response to rapid vertical buildup of cumulonimbus clouds.

Other signs tend to give far less advance notice. Audible thunder typically comes from lightning initiated within three miles—a distance a fast-moving storm can cover in a few minutes. Even more urgent signs include hair standing on end and buzzing electrical discharges from equipment such as ice axes, crampons, and trekking or ski poles. The most effective rule for managing lightning risks is to get an early start on any ascent above timberline, so you can be off the mountain and in safer terrain—below timberline if possible—by noon.

Other rules include the following:

» Avoid being or being near the tallest object around.
» Stay away from open water and shallow caves.
» If a metal-skinned vehicle or building is available, it may shield you from lightning-induced currents.
» If caught in the open in a lightning storm, crouch on your heels or on some insulating material, such as a rope.
» Stay away from metal gear, such as ice axes, crampons, and climbing hardware.

Precipitation

Precipitation such as rain, snow, graupel (soft hail), and hail is also potentially hazardous. In all its forms, it lubricates everything, be it solid rock, talus, grassy slopes, snow, or downed timber. Terrain that provides plenty of traction when dry can become treacherously slick and unstable in a rain shower, and the ball-bearing effects of graupel and hail can be even worse.

Precipitation also increases the risk of hypothermia. Rain-soaked clothes can conduct heat away from the body far more rapidly, even in temperatures above freezing, than dry snow on a subzero winter day. Managing precipitation in a mountain setting requires attention to the weather forecast, an adequate system of clothing layers, and scrupulous efforts to keep survival equipment, such as sleeping bags, dry.

Knowing the forecast can allow a party to get out of the steeps before the terrain gets slick. With any luck you can sit out the storm in a dry tent. To help keep survival gear dry, some rescuers and backcountry recreationists line their packs with contractor-strength plastic garbage bags and stuff their sleeping bags in waterproof sacks inside the bags.

Whiteouts

Whiteouts pose special risks in snowy landscapes and on glaciers. A dense fog, possibly compounded by driving snow or condensing mist, can make the world look like the inside of a ping-pong ball. This lack of visibility makes navigation tricky and increases the risk that party members will fail to notice cornices, cliff edges, potential rockfall zones, crevasses, and other dangerous terrain features. The simplest measure for managing whiteouts is to stay put until the weather clears. If doing so is not practical, the best defense against getting disoriented is to have a preestablished, detailed route plan (Figure 10-1).

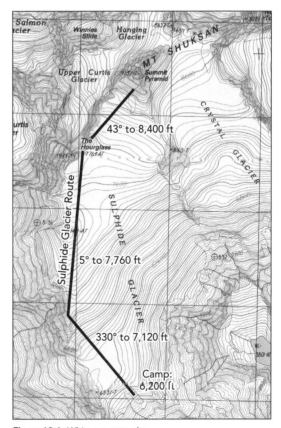

Figure 10-1. *Whiteout route plan*

Wind

Wind can be a potent hazard in the mountains. High winds can blow down standing timber, a factor that deserves serious consideration when selecting campsites. Strong winds, and especially sudden gusts, can cause people to lose their balance. In settings involving roped travel, wind can interfere with audible communications among team members.

The following techniques can be useful in managing high winds:

» Watch for lenticular, or lens-shaped, clouds near mountain peaks, since they indicate that powerful winds aloft may make it unwise to negotiate exposed terrain.
» If possible make camp away from standing timber that can blow over in a wind storm.
» Weight your tent's stakes with rocks to keep them from blowing away.
» Carry handheld two-way radios to aid with communications among members of a roped party.

STREAM CROSSINGS

Swift-running water is common to most mountain ranges. Crossing streams can be extremely hazardous. Swift water has surprising power, and even an ankle-deep creek can sweep a strong hiker off his feet.

When planning a trip, it helps to know the scale and character of the region's watercourses. What the topographic map shows as a small tributary in Wyoming's Wind River Range, located in the dry continental climate zone, may be easily manageable. A similar-looking map feature on the west slope of the North Cascades, where rainfall and glacial melt are prodigious, may pose a practically insurmountable barrier.

Timing may prove critical. In glacier country, stream crossings that seem trivial early in the morning can become steadily more difficult as the day progresses, owing to increased meltwater runoff as the sun climbs higher in the sky. Early in the summer there are additional hazards associated with snow bridges, which tend to weaken rapidly, not only as melting occurs over the course of days or weeks but also each day as snow frozen hard during the night softens.

Managing stream crossings requires good judgment, not only in deciding how to cross but also in deciding whether crossing is really necessary. Keep these points in mind:

» Consider carefully how important it is to cross the stream. Is it possible to accomplish the goals of the trip without crossing? If not, are those goals worth the risks?
» Many established trails cross creeks on bridges or at shallow fords. Even on a cross-country trip it can be a useful investment of time to look for natural

features—such as rocks, stout logs, or wide shallows—that make the crossing easier to negotiate.

» In glacier country, plan to make major creek crossings early in the day.

» When crossing a creek, use trekking or ski poles for balance and support. Undo the hip belt of your pack and your pole straps to allow an easy escape.

» Difficult stream crossings can be made using ropes and harnesses, though these techniques require study, practice, and experienced rope handling. A poorly executed rope crossing can lead to a party member's being inadvertently held underwater by a well-meaning belayer.

GLACIER HAZARDS

Glaciers, distinguished from permanent snowfields by the presence of flowing ice, are among the most dynamic landforms on Earth. They can serve as highly efficient routes, especially compared with boulder fields and talus slopes. But they also challenge the backcountry recreationist with special hazards that may not be apparent to the inexperienced eye. These hazards include crevasses, moraines, meltwaters, and ice avalanches.

Any group planning to spend time on glaciers, either for recreation or as part of SAR operations, should seek hands-on professional training in glacier travel techniques and the fundamentals of crevasse rescue.

Crevasses

Crevasses form as a result of spatial variations in ice velocity, which subject the ice to tension or shearing forces. Cracks form in the ice mass, ranging in width from a few millimeters to yawning "gapers" that can span tens of meters, reach staggering depths, and pose frustrating barriers to travel. In many North American mountain ranges, crevasse danger varies with the season. In mid-winter, new snow tends to cover the crevasses, forming snow bridges that often persist well into the summer, when they metamorphose from hard, frozen structures at night and early in the morning to soft, wet "corn" snow later in the day.

Bergschrunds and moats

Related to crevasses (and similar in the dangers they pose) are bergschrunds and moats. A bergschrund (German for "mountain crevice") marks the zone near the top of a glacier where flowing ice separates from the stationary ice above. Moats form where the ice meets the rock at the crown of a glacier along its flanks. Heat from the rock tends to melt the ice at the edge of the glacier. Crossing a bergschrund or moat can be easy, but in some cases they feature high, steep walls that require special equipment such as ice tools, crampons, and ice screws. Bergschrunds and moats are insidious because they tend not to appear on topographic maps.

Conscientious glacier travelers remain roped together and spread apart to minimize slack in the rope until they are on solid ground. When setting up camp on a glacier, the party should remain roped until party members have carefully probed and marked the boundaries of the prospective camping area to establish a well-defined zone in which they can move about safely while unroped.

Moraines

Also associated with glaciers are moraines, which are piles of rock fragments pushed together by the snowplow-like effects of flowing ice. Moraines tend to persist, remaining in place for thousands of years after the glacial ice has retreated. They can be highly unstable, with large boulders poised to tumble at the slightest provocation.

Moulins

Large glaciers collect rain and shed meltwater. As a consequence they often have complex drainage systems of their own, with rivulets, streams, and lakes that may be connected via large channels with the hydraulics hidden beneath the glacier's surface. The hidden hydraulic connections within the glacier's subsurface can be treacherous. Known as moulins (French for "mills"), these features often take the form of vertical shafts draining deep into the glacier. Stepping into a moulin is like stepping onto an ice-water trapdoor, with

virtually no chance of climbing out under your own power. Managing the risks associated with glacial meltwater is largely a matter of rigorous adherence to good roped travel practices.

Rock glaciers

Slowly flowing mixtures of rock and ice, with rocks constituting the most visible part, have hazards similar to those of moraines. Instability, loose footing, and rockfall tend to be common. Collapse of the surface structure is an additional hazard, as meltwater flowing beneath the surface erodes the supporting ice-rock bridgework. Travel on rock glaciers tends to be slow, tedious, frustrating, and dangerous, especially with heavy packs, so it is almost always worthwhile to look for alternative routes.

Ice avalanches

Ice avalanches can be a serious threat on steep glaciers. They typically occur in icefalls, where the glacier is so densely crevassed that the ice forms bizarre, jumbled arrays of poorly supported towers called seracs. Ice avalanches can affect mountain travelers on dry ground, especially beneath the snout of a glacier where large calving ice chunks can crash down at random.

The most effective method for managing ice avalanches is to avoid icefalls and the runout zones below them, which can extend for thousands of vertical feet. Moving quickly through these zones is an alternative management strategy. There are really no safe times to negotiate this type of terrain. Because ice avalanches result from the steady movement of flowing ice, they can occur in any season and at any time of day.

AVALANCHES AND SNOW HAZARDS

Snow avalanches are such a prominent hazard in the mountain environment that the National Ski Patrol has developed a separate curriculum for avalanche safety and rescue. The rule is simple: An avalanche rescue must occur within minutes. The probability of a live rescue drops to less than half after a victim has been buried for 30 minutes. Therefore, in most settings, the only real hope is for a party to rescue its own victims. That's why every member in a party traveling in avalanche terrain needs to carry standard tools of the trade: a shovel, a collapsible probe pole, and an avalanche transceiver.

Aside from ice avalanches, mentioned above, avalanches fall into two categories: loose snow avalanches and slab avalanches. While either type can be deadly, the vast majority of avalanche deaths occur in slab avalanches, in which an entire block of snow comes loose from the snow around it and slides downhill.

The avalanche triangle

The most important measure for managing avalanche hazards is to get training. A level-one avalanche course that meets the standards of the National Ski Patrol or the American Institute for Avalanche Research and Education (AIARE) reviews the physics of snow and the effects of three major factors known as the avalanche triangle:

1. Terrain. Most avalanche accidents occur on or below slopes in a trigger zone between 30 and 45 degrees in steepness, with a sharp peak in the frequency distribution near 37 to 38 degrees. The runout zone typically extends outward to a point where the angle to the top of the trigger zone is 19 degrees (Figure 10-2). A party traveling in avalanche country should become familiar with the slopes by using an inclinometer, found on many compasses.

2. Weather. The most important weather factor for avalanche forecasting is snow deposition. Any weather event that deposits snow more rapidly than about an inch an hour can add stress to the snowpack faster than it can adjust, leading to instability. Strong wind also tends to form highly coherent slabs that can store the potential energy associated with the added snow load, until additional stress, such as the weight of a skier, triggers catastrophic failure.

3. Snowpack. The classic recipe for a slab avalanche is a strong layer on top of a weak layer. A strong snow layer is

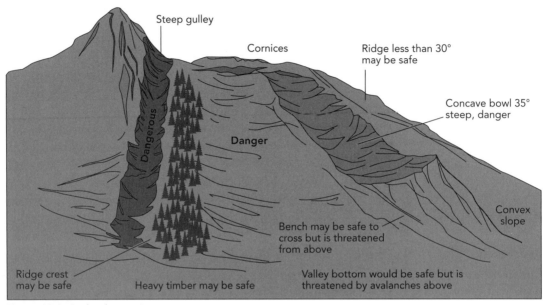

Figure 10-2. *Avalanche terrain*

any layer that is consistent enough to move as a unit, at least for a few seconds after a slide begins. A weak layer is any layer that can fail or collapse under the shearing and compressive forces exerted by new loads, including skiers, snowboarders, snowmobiles, or new snow.

Cornices

Cornices pose a special problem resulting from a combination of all three factors: terrain, weather, and snowpack (Figure 10-3). They are a hazard to ridgeline travelers, who may be tempted to walk or ski out over the unsupported snow; and to those below, who may be vulnerable to tumbling car- or house-sized blocks when the cornice collapses.

In avalanche terrain, cultivating good travel habits, such as the following, helps reduce risks:

» Stick to low-angle slopes or take advantage of terrain features, such as thick timber, that help anchor the snowpack.
» Stay alert to the effects of wind. Windward sides of slopes are usually safer than leeward slope sides.
» Steer clear of gullies, cornices, and obvious avalanche paths.
» Cross suspect slopes one person at a time, with each person moving from one safe zone to another.
» Keep an eye on the terrain above. Avalanches routinely kill people traveling on low-angle slopes beneath unnoticed hang fire looming above.

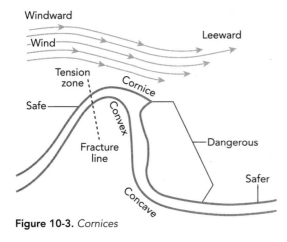

Figure 10-3. *Cornices*

TREE WELLS

Tree wells are depressions that form around tree bases. Evergreen trees in particular can have large, deep tree wells that form when low hanging branches prohibit snow from filling in and consolidating around the base of the tree. These holes are hidden from view by the tree's low hanging branches.

There is no easy way to determine by sight whether a particular tree has a hazardous tree well. Therefore, treat all tree wells as dangerous. Even very small trees with just their tops visible can be lethal; a fall into a tree well can lead to a snow immersion suffocation (SIS) accident.

To prevent a snow immersion accident,

» avoid tree well areas.
» consult local resources and be aware of local snow conditions that may increase the risk of a tree well accident.
» travel in control and give tree wells a wide berth. Look at the open spaces, not the trees.

» remove ski pole straps, if applicable.
» keep fellow recreationists or rescue personnel in sight at all times. Most recorded SIS victims have had a part of their body or equipment visible at the snow surface.

ENVIRONMENTAL HAZARDS

The high mountain environment tends to be dry, cold, and physically taxing. These hazards threaten human health, and backcountry travelers and rescuers are vulnerable to their effects. Some of the adverse health conditions that can arise from exposure include the following:

» Chronic hypoxia
» Dehydration
» Inability to acclimitize
» Frostbite
» High altitude pulmonary edema (HAPE)
» High altitude cerebral edema (HACE)

These health concerns and others are discussed in Chapter 14, Backcountry Medical.

GOOD JUDGMENT

Managing hazards in the mountains requires not only an understanding of objective hazards but also the good judgment required to recognize subjective hazards, or those associated with human decisions. Good judgment is also dependent on cultivating effective group interaction and relies as well on the following factors.

KNOWLEDGE AND AWARENESS OF BACKCOUNTRY HAZARDS

Knowledge is the most important element in managing risks. Accomplished patrollers, rescuers, and recreationists spend years learning about alpine hazards, not only through coursework and study but also through constant, observant experience. Much of this experience has to be personal, and it tends to be hard won because of the physical effort required to spend time in the high mountains. Nevertheless, the experiences of others can be extremely instructive. Serious American mountaineers and rescuers make a practice of reading *Accidents in North American Mountaineering*, edited and published annually by the American Alpine Club. These accounts of major climbing accidents highlight the most common and consequential errors, not only in technical climbing but also in more general mountain settings, where rockfall, crevasses, routefinding errors, inattention, and fatigue play prominent roles.

TIME MANAGEMENT

According to an old mountaineers' adage, "Speed is safety." The point is not simply speed itself but the flexibility in time management that comes with expeditious, efficient travel. Speed in the mountains is only partially a matter of physical strength and aerobic fitness. It also hinges on the party's behavior.

For a party to be successful on a long route, synchronicity must be a key concept on every party member's mind. In a synchronous party every stop by one party member becomes a stop for everyone: a urination stop, a moment to drink water, a boot tightening opportunity, a chance to peel a clothing layer. Done in parallel these inevitable activities, none of which takes much time in isolation, can get done quickly. Done in a series, with every member choosing a different three-minute time slot for map checks, pit stops, and other minor adjustments, the delays can add significant amounts of time to the trip.

Speed is not the only way to build time management flexibility into an itinerary. Among the most common motifs in mountaineering is the alpine start, often requiring a party to be underway in the dark hours before sunrise. Alpine starts

» allow a party to cover easy ground during the dark, thus maximizing the amount of daylight available for negotiating steeper, more hazardous terrain.
» minimize the risks associated with traveling in the darkness at the end of the day, when the party is tired and more prone to errors.
» allows the party, in many ranges, to travel through the most weather-exposed

terrain of a route during morning hours, when winds tend to be calmer and thunderstorms less common.

Another time management element is the ability to analyze a party's slow progress and to compensate for it—or adapt to it—on the fly. It may be possible to correct slow progress attributable to asynchronous stops, but it is harder to move more quickly when a party member's fitness limitations or equipment failures are the problem. The proper time to fix these issues is during the weeks and months preceding the trip. A broken crampon or a party member who is not physically capable of moving faster may require a significant change in plans to accommodate less ambitious objectives or even a retreat. Finally, there are few options that allow a party to compensate for a late start.

AVOIDING COMPOUNDED ERRORS

Let's say a party leaves for a backcountry hut trip on a February morning. Owing to the effects of a winter storm, they leave the city later than planned, and slow traffic on the interstate further delays their arrival at the trailhead. Once in the parking lot they shoulder packs in a heavy snowfall, strap on skis, and begin the arduous task of breaking a steep uphill trail through two feet of fresh powder. Five hours later, as they approach timberline, the nearly exhausted party begins to argue over the direction of the trail, which the new snow has by now obscured. They disagree over their location on the single map that they brought, then split into two groups and travel in separate directions, with no positive plans for getting back together.

Darkness approaches. The snowstorm continues unabated. Somebody remembers listening to the avalanche forecast that morning and observes that the surrounding terrain is steep enough to produce avalanches. Temperatures begin falling. One party member starts shivering uncontrollably.

This scenario is a composite of actual events. Several parties have encountered these life-threatening circumstances, not because of a single hazard or error in judgment, but because of the compounding of errors and the resulting failure to manage risks arising from a large constellation of hazards. In such instances a party can find itself confronted with so many serious problems that it becomes difficult to overcome long odds against success.

The dynamic should be familiar to anyone who has spent enough time in the high mountains. Goals seem more important than the barriers that nature has placed in the way, ego clashes take precedence over the safety of the group, irrational optimism about the weather, the terrain, or the group's capabilities leads to yet another error, and then another.

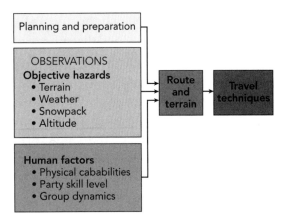

Figure 10-4. *A decision-making framework for mountain travel*

Managing subjective hazards requires the presence of mind and leadership needed to recognize the party's first error in judgment and to make it the last. On recreational outings, these personal attributes can make the difference between a successful expedition and a tragedy. In SAR operations, which tend to unfold in harsh, error-inducing environments, these errors can spell the difference between life and death for subjects and rescuers alike.

A DECISION-MAKING FRAMEWORK

During the past decade, spurred by interest in human factors that contribute to avalanche accidents, many avalanche instructors have proposed a decision-making framework for travel in avalanche country. An analogous concept has utility in backcountry settings more generally.

The idea, as shown in Figure 10-4 is to organize one's thinking about mountain travel into five different components, then to recognize that the components best promote safe travel if they fit into a temporal sequence.

Early in the process are three stages that involve the gathering of information:

1. Planning and preparation. Before the trip, assemble maps and route descriptions; gather and check the required equipment; make decisions about food, water, and shelter; develop a timeline for the trip; review the capabilities of party members; and arrange for logistics and travel to and from the trailhead. Share this information with other party members.
2. Observations. In the field, keep track of objective hazards, weather, terrain features, the group's location and altitude, snowpack characteristics, and other physical variables that may affect the group's travel plans.
3. Human factors. In the field, monitor the group's progress, physical capabilities, equipment, demonstrated skill levels, attitudes, leadership characteristics, and group dynamics.

After implementing the three stages above, two other stages come into play:

4. Route and terrain. Many aspects of this stage get settled during preparation and planning, but subsequent

observations of the objective hazards and human factors may lead the group to refine or make adjustments to its route selection in the interest of ease of travel, safety, or group preference.

5. Travel techniques. The fifth stage is appropriate only after the party has used the information gathered in the first three stages to make an educated choice of routes. Next comes making decisions about travel techniques. Here is where technical mountaineering choices get made. Do we need to wear harnesses and ropes? Will we climb on snow or rock? Are crampons necessary? Is it better to ski on the ridgeline or in the drainage below? To gain the ridge, will it be easier or safer to make a single long traverse or to switchback up through timber? Is it safer to rappel or to downclimb?

It is impossible to avoid all hazards when traveling in the mountains, but recognizing the hazards and knowing techniques for mitigating the attendant risks can help a party minimize threats to the group's success and safety. By organizing one's knowledge and skills into a decision-making framework, a group leader can keep an analytic and systematic frame of mind during all of the stages of an expedition.

SUMMARY

o Objective hazards exist independent of the backcountry recreationist's decisions. Subjective hazards are those over which the recreationist or rescuer has direct control.
o Nationwide, lightning is second only to flash floods among weather-related causes of death, surpassing hurricanes, tornadoes, and blizzards.
o Managing precipitation in a mountain setting requires attention to weather forecasts, adequate clothing layers, and scrupulous efforts to keep survival equipment dry.
o To learn how to mitigate avalanche hazards, enroll in a level-one avalanche course that meets the standards of the NSP or the AIARE.
o The most important element in managing risks associated with mountaineering hazards is knowledge.

PART THREE

BACKCOUNTRY CONSIDERATIONS

CHAPTER 11

ENVIRONMENTAL AWARENESS AND CAMPING

Bob Hollingsworth, Mount Baker Ski Patrol, Glacier, Washington

Candace Horgan, National Ski Patrol Communications Director, Lakewood, Colorado;
*   Arapahoe Basin Ski Patrol, Summit County, Colorado*

Frank Rossi, Summit East Ski Patrol, Newcastle, Washington

Chuck White, Mountain Travel & Rescue Manual Coordinator, Mount Holly Ski Patrol,
*   Holly, Michigan*

OBJECTIVES

o Identify camping techniques and procedures that minimize adverse impacts on the environment.

o Describe various accepted methods of waste disposal.

o Be aware of, understand, and follow regulations designed to protect the environment.

The old adage, "Take nothing but photos, leave nothing but footprints," still holds true today in the backcountry and has recently expanded to include minimum-impact camping and wilderness ethics. Whenever people enter the wilderness it is important to be cognizant of the environment, of wildlife, and of others who are in the area or will be in the future. Everyone needs to do his and her part to preserve and conserve the delicate balance of our natural resources.

Whether the goal is to enjoy a safe backpacking trip or rescue a lost skier, all of us who visit and work in the backcountry need to maintain an awareness of how our actions affect the natural environment. There's nothing more disheartening than hiking into a remote area only to find human waste and/or garbage ruining what should be an inspiring vista.

Poor preparation and planning can and often does harm the environment. Not adequately preparing for a search-and-rescue

(SAR) mission or a recreational backcountry trip may result in sloppy decisions that place unnecessary strains on the environment.

Nevertheless, caring for and safely transporting injured patients is the number one priority for rescuers on SAR missions. At critical times, decisions made in the interest of preserving and sustaining human life may adversely affect the natural environment. Still, rescuers should work toward bringing proper equipment for low-impact camping. They should plan for proper trash removal and have the expertise and skills required to perform quality emergency care while limiting environmental impacts (Table 11-1).

MINIMAL IMPACTS

Minimal-impact backcountry travel means accessing the environment with care and forethought. Campers must respect others and be thoughtful wilderness visitors. Groups should be kept small and consideration given to leaving pets at home.

Each backcountry recreationist and rescuer needs to be aware of and abide by the regulations applicable to the area of travel, since they were established to allow for recreational and environmental sustainability. Regulations vary by season, by region, by government agency, and by area, so be sure the information is current and applicable.

TABLE 11-1. LEAVE NO TRACE

Leave No Trace (LNT) is an international program that assists outdoor enthusiasts in minimizing their environmental impacts. LNT offers these guidelines, called the Seven Principles, to all who venture into the outdoors. Although the well-being and emergency care of backcountry recreationists takes priority with patrollers and rescuers, all visitors to the outdoors are encouraged to consider these suggestions:

1. Plan ahead and prepare.

2. Travel and camp on durable surfaces.

3. Dispose of waste properly.

4. Leave what you find.

5. Minimize campfire impacts.

6. Respect wildlife.

7. Be considerate of other visitors.

The Leave No Trace Seven Principles are printed with permission from the Leave No Trace Center for Outdoor Ethics.

It is important to be familiar with the area in which one is traveling. At serviced ski areas most people are generally familiar with the terrain, but if they venture into unfamiliar areas, they should consult local guidebooks and people who are familiar with the region, such as park personnel and those in local outfitting and mountain shops. This will provide valuable information about locations, such as the type of terrain, location of existing campsites, and regulations. Research the area thoroughly, checking for issues such as typical weather patterns, possible danger areas such as stream crossings during high runoff or avalanche paths during winter. Research how long it takes to arrive at a particular camping area and ensure that you arrive there with plenty of daylight to spare so that you are not trying to set up camp in the dark.

Whenever possible travel on established trails. This means not making or taking shortcuts, especially on switchbacks. Use footwear suitable for the terrain and the loads being carried. During summer, boots with deep lug soles can provide superior traction but may cause more erosion than is necessary. Make sure your footwear does not exceed what is needed for safety and control on the trail. When resting, hikers should stay on the trail or on rocks so as not to further trample nearby areas. This is particularly important if the group is large.

During the summer, walk in the middle of trails to avoid damaging vegetation adjacent to the trail. In areas where it is possible, travel on rock. In the winter, routes may change due to deep snow cover. Use skis or snowshoes, which do not punch through the snow and damage plants underneath. Check ahead of time to see if there are established winter routes to follow.

Minimum-impact camping means blending both campers and camps into the surrounding environment to reduce visual pollution to others. Natural-colored gear blends in to the surroundings, but in a SAR situation brightly colored items are more easily seen by searchers. Check your region's hunting regulations because some states require that a minimum of 400-square inches of blaze orange be worn during hunting season.

When moving off trail, whether a quick excursion for a bathroom break or traveling in an area without an established trail system, travel on durable surfaces such as rock, snow or ice, or on durable vegetation such as dry grasses. This is especially important in sensitive areas such as high mountain tundra or wetlands.

For many who camp in the mountains or forests, the beauty is matched only by the solitude. Travel quietly since others may be enjoying the silence. The exception is in areas where dangerous animals need to be avoided, such as grizzly country; in this case making a lot of noise may warn the animal of your approach and avoid surprising it.

CAMPING

Whether on a backcountry trip or a SAR mission, you need to carefully consider where and how to camp. It's important to remember that the effects of human habitation linger long after a trip or mission has concluded.

CAMP SELECTION

The prospective camper should use knowledge and experience to examine the location of the camp as it applies to the local ecology, the safety of the campers, protection from the elements, and convenience to both the goal and a reliable water supply. Consider potential impacts when selecting campsites (Figure 11-1).

It is best to use a preexisting site. This helps to eliminate further expansion of the site and damage to the nearby environment. Remember that the natural growth is fragile and it may take months or years to recover from use, so leave flowers, rocks, and other natural features undisturbed. Pine boughs should not be cut for beds or fires except in circumstances where survival is truly at stake.

Avoid camping close to water, trails, or animal trails. Obey any regulations regarding campsite selection. For instance, in most national parks there are designated sites for tents. If you don't stay in those areas, you may need to bivouac. If so, avoid creating new disturbances; camp in existing tent or bivouac sites, and whenever possible use existing pit toilets.

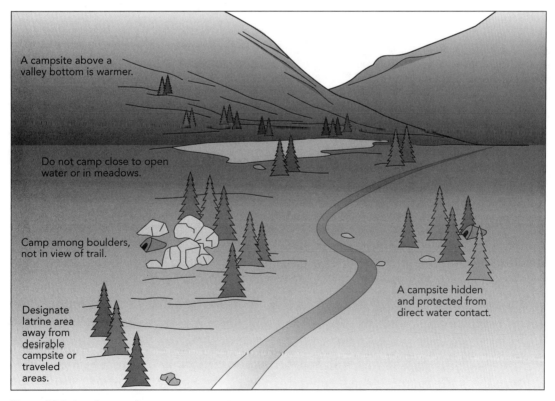

Figure 11-1. *Low-impact sites*

Campers should also be aware of natural hazards when selecting a site. Depending on the season, potential risks include widow makers (dead trees or tree tops that may fall in high winds), avalanches, rockfall, lightning, and flash floods. Never set up camp on avalanche slopes or runouts, or under cornices. Be aware of potential rockfall from cliffs, and debris falling to the bottom of couloirs. Ridges may have excellent views but are cold, windy, and attract lightning. Large open areas like meadows, frozen lakes, and flat valleys can also be windy. Choose an area that will not flood if it rains. If rain is expected, tents or other shelters should be positioned so water flows naturally away from them; avoid digging moats or ditches.

When setting up your campsite, some organization makes things easier and more efficient. This is especially true in the winter when cold and darkness are constant issues. Sorting out equipment, setting up the kitchen area, and laying out the sleeping bags should be done early while it is still daylight.

The group needs to know where the latrines are, or where they will be set up. It's important to know who will set up shelter and also which snow will be melted to obtain water. To help avoid any confusion, a camper might want to immediately fill a large, clean plastic garbage bag with snow to use as the water source. It can be placed at the opening of a tent or shelter for convenience when preparing the meals. This may help prevent accidental contamination as campers relieve themselves during the night.

CAMPING ESSENTIALS

Whether on a recreational backcountry trip or on a SAR mission, travelers need to have basic supplies in order to keep themselves alive and to help others.

SHELTERS

Chapter 6, Emergency Shelters, details the uses of bivouacs, tents, hasty shelters, and snow caves when backcountry recreationists and rescuers must take cover quickly. Those shelters are also useful for non-emergency mountain travel.

Igloos

Igloos are not emergency shelters because they take more time to build than is practical in critical circumstances. However, when time is not a factor they provide comfortable winter shelter and can be pleasurable and rewarding to build. The interior can be spacious and can reach a temperature of 50 degrees F.

Building an igloo requires advance planning since it may require more than four hours to construct. First, a circular or oval outline is made in the snow as a guide for placing the first row of blocks. An inside diameter of eight feet is large enough for four people. The blocks can be cut with a snow saw, machete, ski, or flat snow shovel. They should be at least 4 inches thick, 1½ feet wide, and 2 or 3 feet long.

As the blocks are placed, each one is undercut so that they lean toward the inside. The height of the roof determines the amount of undercut each block receives, which is where practice pays off. Blocks are placed in layers around the wall until there is only a hole left at the top for placement of the key block. During placement, the cracks between the blocks are caulked with snow. If possible the opening should be below the level of the floor.

The igloo may be used at this point, but for more strength and warmth it should be fired inside to glaze the interior with ice. To do this, a stove or fire is lit inside and the entrance covered until the snow on the walls begins to melt. The fire is then extinguished and the cold outside air allowed to enter and refreeze the walls. Ventilation is made at the top and a door closure is prepared, which should allow for a little circulation.

FOOD STORAGE

Backcountry travelers and rescuers need to keep food fresh and secured from scavenging animals. In the winter, cold temperatures prevent spoilage, so perishable items can be included. However, during winter, foods may need to be thawed before being eaten, which requires extra fuel.

Depending on the region, animals such as mice, squirrels, pikas, raccoons, and bears may be bothersome. For this reason the use of bear-proof food canisters is mandatory in a number of national parks and backcountry areas. Although certain types of wildlife are clearly more dangerous than others, even small creatures are likely to chew through a backpack to get at food.

To protect food supplies it may be necessary to suspend food bags or packs from a tree or—where the local bear population has acquired expertise—between two trees or in portable bear-proof containers. Food and garbage should be sealed in plastic bags to cut down on food odors. The bag should be suspended from a tree approximately 10 feet from the ground and at least 4 feet out on a limb or between trees that are 20 feet apart (Figure 11-2).

Cooking near sleeping bags or while wearing the same clothes that are slept in is not recommended in bear country as the odors may attract bears to the tent. No food should be kept in the tent, and no wild animals should be fed.

STOVES

For any trip lasting more than a day, a stove is a must. Its most important use is to heat water or to melt snow for drinking water. Small, lightweight backpacking stoves are available at any mountain shop, and selecting a stove that provides reliable operation in a blustery snowstorm is a must.

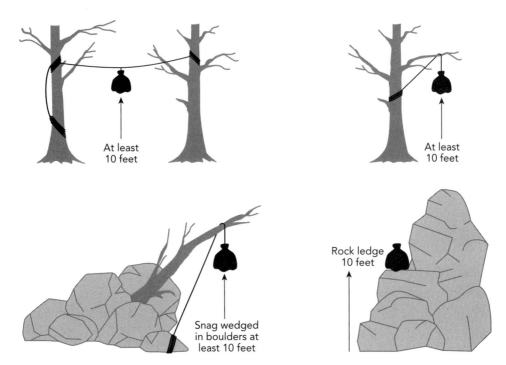

Figure 11-2. *Animal-proof storage*

A camper needs to know the stove well, and how to use the necessary tools to fix it in the field. Thoroughly check and clean your stove before each trip. Since fuel can become contaminated over time, use a fine mesh filter to fill the stove's fuel reservoir. After the trip, drain the fuel from the stove before storing it.

Standard backpacking stoves are powered by butane, Naphtha (white gasoline), kerosene, or regular gasoline. Though all are adequate for summer camping, white gas stoves provide the best performance for winter camping because of their high heat output and ease of ignition in cold temperatures. Butane performs poorly in cold weather because it is difficult to vaporize. Butane-propane mixtures and isobutane perform better than butane. Kerosene burns at a lower temperature than Naphtha. It is important to check the availability of fuel to purchase in the area you are going and to bring enough fuel to meet the needs of the group.

Most stoves require priming, which can be dangerous. Stoves need plenty of air for adequate combustion, so they should not be closed off too much. Prime the stove in an open, well-ventilated area; many a closed tent has gone up in flames from a stove being lit inside. Because of the additional danger from carbon monoxide poisoning, stoves (or any fire) should not be used inside tents or snow caves, since less than 10 percent of all stoves have low enough carbon monoxide emissions to be considered safe to use in a confined space.

Some stoves have an additional hand pump to aid in priming and to keep the gas pressure high. The heat from this burning gas heats the fuel line, vaporizing the gas in the line, and starting a flame from the main burner. Some stoves come with wind guards, which shelter the stove and allow them to burn more efficiently. A wind guard can be constructed out of heavy-duty foil placed around the outside of the stove.

Spilled fuel is highly volatile and can flame up and burn skin, clothes, etc. Even if it does not ignite, fuel evaporating off of exposed flesh can cause frostbite.

WATER

Water is critical for survival. (Chapter 2, Water and Hydration, details hydration, safe water sources, and purification.) Even in the winter, running water can sometimes be located under the snow, on rock faces, and under frozen streams. It may be worth looking for as it is more convenient and efficient than melting snow.

Water pollution, even in the wilderness, is an increasing problem. Many mountain travelers are infected with giardiasis, which is thought to be spread by humans as much as by the once-maligned beaver. All water should be considered potentially contaminated. When camping it is important to treat drinking and cooking water, and to protect the surrounding water sources from human and food wastes. Water may be treated by filtering, ultraviolet stirring, chemical additives, and boiling.

Melting snow

Melting snow is much more efficient with a good size pot (at least two to four quarts). Since the stove may be placed on a snow surface, it should be a stable design and have a base that stays cool. A small insulating pad may be used to keep the stove off the snow to prevent melting.

WASHING

Bathing is not always needed on short trips. When it is, washing up can be best accomplished by a sponge bath using just hot water or with moist towelettes (which are packed out after use). Even though a cold swim in a stream is invigorating after a hot hike, you should not bring soap—even biodegradable soap—into a stream or lake.

Dishes should be cleaned without soap because soap is a contaminate when dispersed in the environment. Clean-up can be made easier by choosing meals that require fewer pots. With a little forethought, one can become quite efficient in one-pot cooking. Many prepackaged foods can be cooked in their bags. In the winter, pots can be left to freeze and then scraped out the next day. Be sure to contain the debris to avoid leaving scraps for animals.

Spoons, bowls, and dirty pots can be cleaned by immediately rinsing them in hot—preferably boiling—water before food dries on them. Sand can also be used as an abrasive cleaner if it does not harm the cookware's finish.

If necessary, use small amounts of biodegradable soap, keeping in mind that even biodegradable soap must be broken down by organisms in the environment. Dish washing and tooth brushing should be done at least 200 feet from streams or lakes. Disperse toothpaste or strained dishwater. As with food, odors from toothpaste, soap, and even cookware can attract wildlife, especially bears. Consider adding these items to any food bags you may hang from trees.

Solids can be screened out of wastewater by using a strainer. Wastewater should be emptied into highly absorbent soil at least 200 feet away from water supplies and not dumped on plant life. Wastes should not be placed near natural water supplies, and the solids should be carried out with other garbage.

GARBAGE

Pack out all garbage, even if it is not yours. Plastic bags are an essential part of a backcountry recreationist's gear. In the winter,

solid waste can be frozen and carried out for better disposal.

Camping areas should always be left cleaner than found upon arrival. If garbage is burned, little scraps of foil that do not burn should be packed out. Even better, don't burn food waste; pack it out. Never burn plastic. Campers should not discard items that may be biodegradable as they are an eyesore to others. Banana skins and orange peels in particular are not very biodegradable. The cold tends to preserve these items, and wild animals do not always eat what is thrown away. Many human foods are not nutritionally appropriate for animals. Campers should try to eat everything, or pack it out and plan better the next time. Garbage should never be dumped into latrines or outhouses.

SANITATION

Improper disposal of human waste can lead to water pollution, the spread of illnesses such as giardia, and unpleasant experiences for those who follow. It can also attract animals.

Whenever possible take time to locate and use bathrooms, outhouses, and other developed sites for human waste disposal. They provide more comfort and privacy, and damage the environment less.

So, what do you do if there are no outhouses? Some very popular backcountry areas, such as Denali, Mount Hood, Mount Shasta, and Mount Rainier require you to carry a "poop tube" or "wag bag" (waste alleviation and gelling) to pack out all human waste.

However, in many wilderness areas, the cat hole method of disposal is preferred. When determining the location of the cat hole, consider soil drainage, privacy, and proximity to the camp and water supply. Latrines should be at least 200 feet from any water source.

Cat holes entail digging a hole in the ground approximately eight inches deep, where the highest concentration of organisms is located, providing for rapid breakdown. The waste should be buried with the removed soil and stamped down.

Winter sanitation requires further skill. Campers should dig through the snow until the ground is reached. This method facilitates bacterial decomposition. If this is not possible, use a separate cat hole each time or let the feces become frozen and carry it out with the garbage. In contrast, if one hole is used, large concentrations of urine and feces freeze into one big mass, which takes a long time to decompose and becomes an ugly eyesore when the snow melts. Winter campers should avoid using flat spots for toileting unless they are familiar with the terrain because they may be on top of a pond, lake, or stream.

Whatever the season, whenever possible use a remote location during the day's travel to help prevent high concentrations of cat holes near campsites. Plan ahead:

Toilet paper can be burned or packed out with you in a plastic bag. Always pack out feminine hygiene products because they decompose slowly and attract animals. Human urine may attract deer and mountain goats. Urinate well away from camps, water sources, and trails.

FIRE BUILDING

The delicate ecology of the backcountry dictates that fires be built only in emergencies unless at designated campsites in established fire rings where regulations permit. That's because, in general, stoves are much more efficient for cooking than open fires. They cook faster and keep pots cleaner. Stoves do not require searching for wood, do not leave campers smelling of smoke, and do not scar the environment.

Although fire building is discouraged, in emergency situations campfires may be essential. Fires provide warmth, raise the spirits of those in difficult situations, and may be of some benefit for distress signaling.

If you must build a fire in an emergency, follow these guidelines:

» Pick a location that is sheltered from wind and precipitation and where wood fuel is in ample supply.
» If building a fire on bare ground, surround it with rocks or wet wood to keep it from spreading to nearby vegetation.
» Pile tinder such as dry grass, paper,

pine needles, lint, very small sticks, and dead kindling wood.

» Use firestarters such as waterproof matches, butane lighters, candles, Vaseline-coated cotton balls, hand sanitizer, fire ribbon, and dead kindling wood. White gas should not be used as it is extremely flammable.

» Use dry, dead wood, which snaps and breaks when bent; green and wet wood does not.

» Keep the flames small.

» Water should always be available to put the fire out.

» After the fire has burned out, saturate the ash with water; make sure it is thoroughly cold to the touch. Scatter the ashes widely and restore the ground to its normal appearance.

CONSIDERATIONS

Striving to be considerate of the environment is especially important in the backcountry where ecosystems are fragile and wildlife can be easily disrupted. And while it's often difficult to remember to be mindful in the midst of an emergency situation, being aware of how you are affecting your surroundings is a goal to always keep in mind.

RESPECT WILDLIFE

One of the true joys of backcountry travel is seeing wildlife, from the tiniest pika to a large moose or raptor. You may even see wolves or lions, preferably from a distance! Unfortunately, many species of wildlife are currently threatened or endangered. It is up to you to manage your interactions with wildlife so that you do not harm them.

Quick movements and loud noises are stressful to animals, so be aware of noise levels and do not pursue or force animals to flee. One exception is in bear country, where it is often advantageous to make noise so as not to startle bears. It is best to view wildlife from afar, for both their safety and yours, so don't mistake wildlife's apparent passivity as an invitation to pet it, pick it up, or feed it. These activities are all stressful to the animal, and it is possible that the creature may harbor rabies or other diseases. Sick or wounded animals can bite, peck, scratch, or otherwise injure you, and young animals removed or touched by well-meaning people may cause the animals' parents to abandon them. If you find sick animals or an animal in trouble, notify a game warden as soon as possible.

It bears repeating: Never feed animals. This can make them less sensitive to human presence and result in more aggressive behavior. It can also damage their health, alter natural behaviors, and expose them to predators and other dangers. Store all food and garbage securely. If your camping area has bear-proof containers, use them.

Although taking your dog with you into the backcountry is generally discouraged—exceptions are made for working dogs on SAR missions—it's important that if you do decide to bring your pet, you are completely in control. Wildlife and pets do not mix well, since dogs sometimes harass wildlife and disturb other recreationists. Use a leash to keep your pet in check when hiking, and make sure to properly manage the waste.

BE CONSIDERATE OF OTHER VISITORS

You would not want to have your backpacking or ski trip ruined by loud, inconsiderate recreationists who clog the trail, so show others the same courtesy. When passing another group of hikers, make sure to share the space. Offer friendly greetings. Yield to downhill traffic, faster traffic, and horses, which sometimes spook at the sight of pack-laden humans. Avoid hiking on ski or snowshoe tracks. Take rest breaks a short distance from the trail on durable surfaces, such as rocks or bare ground. If the vegetation around you is thick or easily crushed, pick a wide spot in the trail so others can pass by. Use established campsites out of sight and sound of trails and other visitors.

SUMMARY

o The backcountry environment is fragile. Field conservation is dynamic and changes as we learn more about our ecosystem. It is important for recreationists to be knowledgeable about current low-impact camping methods and techniques.

o Winter camping often means cold temperatures, early darkness, and challenging snow conditions. These can be managed with proper training, the correct equipment, and a woll planned trip.

o No matter what season, minimal-impact backcountry travel means moving through the environment with care and forethought.

CHAPTER 12

WEATHER

Karl Auerbach, Bristol Mountain Ski Patrol, Canandaigua, New York

OBJECTIVES

o Explain characteristics of weather patterns on a regional and local level.

o Describe the significance of cloud formations in forecasting weather.

o Describe other indicators of changing weather.

o Discuss the influences of local topography on weather.

o List sources of current weather forecasts for the intended trip area.

o Recognize the impact of weather on trip planning, execution, and search and rescue.

Weather can be one of the most disruptive and dangerous forces for the backcountry recreationist. Visibility, mobility, communications, and gear and shelter requirements are impacted by the weather. Violent weather conditions such as blizzards or thunderstorms can develop suddenly. Weather can impact terrain conditions, including surface characteristics, avalanches, or flooding. Thus, recreationists' enjoyment in the backcountry and the success and safety of rescue missions depends on good weather information and assessment.

Prior to a trip the diligent backcountry traveler should acquire a general understanding of anticipated weather. While traveling in the backcountry, a good "weather eye" must be maintained by observing changing weather conditions and understanding local factors that impact weather.

BASIC CONCEPTS

Most weather occurs as a result of air masses coming together. Movement of air masses on a regional and local basis impact weather and create conditions of concern. This may occur horizontally across the terrain or vertically as air masses rise or fall.

Converging air masses differ in temperature, moisture content, and/or air flow direction. The characteristics of an air mass can change as it moves across terrain or as it rises or falls. These differences and changes create a wide variety of conditions that we call "weather."

Generally, warmer air rises and cooler air falls. While this may seem simplistic, it is a good way of understanding weather changes. Warmer air can hold a greater amount of moisture than cooler air. But as it rises, the air cools, releasing that moisture in the form of clouds or precipitation. The more moisture in a mass of air, the greater the potential for unsettled weather.

Warmer air also tends to have lower pressure than cooler air. As these air masses of different pressures interact, a pressure gradient develops. Again, simplistically, the sharper the pressure gradient, the stronger the potential is for air movement such as wind. The faster the

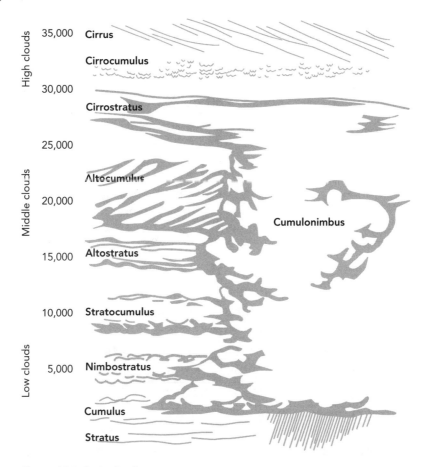

Figure 12-1. *Basic cloud groups*

change in characteristics of air masses, the more likelihood there is for violent weather.

CLOUDS

Clouds form when the air is sufficiently cooled to allow the moisture it contains to condense. Since air is generally cooler at higher altitudes, any factor that lifts air may lead to cloud formation. This lift may occur because of regional movement of air masses or because of local topography.

Clouds are probably the best indicators of weather conditions. They are also one of the most easily observed phenomena in the field. They fall into three basic categories:

» cumulus (lumpy, rounded, like cotton balls)
» stratus (layered, fuzzy, hazy)
» and cirrus (feathery, often horizontal)

Various types of clouds occur in different combinations and at a range of altitudes (Figure 12-1). Each can be generally associated with specific weather events. Often clouds warn of an approaching change in weather long before the temperature or wind changes.

In addition to cloud development from moving air masses, local factors such as heating effects often impact cloud formation. It is not uncommon for cumulus clouds to develop over the course of a day. If the lifting effect is sufficient, such clouds can develop into rain or thunderstorms. Cumulus clouds also form over lakes, especially in the spring.

When clouds are in contact with the ground surface, they are called "fog." This contact with the surface can occur as a cloud passes over a high point in the terrain. At night, valley bottoms trap cool air as it sinks. This can result in fog or low clouds in the morning. Depending on the general air mass characteristics, such fog may dissipate with heating during the day.

Different clouds and patterns of clouds can be associated with varying weather patterns, depending on regional and local considerations. The following are general weather patterns and the cloud patterns associated with them.

Fair weather is characterized by

» a cloudless blue sky with possible low fog or a layer of haze at valley bottom.
» small cumulus clouds appearing in a clear sky before noon but decreasing or vanishing during the day.
» clear skies except for a low cloud deck, which does not rise or thicken during the day.

Local disturbances such as local thunderstorms, showers, or squalls are indicated by

» scattered cumulus clouds that increase in size and rapidly thicken during the afternoon.

» the approach of a line of large cumulus or cumulonimbus clouds (thunderheads) with an advance guard of altocumulus (uniform layer of cumulus at 9,000 to 16,000 feet). At night, increasing lightning to the windward of prevailing wind gives the same warning.

The approach of a storm is characterized by

» clouds that tend to thicken and darken.
» changes that can be seen over a couple of days or over hours, depending on the nature of the storm.

Since increased moisture occurs in air masses during storms, the old adage "red sky at night, sailors delight; red sky in the morning, sailors take warning" can be useful even in mountainous regions. High moisture caused by local heating during the day can cause a refraction of sunlight as the sun sets, causing the sky to look reddish. But if the same occurs in the morning before heating, it is a sign that there is increased moisture in the air, heralding the potential for unsettled weather.

Typically clouds start at a high level as a thin veil of cirrus clouds and take form as they lower in elevation. As they thicken, a smooth-bottomed layer of mid- to high clouds are formed that can block out much of the sun during the day and the moon and stars at night.

Over time lower decks of clouds will form. If there have been lower clouds due to local conditions, they can merge with the lower clouds from the approaching storm. Confused layers of clouds develop and the smoother clouds lose their streamlined shape. These changes are often accompanied by strong winds.

Lens-shaped clouds that are generated by strong winds can appear often at the top of developing, cumulus-type clouds. Also called lenticular clouds, these clouds are indicative of strong winds and forces at altitude; they are often harbingers of violent weather.

As a storm moves past, the cloud cover starts to break up. Lower level clouds, often cumulus, move in. An upper cloud level can often be seen through broken lower layers.

FRONTS

A front exists where air masses with different properties, such as temperature and humidity, meet.

A warm front develops when a warm air mass overtakes and slides up over a cooler air mass. The contact zone between the warm and cold air masses is usually low angled and long. A warm front is slow moving, with cirrus clouds the first indicators of its approach. As the main part of the front approaches, the clouds thicken and precipitation is likely. Typically warm fronts are less violent than cold fronts, but because they are slow moving they can result in significant precipitation over time. While the term "warm" is used, the precipitation can be in the form of snow if the lower level air temperature is cold enough.

A cold front forms when a cooler air mass slides under a warm air mass, pushing it up steeply. If the speed of the cooler air mass is fast enough the cooler air can crest like a wave and come crashing down on the warmer air. Cumulus clouds form along the contact zone between the air masses. Thunderstorm activity frequently accompanies cold fronts. Though often passing faster than warm fronts, the cold front is often accompanied by sudden severe weather in the form of winds and heavy precipitation.

When a warm air mass is trapped between two cold masses, an occluded front forms. This front is usually found in the heart of a storm system and is accompanied by large amounts of precipitation.

Depending upon the movement of air masses, a given location can remain in a frontal zone for a long time. This is referred to as a stationary front. It may be due to the front moving relatively small distances from north to south, or it may be that the front is at the same general location but the system is moving to the east, sliding the frontal zone past a particular location.

The greater the difference between the temperature of the air masses and the speed of movement of the air masses, the greater the chance of violent weather.

Watching cloud formations and observing the changes in temperature and wind direction provides information about the nature and possible severity of the approaching front.

WIND

Wind is air moving between areas with different temperatures and pressures. In the Northern Hemisphere the prevailing winds usually blow from the west or southwest. In storm systems the air circulates counterclockwise so that the direction of the wind changes as a system passes. Generally, the longer a storm takes to arrive (indicating a large, slow moving front), the worse it will be in terms of persisting stormy weather.

On the other hand, a rapidly moving storm may arrive abruptly, bringing with it brief but often violent winds and precipitation, typically generating its own winds. As a thunderstorm passes, wind shear can occur, where the wind is gusty and changes direction suddenly. A 180-degree change in wind direction and a rising barometer are both indicators that a storm has peaked.

Wind affects visibility, especially when blowing and drifting snow causes a ground blizzard. Winds of 40 miles per hour or more can knock a person off balance. If the visibility is limited, following a route with known landmarks is advisable. In severe wind conditions, making camp and waiting out the storm may be the wisest decision.

HUMIDITY, DEW POINT, AND PRECIPITATION

Air at elevations up to 25,000 feet contains water vapor, which is responsible for clouds and precipitation. How much water vapor the air can hold depends on temperature and is expressed as a percentage of humidity. The quantity of water vapor in the air approximately doubles for each 25 degree F increase. As warmer, moisture-laden air cools, the amount of water it can hold decreases.

The temperature at which it is cool enough for water to condense out of the air as dew, fog, or frost is called the dew point. Low dew point indicates dry, stable air. If an air mass is quickly cooled or if it absorbs too much moisture, precipitation in the form of rain or snow will occur.

Precipitation has a direct bearing on the comfort and safety of a backcountry trip. After rain, creeks and rivers rise, making previously benign crossings a serious hazard. Rain on snow makes the snowpack unstable, as does a large amount of snowfall. The effect of precipitation must be considered when planning a trip route, considering retreat, or deciding to stay put.

TEMPERATURE

As altitude changes, so does temperature. For moist air, a 3.5 degree F decrease per 1,000 vertical feet of rise is typical. For dry air, 5.5 degree F is typical. These temperature gradients are called the adiabatic rates. Temperature gradients outside this range indicate unstable air.

As fronts pass, the nature of the temperature change indicates how much of the storm has passed and what further changes may be expected. Temperature will gradually rise with an approaching warm front, though it may still be below freezing. A cold front often produces sudden and dramatic drops in temperature.

Even when there is no storm system approaching, the rise of air over high terrain can cause a change in the temperature and moisture-carrying capability of the air.

When there is cloud cover, nights are warmer than they would otherwise be. This is caused by a cloud blanket blocking normal radiation loss of heat from Earth's surface. On the other hand the clear night air following a storm can be extremely cold because of the loss of the insulating cloud layer and the lower air humidity following precipitation.

The temperature pattern during the course of a day, as well as over the past days and weeks, has a direct impact on the quality of snow, on avalanche danger, and on travel conditions. The temperature effect on snow should be taken into consideration when planning each day's route. An early start may be needed to cross steep, unstable slopes before the sun warms them. Rockfall potential also increases as the sun melts away ice. Travel becomes slow and uncomfortable when snow is slushy. Backcountry recreationists may wish to set up camp or enjoy a prolonged rest stop during this time.

REGIONAL AND GENERAL WEATHER PATTERN CONSIDERATIONS

Surface conditions involve a complex interaction of air masses and movement. Air masses near the surface of the earth tend to be "steered" by high altitude air movement. The strongest movement of air occurs in the jet streams, which are relatively narrow bands of air flow that occur as a result of both planetary rotation and heating of the atmosphere.

The jet streams in both the Northern and Southern hemispheres generally flow west to east at an altitude of about 23,000 feet in the Arctic region to 50,000 feet in the subtropical regions. Wind speed in the jet stream can be in the range of 150 to 300 miles per hour. There may be more than one jet stream as flows can split and rejoin. The jet stream also has north-to-south dips in the Northern Hemisphere, and south to north in the Southern Hemisphere, shifting slowly away from and toward the poles.

Air cells of varying composition can be thought of as riding the jet stream. Thus the weather system in a region can be roughly predicted by looking at the location of the jet stream and calculating where it will move along the general flow. Depending on the configuration of the jet stream, weather systems can be expected to come from the west if the jet stream is straight, or from the north or south depending on where the dips in the jet stream occur. These air cells interact as they come into contact with one another. These fronts produce the type of weather outdoor recreationists need to pay attention to.

A first pass forecast can be made based on the general flow of systems. There are exceptions, since land masses and local intense heating can change the general rule. The best example of this is found in tropical storms, which often take atypical courses.

Another regional concept concerns cyclonic flow. In the Northern Hemisphere air tends to move in a counterclockwise pattern around low pressure systems. In the Southern Hemisphere this flow is clockwise. Since low pressure systems or storms tend to be a major factor in weather conditions, knowing where you are in relationship to an approaching low can be determined by wind direction. While each storm is unique, there are patterns of events that can help make a forecast for a given location.

Meteorologists have developed complex computer models to predict these movements of both the jet streams and the surface air masses they impact. These predictions are increasingly accurate but far from perfect. Before setting out, the mountain traveler should check the forecast based on these movements.

LOCAL CONSIDERATIONS

The weather pattern in a region is often altered by local geography, so in a sense all weather is local. Each area has its own unique weather patterns, and understanding and respecting those patterns is important for route planning and safe travel. Seasonal patterns exist as well. For example, in the Pacific Northwest most precipitation falls in the winter. Storms move through nearly daily, while during the summer longer periods of fair weather are common. If planning an extended trip in unfamiliar country, talk to local residents, check weather reports, and research weather websites.

The hills and valleys that make up mountains impact both regional and local weather. Whenever an air mass moves over a mountain, adiabatic heating and cooling occurs (Figure 12-2).

As the air mass rises it loses pressure and is cooled at the moist air adiabatic rate. As air cools it also loses excess moisture. Thus the west side of the major mountain ranges experience more wet weather than the east side. As the lighter air spills over the mountain crests it increases in pressure and becomes much warmer at the dry air adiabatic rate. This warm, dry air rushing down the slopes is sometimes called a Chinook. Areas immediately leeward of major mountains experience more dry, fair weather than other areas in the region.

12,000 feet   33° F

5,000 feet   Chinook   68° F

34° F

Figure 12-2. *Adiabatic lapse rate in an air mass moving over a ridge*

During the course of a sunny day, local winds develop. When the sun first rises it warms the tops of eastern-facing ridges. The warm air rises and a light up-slope and up-valley wind develops. During the day the rising warm air may lead to cumulus cloud development above ridge crests. In northern latitudes northern and eastern slopes receive less sun than southern and western slopes. Thus, afternoon thunderstorms often develop over mountain ridges with large southern or western exposures. As the sun sets, the air cools and starts to settle in the lower elevations. The wind shifts down-slope and down-valley. Just prior to the shift is a period of calm. Local clouds usually dissipate. Because the cooler air settles into valley bottoms, the warmest campsites are found about a third of the way up the slope, above the cold air pocket and below the windy ridge. These local winds make assessing larger, regional weather patterns more difficult and can accentuate any weather disturbances.

Oceans and large lakes influence local weather. Besides being a source for additional moisture that can evaporate into the air, the water absorbs warmth and influences the air passing over it. Areas around the Great Lakes and near coasts experience far different weather than inland areas in the face of similar regional factors. To some extent smaller lakes influence the micro-weather around them.

FORECASTING

Weather forecasting has improved with satellite technology and improved computer models, but mountain topography and bodies of water reduce forecasting accuracy for specific localities. Prevailing seasonal weather data for specific locations is available from local weather records and past experience. Local residents, the media, and government agencies are valuable sources of current weather information.

One such agency is the National Oceanographic and Atmospheric Administration (NOAA), which broadcasts information continuously throughout the day on the following frequencies (MHz) from more than 100 different sites: 162.400, 162.425, 162.450, 162.475, 162.500, 162.525, and 162.550. Small, pocket-sized receivers for these frequencies are available at most retail consumer electronics stores. Nearly all urban areas receive transmissions on one of these frequencies, but reception in the mountains may be spotty and uncertain.

Forecasts for nearly all locations are available on the internet. Satellite internet service or cell phone–based service make this available in some of the most remote areas. A wide variety of websites such as local news services or NOAA (www.noaa .org) can provide weather information on a real-time basis. Links are also available to local observation stations. However, as with the weather radio, connectivity can be spotty in mountain regions. Avalanche forecasts can be obtained from state highway departments, state forestry departments, and the US Forest Service.

Many mountain states have dedicated state avalanche forecasting agencies. It is wise to monitor avalanche forecasts over time to understand the avalanche history of any given area.

SUMMARY

o The passage of a weather front results in a major 180-degree shift in wind direction and velocity. Stronger winds usually indicate more rapidly moving storms.

o Air temperature decreases with elevation gain in the ratio of 5.5 degrees F for dry air and 3.5 degrees F for wet air, every 1,000 feet of change.

o All weather is local. While regional and general forecasts are important, local topography and features can significantly impact the weather at any given site.

CHAPTER 13

GROUP DYNAMICS

Myron Allen, Medicine Bow Nordic Ski Patrol, Laramie, Wyoming

OBJECTIVES

o Explain the differences in group dynamics between a party of backcountry recreationists and a team of rescuers on an Incident Command System operation.

o Identify at least three leadership skills.

o Describe four good group habits.

o Explain decision-making traps in group settings, and identify at least three.

A party of backcountry recreationists typically takes a far less formal approach to group interactions than do rescuers on an emergency operation. A search-and-rescue (SAR) team involved in a multi-jurisdictional SAR mission, in contrast, is mandated to follow Incident Command System (ICS) protocols. (For more on ICS and its protocols, see Chapter 15, Search and Rescue Basics). Regardless, any time a group enters the backcountry, either for recreation or rescue purposes, one element remains central: critical to that group's success is the group itself.

LEADERSHIP

Leadership is a commitment to the success of the group. It has particular relevance to ski patrollers who, by virtue of their training and experience, have special responsibilities in the mountains and in rescue operations. In these settings patrollers often serve as leaders and help others succeed as leaders.

Much of what concerns leaders in backcountry settings focuses on hazards and how to manage them. As discussed in Chapter 10, Backcountry Hazards, objective hazards exist independent of group or individual decisions. Subjective hazards are those over which the group has direct control. To manage either type of hazard a leader must recognize it and make decisions that minimize the risk.

Cultivating leadership skills is a lifelong process. It requires, among other attributes, an awareness of one's own leadership style and the styles of other leaders, attention to group dynamics and teamwork, and an ability to steer clear of common decision-making traps.

When you are a leader of a backcountry trip, the trip itself is not about you. This simple observation has three important implications:

» First, leaders in the mountains need a high level of personal skills and fitness, not only to ensure that they have the reserves needed to help a struggling team member but also to minimize the temptation to focus on their own struggles.
» Second, leadership requires preparedness. The leader is responsible for the prior research needed to understand the route, terrain, equipment needs, and weather. The leader must also make sure that team members are prepared with this information.
» Third, to foster effective group intelligence, it is important to share credit for the success of the trip liberally, not just after it is over but during the decision-making dynamics that play out as the trip unfolds.

Also critical is how the leader defines success. How we measure the success of an excursion in the mountains depends on the context, but one element is common: the safe return of everyone in the party. In recreational outings—which are important in the context of backcountry travel because these trips cultivate our interests and solidify our expertise—the safe return of party members is the only essential criterion for success.

In SAR training exercises, additional criteria include acquiring specific skills and the development of teamwork. In real SAR missions the criteria for success are complex. They include smooth functioning of the operation, effective organization of people and equipment, clear communication, and optimizing efforts to locate and care for the incident's subjects. Still, even if finding and saving the subjects proves impossible, the safe return of everyone in the party remains an essential element of the group's success.

LEADERSHIP STYLES

To be a leader does not take a specific personality type or leadership style. Instead it requires attributes that most people must cultivate: a willingness to promote the success of the group, an ability to manage stress in oneself and in others, and a set of skills and expertise that wins the group's respect and serves as a reservoir when the going gets tough.

Whether you are leading a private backpack trip or a large SAR operation, your leadership style depends in part on your natural inclinations. The ICS framework encourages leaders to delegate responsibility so as not to bottleneck operations.

Regardless of the setting, leadership requires careful attention to the tone displayed at the top. An effective leader strives to be calm, dignified, analytic, optimistic, and flexible. A leader should instill in the group a sense of control over its destiny. A team that has "bench depth," meaning several team members who possess these attributes and who support the leader's overall objectives, is indispensible.

TEAMWORK

Whether on a recreational or SAR excursion, if the leader is the only one working for the success of the group, failure lurks at every turn. Marshalling everyone's contributions requires good group dynamics and teamwork, which in turn requires communication. Teamwork also means generating accurate assessments of team members and good group habits and effectively managing stress within the group. Important, too, is the cultivation of group intelligence, a synergy among team members in which the training, experience, and judgment of each member contributes to a cumulative wisdom that is greater than that of even the most expert team member.

Effective communication means that everyone must understand the trip's goals, the equipment required, the weather forecast, the route and its objective hazards, and the levels of skill and fitness needed. An ICS principle, called the span of control, limits the number of people one person can manage to no more than seven subordinates (see Chapter 15, Search and Rescue Basics). Span of control can reduce the potential for miscommunication within any group.

Communication outside the group is also important. On recreational outings and training exercises the itinerary needs to be relayed to a source, including a time limit beyond when an absence of communication from the group may indicate trouble. Depending on the size of a SAR operation, ICS provides a structure for clear and complete communication channels.

Accurately assessing your team members is one of a leader's most difficult tasks. During recreational outings the group may include people of varying fitness levels, skills, and personal motivations. The success of the group may demand that you pay more attention to whether people enjoy themselves safely than whether you complete a preconceived itinerary. Still, tension within the group can arise when the jackrabbit faction's agenda is more ambitious than what the turtle faction can enjoyably or safely pursue. In this situation the only way to ensure success is to make sure everyone understands the physical demands and skills required before they show up at the trailhead.

Sharing this information effectively and in a timely manner, especially with a group defined by social relationships instead of common outdoor interests, can be a delicate balancing act. It pits tact against firmness, and friendship against good judgment. In many cases tact and friendship win, and group success requires scaling back the itinerary. It's better to recognize this need before you have gotten too far beyond the trailhead to make adequate adjustments.

In training exercises and SAR missions, team member assessment is an integral part of choosing the team, because it can prove critical to the group's success. In a training exercise, team members must have sufficient fitness levels to complete the exercise. They need to be sufficiently prepared to work effectively with each other, and they must have the motivation and sense of purpose to stay on task. In a SAR mission all of these attributes are essential. In addition, everyone in the team must already possess—and not just be ready to practice—the specific skills and knowledge needed to carry out the mission. In these settings a leader may face the unpleasant task of telling a volunteer that he or she cannot be part of the team or must find another way to contribute.

GOOD GROUP HABITS

Even with a group that seems ideally matched to its itinerary, it is essential to monitor team members. Mountain travel is strenuous, and the inherent physical stresses can provoke unexpected difficulties: overuse injuries, forgotten or malfunctioning gear, acute mountain sickness (AMS), emerging cold injuries, and unacknowledged medical problems. Among the most subtle difficulties can be lapses in mental orientation to the alpine environment, as those with indoor careers negotiate the sudden transition to a high, wild, and chilly mountain realm. Leaders have a responsibility to check even the most robust-seeming team members for signs of fitness deficits and other problems.

Several group habits can help ensure success:

Establish trailhead protocols. Get a head count. Know who is in the group. Remind group members of essential personal and group equipment (see Chapter 7, Essential and Group Equipment). Check radio communications. Report to your appropriate leader. Review the weather forecast and the itinerary on a map. Establish group decision-making dynamics, including every person's right to express safety concerns at any time. Wait until everyone is ready to go before starting.

Practice time management. Establish a turn-back time to help promote good judgment if the party turns out to be slower than expected. Encourage team members to make the best use of every stop.

Periodically regroup and sweep. Place someone strong at the front of the group, and someone at the end to serve as sweep. The lead person and sweep should have radios if possible. Reassemble the group periodically to make sure party members don't get too spread out. It is an especially good idea to regroup at every fork in the trail to keep the group from getting separated.

Verify protocols at trail's end. When on an ICS mission, follow ICS protocol. Recreation team members should get a head count. Take stock of equipment and make sure it goes home with the right people. Don't leave for home before accounting for all members of the party, and before knowing that they are safe and that they understand that they are on their own.

STRESS MANAGEMENT

Even with the best communication, team member assessment, and group habits, the mountain environment can produce unexpected challenges for recreationists and rescuers alike. Harsh weather, rugged terrain, equipment failure, or injury can change a group's prospects with surprising suddenness. A leader's skill at managing these stresses can be critical to the group's success.

Two principles underlie stress management in mountain travel and rescue settings:

Maintain a flexible, analytic frame of mind. When a stressful circumstance arises, stop for a moment, take a breath, and evaluate the situation. Note the time and your location. Mentally catalog the principal threats to group safety. Review the elements of your training that can help reduce these threats. Avoid getting wedded to preconceived notions. It is important that you arrive at an accurate appraisal of the situation and that you adopt an effective plan for dealing with it.

Avoid compounding errors. Compounding errors can turn minor problems into disasters. Most serious backcountry accidents arise not from a single erroneous judgment but from a sequence of bad decisions. If you find your group confronting an unanticipated problem, immediately stop, take a breath, and tap into your common sense to avoid adding to the difficulties.

THREE RULES BEFORE SEPARATING

» Have a purpose. Recognize when the group is drifting apart and take measures to assess the situation. If there is a good reason to separate, do it consciously and make sure everyone in the group knows why.

» Check each subgroup's preparation. If your group decides to split, make sure each subgroup has more than one member and appropriate navigation tools. Conduct a radio check. Look at maps to make sure everyone understands where the different subgroups plan to go. If you are separating to manage an injury, make sure the people staying with the injured have shelter, medical gear, and expertise. Make sure the people going for help have both a map with the injured party's location marked and written notes describing the party's medical and physical conditions.

» Make a plan for getting back together. The plan should include a time, place, and backup plan in case the reunion doesn't occur as anticipated. As simple as this step seems, it is the most critical—and most commonly forgotten—element of a group separation.

DECISION-MAKING TRAPS

It is also helpful to stay alert to a set of lapses in judgment commonly observed in backcountry accidents. In "Evidence of Heuristic Traps in Recreational Avalanche Accidents," published in *Avalanche News* (Spring 2004), renowned avalanche authority Ian McCammon, Ph.D., identified and analyzed the following four categories of traps that are equally relevant to other mountain settings:

1. Familiarity. Objective hazards—those natural forces that cannot be controlled—can seem less risky as one becomes familiar with the terrain. The effect is purely subjective: our sensitivity to these threats may be diminished, but the threats themselves have not changed. A related psychological phenomenon is our tendency to underestimate all hazards—even those that are largely unrelated to weather—when the sun is out and the winds are calm.

2. Social proof. In avalanche country, social proof refers to the reasoning that a slope is safe simply because other people are on it. In more general backcountry settings this trap refers to the tendency to underestimate

the hazards associated with an activity when we see others engaging in it.

3. Commitment. Sometimes known as tunnel vision or summit fever, this trap poses its greatest threat when a party is so determined to achieve a preconceived goal that they ignore or dismiss critical danger signs. In mountain settings commitment can cause a party to overlook obvious hazards or evidence that the terrain is beyond the group's technical skills. Many people visit the mountains precisely because of the challenges they present, and overcoming these challenges with knowledge and physical skills can be immensely rewarding. Managing the commitment trap without abandoning this sense of adventure requires constant attention to one's surroundings and a keen understanding of the party's limitations.

4. Scarcity. For many people a visit to the mountains is a rare treat. Even for seasoned mountaineers, special events such as perfect snow conditions and trips to remote peaks lend a sense of urgency to a ski or climb. It is crucial to avoid the sense that an event of this type is the last chance and hence must be pursued at all costs. The mountaineers' adage, "Getting up is optional; getting down is mandatory," is an effective reminder for managing this trap.

Beyond McCammon's taxonomy, there are at least five additional conceptual traps that parties can fall victim to in the mountains:

1. Fear of being a party pooper. A common dynamic in groups is for group members to be reluctant to express concerns about the wisdom or safety of a proposed undertaking. The natural consequence is that the group tends to do what the most risk-tolerant member proposes.

2. Poorly matched abilities. Groups whose members have a wide range of mountaineering skills and physical abilities pose special problems. Mismatched groups are quite common, since people tend to gather on the basis of relationships established in other settings, such as work, school, family, or other organizations. The problem here is not the wide variation in abilities per se; it is the potential for serious problems to arise when the group embarks on an outing that not everyone can or is willing to complete. It's wise not to join a group that seems likely to undertake an outing beyond your abilities, and if you lead a group of mixed strengths and abilities, it is critical to adapt the itinerary to the group, not vice versa.

3. Guide-client mentality. It is especially easy for recreational groups to

fall into the guide-client dynamic, in which one person is perceived to be the expert to whom the others cede all decision making. This configuration has two dangers. First, it leaves untapped a great deal of the group's reservoir of judgment and caution. Second, it can exert subtle pressure on the "guide" to take risks that he would not ordinarily take, in the interest of satisfying the "clients." Even if there is a formally designated leader with more expertise than other group members, the chances for group success are greatest when everyone in the group is thinking critically about the route, the weather, the group's condition, and the level of preparation.

4. Separating the group. Before separating a group, review the purpose, each subgroup's preparation, and the plan for getting back together. Among the most common sources of trouble in the backcountry is separating the group. The conventional admonition—to keep the group together at all costs—is too inflexible for some recreational outings and for many SAR operations. Legitimate reasons to separate a group include temporary differences in recreational interests, accommodating varying abilities within the group, and managing a backcountry injury that requires additional help. In SAR operations, circumstances sometimes require team members to be in different places.

5. Failure to put the rescuers first. Specific to every ski patrol and rescue setting—whether it involves injuries on the hill, avalanche terrain, mountain travel, or search and rescue—the rescuers' safety is the highest priority. An injured or lost rescuer is of no utility to the mission, adds unnecessarily to the mission's scope, and compounds the risks that other rescuers must manage. This guideline bears explicit and repeated mention especially when SAR operations are in progress, because patrollers and rescuers tend to focus attention solely on the welfare of the injured or lost subjects.

SUMMARY

o Whether a group is made up of friends on a backcountry ski trip or team members on an ICS-mandated multi-jurisdictional SAR operation, a group's success relies in part on leadership abilities, group dynamics, and avoidance of decision-making traps.

o The hallmark of an effective leader, in the mountains and elsewhere, is a commitment to the success of the group.

o An effective backcountry group has "bench depth," meaning several team members who support the leader's overall objectives and are calm, dignified, analytic, optimistic, and flexible.

CHAPTER 14

BACKCOUNTRY MEDICAL

Colin K. Grissom, M.D., Critical Care Medicine, Intermountain Medical Center,
*   Murray, Utah; Wilderness Medical Society President; Park City Ski Patrol, Park City, Utah*
J. Michael Wallace, M.D., Division of Emergency Medicine, University of Utah,
*   Salt Lake City, Utah*
David R. Sutherland, M.S., EMT-I, University of Utah School of Medicine,
*   Salt Lake City, Utah, Park City Ski Patrol, Park City, Utah*

OBJECTIVES

o Explain the differences between providing emergency medical care in a backcountry setting versus a serviced ski area or other accessible location.

o Describe what high-altitude illness is and how it can be treated in the backcountry.

o Explain some of the symptoms of both heat-related illness and cold-related illness.

o Describe the more common traumatic injuries that occur in the backcountry.

o List a few of the items that can be used for improvised splints and stabilization devices when treating fractures and other injuries.

Injuries and accidents that occur in the backcountry can be especially challenging because access to medical care may be very limited or nonexistent. In addition the mountain environment may worsen pre-existing medical conditions or predispose some backcountry recreationists to specific medical problems.

It is important that those entering the backcountry anticipate medical situations and prepare accordingly. This preparation should consist of the following:

» Taking steps to prevent injury or illness
» Contemplating means of addressing various injuries or illnesses

» Determining how evacuation of a patient may be accomplished

It is impossible to prepare for every possible situation and it is impractical to pack enough equipment for all potential scenarios, so improvisation is emphasized in backcountry settings. Outdoor Emergency Care (OEC) technicians are well trained in the use of dedicated splints, dressings, and patient packaging; however, in the wilderness such equipment is often unavailable. Instead rescuers should use their training to utilize whatever materials are available.

This chapter is not meant to be comprehensive but serves as a supplement to prior medical training by shifting the focus from the acute "stabilize and transport" model to the real possibility of an extended evacuation where advanced medical care is several hours to days away. An understanding of pathophysiology—that is, the functional changes associated with an illness or injury—allows the rescuer to better treat a patient in a wilderness setting. Recognize that the following information is condensed. More complete explanations can be found in the fifth edition of the National Ski Patrol's *Outdoor Emergency Care* manual. Additionally, understand that the following techniques are meant as examples of treating backcountry patients and may not be the preferred treatment for all situations.

A rescuer should not provide care beyond his or her level of training. Be aware, too, that administering any medication beyond oxygen is outside OEC treatment guidelines. Ethical exceptions to this rule will undoubtedly arise in the backcountry and should be dealt with cautiously. Some of the content of this chapter exceeds the scope of practice of an OEC technician and is provided for background information only.

ASSESSMENT

No matter what the illness, emergency, or accident, proper assessment is essential to a successful rescue.

The primary assessment of an accident scene and initial patient assessment are extremely important in the timely triage, care, and rescue of patients in the outdoor environment. Good patient care is directly linked to good patient assessment.

When approaching the scene of an accident, the first step of the assessment process is scene size-up consisting of four components:

1. Scene safety. Determine that rescuer and patient are not in danger.
2. Mechanism of injury. Determine how the illness or injury occurred.
3. Total number of patients involved. In a multiple-patient accident, triage may be necessary to determine who

is to be cared for first. Immediate care is determined by the ABCs: airway, breathing, and circulation.

4. Need for additional resources. Assess how badly injured the patient is, and decide if additional help is needed.

HIGH-ALTITUDE ILLNESS

Unique to those involved in mountain travel and rescue are medical issues concerning the effects of altitude on the human body. Ascents to altitudes above about 7,000 feet may result in high-altitude illness.

High-altitude illness is caused by a lack of oxygen because of a lower barometric pressure at high altitude. Cold, fatigue, and dehydration may play a role. Individuals vary in their tolerance to high altitude.

The best predictor of who will get high-altitude illness is a prior history of the condition during similar rates of ascent to similar altitudes. In general, risk of altitude illness increases with faster rates of ascent to higher altitudes. Some people can reach very high altitudes with little or no distress, while others become ill at moderate altitudes.

Symptoms can occur in people who fly or drive from low to high altitude, and in those who travel to high altitude under their own power. Symptoms may come on rapidly, and they usually disappear quickly upon descent, or slowly during one or two days at the same altitude as acclimatization

occurs. Rest, over-the-counter analgesics (ibuprofen and acetaminophen) for headache, hydration (but not forced overhydration), and a light diet are helpful. Oxygen is useful but generally unnecessary.

ACUTE MOUNTAIN SICKNESS

The most common form of high-altitude illness is acute mountain sickness (AMS). Acute mountain sickness can occur within hours of ascending to high altitude. Predisposing factors to AMS include a too-rapid ascent and a prior AMS history. Children and adolescents seem to be more susceptible than older individuals.

AMS signs and symptoms

AMS symptoms may mimic other general ailments, initially misleading companions about a person's condition. Some of the signs of AMS include the following:

» Generalized throbbing headache that's worse at night and when bending over
» Apathy, weakness, and fatigue
» Lightheadedness
» Loss of appetite, nausea, and vomiting
» Insomnia

Additionally, periodic breathing during sleep, known as Cheyne-Stokes respirations, may develop and are characterized by intermittent periods of alternating deep and shallow breathing during which the patient may stir or awaken with a sense of suffocation.

Symptoms appearing early on the first day of attaining altitude are more likely to be caused by mild AMS. A day or two of rest at the same altitude without ascending any higher may be appropriate. If symptoms worsen with rest, descent should be considered. If confusion or ataxia (the loss of muscle coordination) develop, immediate descent is mandatory. Do not ascend in the face of persistent AMS symptoms.

Headache should be treated with a nonprescription medication such as acetaminophen, ibuprofen, or aspirin. A number of prescription medications are available that have some value in the prevention and treatment of AMS but do not replace descent. A drug called acetazolamide (Diamox) can prevent the condition but requires a prescription from a physician. It is recommended for people who have a recurrent history of AMS during prior similar ascents to high altitude. Acetazolamide also effectively eliminates periodic breathing during sleep at high altitude.

Signs and symptoms of AMS that mandate immediate descent include any of the following:

» Ataxia
» Altered level of consciousness
» Respiratory distress associated with persistent cough and gurgling in the chest
» Inability to eat or drink due to nausea, and vomiting that lasts for more than a few hours

Descent should be at least 3,000 feet below the altitude where symptoms began. The group should descend early while the patient can still walk. If the patient can no longer walk, the rescuers should carry him in a sitting or upright position. If the patient becomes unresponsive, care must be appropriately provided.

These guidelines are not absolute. If there is any question about whether to evacuate, always evacuate. The risk of severe, advanced altitude illness is quite low after the fifth day at altitude, but symptoms can still be precipitated by stressors such as swimming in a cold stream, a hard fall, hypothermia, or a respiratory infection.

Assessing AMS

When assessing AMS, the rescuer should

» consider AMS in anyone who is not feeling well at altitudes of 7,000 to 8,000 feet or above.
» assess vital signs, especially the pulse and respiratory rate, and compare these with other members of the party.
» carefully question the patient about headache, nausea, vomiting, and shortness of breath.
» assess the level of responsiveness; if it is decreased, assess ability to move and the patient's perception of pain and touch.
» listen for abnormal lung sounds such as wheezes and crackles.
» assess for ataxia and mental alertness.

AMS emergency care

The most common practical problem is distinguishing mild AMS from moderate and severe AMS. Mild AMS may improve with rest alone if the ascent is halted. Those with moderate and severe AMS require immediate evacuation to a lower altitude.

HIGH-ALTITUDE PULMONARY EDEMA AND HIGH-ALTITUDE CEREBRAL EDEMA

Two more serious types of high-altitude illness are high-altitude pulmonary edema (HAPE) and high-altitude cerebral edema (HACE). Severe high-altitude illnesses—HAPE and HACE—appear following a lag period of 6 to 96 hours after ascent. This is due to the effect of continued hypoxia, a deficiency of oxygen in the lungs and brain causing increases in circulatory pressure that leads to blood vessel damage, swelling, and edema. In the lungs these changes cause some of the alveoli to fill with fluid, leading to life-threatening HAPE. In the brain, generalized swelling and increased intracranial pressure can lead to life-threatening HACE. High-altitude pulmonary edema is more common than HACE and occurs after acute ascent to sleeping altitudes above about 8,000 feet. High-altitude pulmonary edema is more common in the winter months and typically affects males who have ascended from low altitude to over 8,000 feet rapidly. High-altitude cerebral edema generally occurs at higher sleeping altitudes above about 10,000 feet, but it can occur as low as 8,000 feet.

HAPE signs and symptoms

Early signs and symptoms include the following:

» Persistent cough
» Respiratory distress that is worse with exertion
» Increased pulse and respirations
» Weakness
» Noticeably decreased exercise capacity

Late signs and symptoms:

» Cyanosis, or bluish skin coloration due to poor circulation
» Cough that produces large amounts of frothy, pink sputum
» Rapid pulse and respirations
» Crackle sounds in lung
» Severe respiratory distress
» Severe inability to exercise

HACE signs and symptoms

Early signs and symptoms are the same as AMS, plus the following:

» Ataxia
» Confusion, progressing to stupor, coma, and, in some circumstances, death

The biggest impediments to early recognition of HAPE and HACE are their insidious onsets. Early signs and symptoms frequently go unrecognized or are ignored by patients and their companions, who also may be suffering from some degree of AMS. By the time a serious problem is suspected, nightfall or bad weather may preclude evacuation to a lower altitude. It is also important to recognize that HAPE and HACE may occur together; hypoxia caused by pulmonary edema can contribute to the worsening of cerebral edema.

Emergency care of HAPE and HACE
It is important that group members have an awareness of HAPE and HACE so that the ailment can be addressed:

» Recognize the problem and descend.
» Provide supplemental oxygen if it is available.
» Give care for unresponsiveness.

Descent is the primary treatment for HAPE or HACE. Usually a descent of about 3,000 feet results in marked improvement in symptoms. If symptoms persist, keep descending until they resolve.

HEAT-RELATED ILLNESSES

The body has many complicated regulatory mechanisms to maintain a normal body temperature of 98.6 degrees F. The two most efficient mechanisms are evaporative cooling by sweating and radiation by a dilation of cutaneous blood vessels. It is possible to suffer from heat-related conditions even while traveling in winter and in relatively mild mountain climates.

In the backcountry, individuals may suffer from one of two types of heat-related conditions: heat exhaustion and, less often, heat stroke. The more serious of the two, heat stroke is differentiated from heat exhaustion by persistent profound mental status changes, shock, and profound elevations in temperature. When there is doubt about whether a patient has heat exhaustion or heat stroke, treat it as heat stroke.

HEAT EXHAUSTION
Heat exhaustion occurs after exposure to a hot environment, especially when exercising. It is characterized by exhaustion, dizziness, nausea, headache, leg cramps, excessive sweating, and decreased urine output, but body temperature is less than 104 degrees F and level of responsiveness is normal or mildly confused. The body loses too much water and too many electrolytes through heavy sweating, resulting in hypovolemia. The body responds rapidly to treatment, and mental status changes do not persist or worsen.

HEAT STROKE
Heat stroke is a life-threatening emergency identified by a decreased level of consciousness and a body temperature greater than 104 degrees F. Shock follows with dysfunction of the organ systems such as the brain, the heart and blood vessels,

the liver, and the kidneys. Untreated heat stroke results in death.

Symptoms include a fast heart rate, high respiratory rate, and decreased sweating. Unlike during heat exhaustion, the patient has a decreased level of consciousness that persists or worsens, which should prompt immediate treatment and evacuation.

Recovery from heat stroke depends on the duration of the hyperthermia, or elevation of core body temperature and the speed with which treatment is administered. Emergency treatment should begin immediately in the field and has one objective: Lower the body temperature by any means available.

Take the following steps when treating a patient with heat stroke:

» Move the patient promptly from the hot environment to a cool environment.
» Shade from direct sunlight.
» Remove clothing.
» Keep exposed skin wet with continuous air flow on it.
» Immerse patient in cold water.
» Provide supplemental oxygen.

If possible check the patient's temperature frequently to determine if the body temperature is cooling. When the core body temperature reaches approximately 101 degrees F, taper off the cooling efforts; rapid cooling below this point may lead to shivering (which will generate heat). If the patient returns to a level of responsiveness appropriate for oral hydration, give fluids. Anti-fever medications such as aspirin or acetaminophen are not helpful. Rapid evacuation is indicated. Monitor carefully for rebound temperature increase.

COLD-RELATED ILLNESSES

Just as heat-related illnesses can strike in cold winter environments, cold-related illnesses can afflict those traveling in hot weather. Continued submersion in cold water can be as dangerous as prolonged exposure in freezing weather.

HYPOTHERMIA

Hypothermia refers to cooling of the central part of the body to a core temperature below 95 degrees F as determined by a core thermometer. Factors that control hypothermia are discussed in Chapter 1, Body Temperature Regulation, while this chapter focuses on recognizing hypothermia and providing early emergency care.

Hypothermia can occur at temperatures above and below freezing. The combination of cold wind and water is especially dangerous. The initial drop of one to two degrees triggers shivering, followed by clumsiness, falling, slow reactions, mental confusion, and difficulty speaking. When body temperatures fall below 90 degrees F shivering gradually ceases, muscles become more rigid, and breathing and pulse rate slow. The patient gradually becomes unresponsive and death may occur at body temperatures below 80 degrees F.

When the body is too cold to be capable of shivering, it cannot warm itself without outside help. The most common cause of death from hypothermia is ventricular fibrillation, which can be spontaneous or precipitated by jarring a hypothermic patient. A patient with severe hypothermia may appear to be dead if the pupils are fixed and dilated, pulse and breathing become undetectable, and body rigidity develops. However, the patient still may be saved with proper emergency care. That's why the dictum, "No one is dead until warm and dead" emphasizes that all patients with hypothermia deserve an attempt at rewarming.

Classification of hypothermia

Hypothermia is commonly divided into two classifications: primary and secondary. Primary hypothermia occurs due to environmental exposure and is sub-divided into immersion hypothermia and non-immersion hypothermia, which occurs due to exposure to a cold environment. Secondary hypothermia is frequently associated with traumatized or critically ill patients.

Once the underlying cause of hypothermia is determined, it can be categorized based on the patient's core temperature:

» Mild hypothermia: 95 to 90 degrees F
» Moderate hypothermia: 90 to 82 degrees F

» Severe hypothermia: less than 82 degrees F

Assessing hypothermia

Hypothermia should be suspected when a companion shivers, appears clumsy, stumbles, drops things, has slurred speech, or lags behind. Any person who is found ill, injured, or unresponsive outdoors in cold weather or who is removed from cold water should be considered hypothermic until proven otherwise.

Primary survey. The rescuer should assess the patient's level of responsiveness (LOR), airway, breathing, circulation (ABCs), and should look for obvious injury. Remember that with hypothermia the pulse may be weak and very slow, and the patient may be breathing only a few times a minute. Do not start CPR prematurely.

If a thermometer is available, take the patient's temperature. Accurate diagnosis depends on core temperature, measured rectally; however, it is not always possible to obtain a core temperature. Oral temperature may be substituted if the patient is responsive. The thermometer should be left under the tongue for a minimum of three minutes.

Secondary survey. The first priority is to stabilize the body temperature. Additionally, rewarming methods can be quite limited in the backcountry but may include the following:

» Get the patient out of the weather and to shelter.
» Examine the patient from head to toe, looking for injury or bleeding.
» If the patient's clothing is wet, gently exchange it for dry clothing.
» Avoid unnecessarily handling the patient. It may be better to cut off wet clothing than to undress a profoundly hypothermic patient.
» If clothing is wet and no dry clothing is available, remove the wet clothing and place the patient in a sleeping bag. Alternatively, place a blanket or spare clothing over and under the patient, cover the patient's head, and wrap them in something windproof.
» Use body-to-body contact to rewarm the patient by having one or two rescuers get into a sleeping bag with the patient with as much skin-to-skin contact as possible.
» Fill water bottles or water bladders with hot water. Wrap the containers to protect the patient's skin then apply them to the patient's armpits, neck, and groin while the patient is in a sleeping bag. Note: Chemical heat packs are NOT effective for rewarming hypothermia but if placed in the patient's hands and around the feet, they may help prevent frostbite.
» Place hot rocks wrapped in clothing in a sleeping bag with the patient.
» Treat dehydration with warm fluids if the patient is able to swallow.

» Don't allow the patient to sit, stand, or walk until he or she has been rewarmed.
» Light a stove or build a fire.

Emergency care of a hypothermia patient
The principles of emergency care are to

» prevent further heat loss.
» rewarm the patient as safely as possible.
» rewarm the body core first, prior to surface warming.
» treat the patient gently to avoid precipitating ventricular fibrillation.
» treat any injuries.

The application of these principles depends on the patient's condition, the equipment available, and the presence or absence of complicating factors such as other illnesses or injuries. If a thermometer is not available, the patient is considered to have a core temperature of 90 degrees F or above if he is still shivering and capable of appropriate actions such as zipping a parka. The core temperature is likely below 90 degrees F if the patient is no longer shivering and has an abnormal mental status.

Rewarming a moderate to severely hypothermic patient in the backcountry may not be possible with the equipment available. Therefore, gently transporting the patient rapidly to medical care while instituting the above field rewarming measures is recommended. Before transport the patient should be stable, fractures should be splinted, and other injuries treated using standard methods. A rapid transportation method such as a helicopter is preferable to a long, bumpy, toboggan or snow vehicle ride.

If a patient with profound hypothermia cannot be evacuated, help should be requested and rewarming started in a tent or snow shelter. The best method is probably body-to-body contact and hot water bottles in a sleeping bag.

FROSTBITE

Frostbite, the freezing of a body part, occurs when the heat produced by the part, the heat carried to it by the blood, and the amount of covering insulation are insufficient to prevent body temperature from dropping below the freezing point of body tissue, which is about 24.8 degrees F. The amount of total damage depends on the extent and duration of freezing at the tissue level.

Certain body tissues, such as the hands, feet, ears, cheeks, and nose, have a higher risk of frostbite than others. Factors that contribute to the development of frostbite are related to the restriction of peripheral circulation and include the following:

» Fatigue
» Poor nutrition
» Alcohol
» Tobacco and/or drug use
» Arteriosclerosis, or hardening of the arteries
» Tight clothing

Inadequate insulation, wet clothing, and contact with metal or highly volatile liquids such as gasoline can also contribute to frostbite.

As frostbite thaws, the appearance of the injured part depends largely on the degree of blood vessel injury (Figure 14-1). When vessel injury is limited to minor damage, plasma, but not red cells, leaks out into the surrounding tissues, causing edema in mild cases and large blebs and blisters containing pale or yellow fluid in more extensive cases. More severe vessel injury allows red cells to leak out as well, producing smaller blisters containing dark reddish or purple fluid. When there has been extensive spasm and clotting, very little blood can reenter the injured area. Blisters are small or absent, and the tissues quickly die.

Frostbite types

For backcountry medical purposes the most useful rating is the simplest.

First-degree, or superficial, frostbite, also called frost nip, is the mildest form and presents with numbness and erythema, or reddening of the skin. A white or yellow, firm, slightly raised plaque develops in the area of injury. Mild edema is common.

Second-degree frostbite results in blisters and swelling appearing at the site, surrounded by erythema and edema.

Third-degree, or deep, frostbite is a much more serious injury because of the danger of tissue death. It commonly involves the hands and feet and creates deeper blisters. It should be suspected if a painfully cold part suddenly stops hurting when it obviously is not getting warmer. The affected part is cold, hard, and numb, with pale, waxy skin. Hypothermia typically accompanies third- and fourth-degree frostbite.

Fourth-degree frostbite extends completely through the skin and involves deeper tissues, with cell death extending into muscle and to the level of bone.

Backcountry frostbite treatment

The best field care for a patient with frostbite is evacuation to medical care—as fast and as safely as possible. Rewarming should not be attempted if the extremity

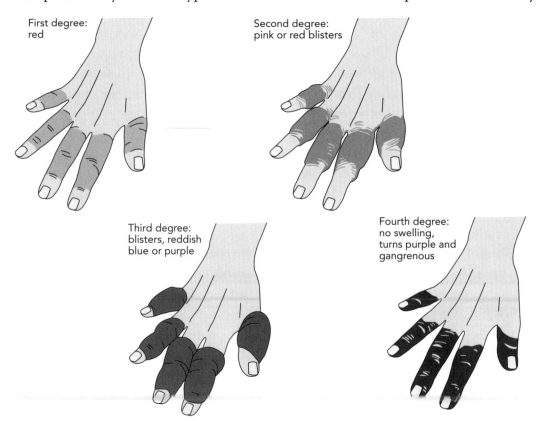

First degree:
red

Second degree:
pink or red blisters

Third degree:
blisters, reddish
blue or purple

Fourth degree:
no swelling,
turns purple and
gangrenous

Figure 14-1. *Categories of thawed frostbite*

has already rewarmed spontaneously, if there is not proper equipment or proper shelter, or if medical care can be obtained soon. Conversely, rapid field rewarming may be advisable if equipment and shelter are available, if the patient can be carried out or evacuated by vehicle or toboggan, and if there is a good chance the part can be protected from refreezing during evacuation.

Rewarming should be done only in a sheltered area where the patient's entire body can be kept warm. One of the worst things that can happen to a frostbitten part is for it to refreeze after thawing. Therefore, it should be protected against refreezing by all means. For a patient who can be transported to medical care, thick layers of sterile dressings should be applied. The rescuer should leave blisters unopened, separate digits with soft cotton or wool pads, and elevate the part to reduce swelling.

BURNS

Caring for burns largely depends on their degree (Figure 14-2). Whether caused by a camp stove or outdoor elements, painful burns acquired in the backcountry generally need to be addressed prior to a physician's consultation.

THERMAL BURNS

Burns are very common and are among the most serious and painful of all injuries. Backcountry recreationists are susceptible to thermal burns from cooking stoves, lanterns, and fires. Upper airway burns can also occur, particularly in enclosed spaces, so assessment of the patient's airway is critical.

Keep these tips in mind when caring for burns:

» Stop the burning process and prevent additional injury.

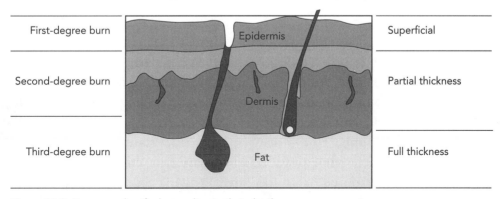

Figure 14-2. *Burns are classified according to their depth.*

» Immerse the burn area in cool, sterile water or saline solution; however, do not immerse the affected area for longer than 10 minutes as this can increase the risk of infection and hypothermia.
» An alternative is to irrigate the area and apply a sterile dressing.
» Prevent heat loss to avoid hypothermia.

Sunburn, windburn, and snow blindness

Humans are more vulnerable to the harmful effects of solar radiation when at high altitudes, on snow, or on bodies of water. Injury to the skin and eyes can also occur on cloudy days when people forget to protect themselves.

Sunburn. Sunburn is a first- or second-degree skin burn. Repeated sun exposure over many years may lead to chronic degenerative skin changes such as wrinkling, thickening, and cancer. Avoiding excessive sun exposure and using proper skin protection, such as clothing or topical sunscreens, can delay these effects.

Sunscreen preparations with a high (at least 30) sun protection factor (SPF) are recommended. Because sunscreens with a cream or grease base are better at preventing frostbite and windburn than alcohol-based preparations, they are preferable for use by skiers, high-altitude climbers, and others exposed to cold, wind, and sunlight. Sunscreen should be applied 15 to 30 minutes before sun exposure and reapplied several times during the day, particularly if sweating is heavy.

Care for sunburn by removing the patient from exposure and applying cool compresses. Later, soothing ointments are useful to control discomfort. A physician should be consulted if the sunburn is extensive or if the skin is blistered.

Windburn. Windburn is an irritation of the skin that resembles first-degree sunburn. It can be prevented to some extent by wearing a face mask or by applying a greasy sunscreen. Treat windburn by applying soothing, greasy ointments or lotions.

Snow blindness. Snow blindness, or sunburn of the conjunctiva of the eye, can be prevented by wearing dark sunglasses or goggles. Because radiation can reach the eye by reflection from the snow, sunglasses should have extensions on each side and below, as found on glacier sunglasses.

Symptoms of snow blindness develop 6 to 12 hours after exposure. The eyes feel irritated (a sensation similar to "sand in the eye") and are sensitive to light. The conjunctivae are reddened, and there may be excessive tearing and swelling around the eye, as well as pain with eye motion.

Emergency care includes covering the eyes or moving the patient to a darkened area, applying cool compresses, and using nonprescription pain relievers. In severe cases the patient should see a physician as soon as possible; medication may be prescribed to relieve the pain and speed healing.

TRAUMATIC INJURIES

Mountain travel exposes adventurers to a wide range of traumatic injuries. In the backcountry, where advanced medical care is often hours and miles away, rescuers need to modify their training in order to provide the most effective support to the sick and injured. The following information serves as a supplement to *Outdoor Emergency Care,* fifth edition, which should be consulted for further detail.

Some of the more common backcountry injuries include the following:

» Blisters
» Strains/sprains
» Dislocations
» Fractures
» Head/neck/spine injuries
» Bleeding
» Internal injuries

BLISTERS

Blisters develop when skin is subjected to increased friction caused by activities such as hiking in ill-fitting boots, rowing a boat, or climbing. When the skin is subjected to excess rubbing, irritation occurs and creates what is often termed a "hot spot." This is an important sign to recognize, because if left unaddressed a hot spot may become a blister. Early recognition of a potential blister or hot spot should be a catalyst for applying dressings to shield the skin from the friction before the hot spot becomes a full-blown blister. Moleskin is most often used to cover the hot spot, but simple duct tape may also work.

When treating a blister,

» clean the area well.
» drain the blister using a sterilized knife or pin by carefully puncturing the roof of the blister near the edge.
» bandage the area sufficiently to prevent infection and further damage.

STRAINS AND SPRAINS

Strains—stretching or tearing of muscle or tendons—are commonly associated with pain and bruising at a site remote from a joint. Treatment for strains consists of RICE:

» Rest
» Ice
» Compression
» Elevation

Typically strains do not require immobilization other than for comfort.

Sprains—stretching or tearing of ligaments surrounding joints—are categorized into three grades:

Grade 1, or minor sprains, have little to no swelling but may be painful. These can be treated with RICE.

Grade 2, or partial-tear sprains, often present with swelling, pain, and discoloration. These injuries may require at least initial immobilization in addition to RICE.

Grade 3, or complete tear sprains/strains, typically are quite swollen and discolored. The pain may be out of proportion to the injury, or may be nonexistent. The affected joint requires immobilization.

DISLOCATIONS

It is important that a thorough assessment is done to ensure the injury is a dislocation and not a fracture. Current OEC protocol is to treat any dislocation like a fracture. In general, do not attempt to relocate a dislocated joint unless you are familiar with proper relocation techniques.

FRACTURES

A fracture in the wilderness presents a unique problem as only rarely can the patient reach definitive medical care within the "golden hour." This requires the rescuer to complete a thorough assessment, including the patient's vital signs, to monitor for signs of shock. In most situations it is advisable to treat the patient for shock as soon as possible.

The general approach for splinting a fracture is to re-create the fractured part's function. For a long bone this means to splint to the joint above and below the fractured bone, re-creating the stability the bone would provide. Similarly, for a fracture near a joint the splint should extend to the bones above and below the injured joint to re-create the role of the joint, which is to connect those two bones. Use whatever materials are available to accomplish this goal, such as branches, tent or ski poles, and sleeping pads.

In two particular fractures—a mid-shaft femur fracture and a cervical spine fracture—traction should be employed whenever re-aligning a fracture and should be maintained by appropriate splinting. There are many objects that can be used for improvising a femoral traction splint, such as paddles, poles, or tree branches (Figure 14-3). These general steps are similar to applying a commercially produced traction splint.

The following describes an improvised traction splint for a mid-shaft femur fracture:

» One rescuer maintains manual traction.
» The other rescuer sizes the improvised splint to the uninjured leg, preferably at least 12 inches beyond the foot.
» Using padding, pass a strap under the injured leg at the groin and affix to one end of the splint.
» Apply an ankle hitch to the injured leg.
» Tie a small rope on the distal end of the splint and pass it through the ankle hitch.

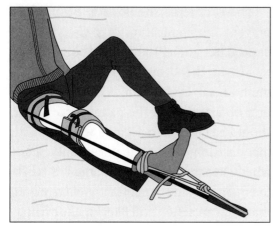

Figure 14-3. *Improvised traction splint*

» Pull tension on the rope until traction is transferred from the rescuer to the splint and the rope is tied off.
» Bandage the leg to the splint in three to four places.
» Reassess distal circulation, sensation, and motor function.

HEAD, NECK, AND SPINE INJURIES

An overlooked spinal fracture may result in permanent loss of limb function or, in the case of a cervical fracture, death from pulmonary failure. However, in the backcountry it is rare that a backboard, C-collar, and head immobilization device are available, making it necessary to improvise a spinal stabilization system (Figure 14-4). Improvised C-collars do not provide as much stabilization as commercially manufactured ones but are essential if a neck injury is suspected, even if they only remind the patient to not move her neck.

Follow this procedure to make a C-collar using a SAM splint:

» Maintain C-spine stabilization.
» Place two to three bends in the SAM splint.
» Pass the splint behind the patient's neck and cross it over the chest.
» Bend the two ends of the SAM splint over each other, "locking" the splint on the neck.
» Flare out the long edges of the SAM splint for comfort and to avoid constriction of the airway.
» Bend the SAM splint further, tightening the splint in place.

Another way of improvising a C-collar is by using a rolled blanket or sweatshirt, but this method provides less stabilization.

Figure 14-4. *C-collar using a SAM splint*

Improvised backboards can be integrated into a litter, and once the patient is secured with a C-collar in place the head can be strapped down using tape and rolled clothing to complete spinal immobilization.

The likelihood of a spinal injury and/or a fracture should be evaluated in every patient. Assessment of these injuries is critical because relegating a previously ambulatory patient to a litter increases evacuation time and potentially exposes both patient and rescuers to increased hazards. In remote settings the following guidelines can be considered.

Patients not requiring cervical spine immobilization in a backcountry setting are characterized by the following:

» Age under 65 years
» Less significant mechanism of injury
» Normal level of consciousness
» No significant painful, distracting injury
» No weakness, numbness, or tingling
» No spinal column tenderness

Patients requiring cervical spine immobilization in a backcountry setting are characterized by the following:

» Age 65 years or older
» Dangerous mechanism of injury
» Altered level of consciousness
» Numbness or tingling in extremities
» Pain or tenderness over the spinal column

These criteria should not be used to prevent the application of a C-collar and backboard. Rather they should be employed to aid in the decision to determine the method of evacuation. Other information obtained from the patient assessment should be taken into account when making this decision. If there is uncertainty about whether to immobilize the patient, it is best to err on the side of caution while realizing that such an action will likely make evacuation significantly more difficult.

Little can be done in the backcountry setting to treat internal head injuries. Close monitoring can help determine if a head injury is a concussion or if it may progress to an intracranial hemorrhage. Patients whose mental status improves following the injury may have a concussion and should be monitored. In these patients it is important that they do not re-concuss their heads as this may result in long-term symptoms. For patients whose mental status is worsening or does not improve, an intracranial hemorrhage should be suspected. Field treatment should include elevating the head, administering oxygen if available, and evacuating the patient rapidly.

BLEEDING

The first priority with a bleeding injury is to stop the bleeding by applying direct pressure, elevating the wound, applying pressure to a pressure point to occlude blood flow, and, in rare situations, applying a tourniquet.

CPR IN THE BACKCOUNTRY

In an initial patient assessment, an injured or ill patient may be found without signs of life or may progress to cardiopulmonary arrest. Initiation of cardiopulmonary resuscitation (CPR) in a backcountry setting has unique implications for rescuers.

The following considerations can help determine whether CPR should be initiated in the backcountry and how long CPR should continue in the event of cardiac arrest:

» Even in urban settings, CPR—with delayed use of an automated external defibrillator (AED) or delayed access to advanced medical care—has success rates of only 1 to 6 percent.

» CPR should not be initiated in patients who have obvious signs of death, such as pooling of blood, rigor mortis, or decapitation.

» Consider that CPR is exhausting to a rescuer, particularly in extreme conditions found in the backcountry where energy may be required for self-evacuation. Safety of the rescuers should be considered in decisions regarding duration of CPR attempts in the backcountry.

» Current American Heart Association guidelines advise discontinuing CPR in patients who have sustained non-traumatic or blunt traumatic cardiac arrest after a trial of advanced cardiac life support (ACLS) has been given. However, since ACLS is generally unavailable in the wilderness, if a patient has been pulseless for longer than 15 minutes with or without CPR, further attempts at resuscitation should not be made (exceptions are lightning or hypothermia victims).

» CPR in the wilderness has the highest success in patients who have been struck by lightning.

» A hypothermic patient is "not dead until warm and dead."

These considerations should not prevent initiating CPR in situations where a helicopter or ACLS is accessible within 15 to 30 minutes even if a prolonged evacuation may follow resuscitation.

CPR may actually precipitate ventricular fibrillation in a patient with a pulse that is weak or slow enough to be undetectable. Therefore, CPR should not be started unless careful examination (palpating for a pulse for at least one minute) reveals no signs of life, or ventricular fibrillation is strongly suspected because of a sudden event such as collapse of the patient or loss of a previously detected heartbeat.

CPR is not indicated if it places the rescuers in danger, if the patient's core body temperature is less than 50 degrees F, or if the chest is frozen and non-compressible. During a technical extrication, it is better to focus efforts on removing the patient from a dangerous situation, such as extrication from a crevasse fall, before starting CPR in a safer location. Adequate CPR usually cannot be performed during a technical extrication.

Sterile dressings and fluids for cleaning wounds may not be available. Water that is clean enough to drink is adequate for cleaning wounds. Clothing may be used for dressing wounds. Patients with substantial blood loss should be treated for shock and given fluids. As always, continue to reassess the patient on a regular basis.

Tourniquets should be employed only in extreme situations because their use generally commits the limb to amputation. Use a tourniquet when the limb is already amputated or nearly amputated and there is massive arterial bleeding that cannot be stopped by pressure points.

INTERNAL INJURIES

Much like internal head injuries, internal abdominal injuries cannot be treated in the wilderness and patients must be evacuated immediately. Assessment of the abdomen and back should be thorough. Traumatic abdominal injuries that have increasing pain or signs of bruising are suggestive of internal bleeding and are particularly unstable. A painful, tender, or pulsating abdomen, vital signs suggestive of shock (tachycardia, rapid breathing, falling blood pressure), and symptoms such as bloody urine or nausea and vomiting may be indicative of internal bleeding and should increase suspicion of an internal injury.

MEDICAL ILLNESS

Most medical illnesses cannot be adequately treated in the wilderness and require evacuation for advanced medical care. Following are those conditions that may be treated in a backcountry setting.

MYOCARDIAL INFARCTION OR HEART ATTACK

Signs and symptoms of unstable angina, myocardial infarction, or heart attack, include the following:

» Severe chest pain associated with radiating pain to the shoulder or arm
» Sweating
» Difficulty breathing
» Nausea
» Lightheadedness

Although it is beyond the scope of an OEC technician to do so, patients with chest pain should be given 325 milligrams of crushed or chewed aspirin or nitroglycerin (if prescribed). A patient with chest pain that resolves during evacuation should still be taken to advanced medical care because unstable angina may progress to a myocardial infarction and heart failure. Arhythmias may occur as well.

STROKE OR BRAIN ATTACK

Any patient with signs or symptoms of a stroke should be evacuated immediately. If, during evacuation, the patient's symptoms resolve, rescuers can consider that the stroke event was a transient ischemic attack (TIA). These types of strokes are, by definition, ischemic, meaning they are caused by an inadequate blood supply, and can be appropriately treated with 325 milligrams of aspirin to help prevent subsequent TIAs or a full stroke while the patient is being taken to advanced medical care.

In a minority of cases, aspirin given to a patient with a hemorrhagic stroke will impair the blood's ability to clot, increasing the bleeding and the potential for a stroke resulting in death. For this reason it is important that patients with strokes do not receive aspirin or any other blood thinner unless it is determined to be ischemic. In general, any patient suspected of having a stroke should not be given blood thinning medications.

ANAPHYLAXIS

Pre-screening of group participants will help identify people with allergies that may lead to anaphylaxis. These people should have access to injectable epinephrine, and others in the group should be made aware of where it is kept and how to administer it.

As stated earlier, administering any medication beyond oxygen is outside OEC treatment guidelines. In the case of anaphylaxis, epinephrine may be the only means to prolong patient survival. The allergic reaction typically outlasts the effects of epinephrine. Therefore, if limited amounts of epinephrine are available, it should be administered when the patient's airway is in danger of compromise. Antihistamines such as diphenhydramine (Benadryl) do not reverse allergic reactions like epinephrine does, but they can act to slow the reaction. Optimal treatment for anaphylaxis includes epinephrine followed by antihistamine when the patient is able to swallow, and rapid evacuation prior to recurrence of anaphylaxis.

DIABETES

Hypoglycemia, or low blood sugar, is generally a more life-threatening condition than hyperglycemia, or high blood sugar. Therefore, a diabetic who has an altered mental status should be given sugar and not insulin. Current OEC guidelines state that nothing should be placed within the mouth of an unconscious patient; however, in a remote setting, applying a small amount of glucose paste or similar non-solid, non-liquid product to the oral tissues may prolong survival and significantly reduce brain damage. Diabetics with an altered mental status should not be given insulin.

....

SUMMARY

o Caring for patients in the wilderness is complex. As resources are frequently limited, rescuers must be able to improvise in order to provide treatment.

o Rather than learning a singular approach to caring for a given problem, a successful wilderness rescuer is able to adapt to any situation and provide the best treatment possible.

....

PART FOUR

SEARCH & RESCUE

CHAPTER 15

SEARCH AND RESCUE BASICS

Dale Atkins, American Avalanche Association President; RECCO Education and Training Manager for North America, Loveland Ski Patrol, Clear Creek County, Colorado

OBJECTIVES:

o Identify the major elements and their sequence in a search plan.

o Describe the five core phases of search and rescue.

o Identify at least two search tactics for locating a subject in the fastest possible time.

o Describe search theory and its components.

o Describe the basic principles of the Incident Command System and its use in search-and-rescue operations.

Increasing numbers of people are venturing into the backcountry, into the side country just beyond a ski area's boundary, and into remotely traveled areas within serviced ski resorts. That means ski patrols and other search-and-rescue (SAR) organizations must contend with a growing number of lost, injured, or sick people.

Factors such as access, distance, terrain, weather, and darkness conspire to complicate rescue and medical intervention. In their local communities ski patrollers might be called upon to assist in the search for anyone lost or overdue in the outdoors.

Lost persons may include not only outdoor recreationists but also community members such as a senior suffering from dementia or a toddler who wanders away during a family picnic. The basic strategies for these SAR scenarios are the same; only the settings differ. The solutions are found in the special tactics that arise from the proper application of manpower, transportation, technology, and safety margins.

Unique problems often challenge mountain SAR operations as a result of terrain and weather conditions. Armed with a fundamental understanding of SAR basics and how the SAR community works, ski patrollers, rescuers, and backcountry recreationists can better solve incidents in their home mountains and better work together with other SAR resources.

SAR RESPONSE

The success of any SAR operation depends on the right people, in the right places, working for a common goal in an organized and systematic way. If any of these factors is incomplete, the effort may quickly become disorganized, ineffective, and possibly dangerous.

In many parts of the United States the responsibility for wilderness SAR is delegated to a local level that is usually the county sheriff, but this varies by region and state. In some parts of the country the official response comes from the state police or land-management agencies like the New York State Department of Conservation, Maine's Warden Service, and some national parks. While these agencies may have jurisdictional authority in wilderness SAR operations, they rely heavily on volunteers to address local SAR problems. Ski patrollers should be aware of the jurisdictional agencies and of their ski patrol's role if they are called to help.

In a 2011 report the Department of Homeland Security identified gaps in emergency response. Four key topics were identified that all ski patrollers can relate to:

1. ambiguity of authority
2. inability to communicate between agencies
3. poor use or no use of specialized resources
4. unplanned negative interactions with news media

THE SAR PREPLAN

To be "at the ready," ski patrols need to identify the types of SAR incidents they have responded to in the past and what they may likely be asked to respond to in the future. Each patrol should also identify its level of involvement in an incident. For a lost skier or an avalanche, the patrol may be the lead organization in conducting the operation.

TABLE 15-1. SAR EMERGENCIES

» Lost skier/snowboarder—in area
» Lost skier/snowboarder—out of area
» Avalanche—in area
» Avalanche—out of area
» Overdue hunter or hiker
» Overdue ATV or mountain biker
» Crashed airplane
» Injured skier/snowboarder—out of area
» Injured hunter/hiker
» Missing mental patient
» MCI—lift accident
» MCI—base lodge
» Mudslides or floods
» Other

If called to assist in the search for a missing hunter or hiker, the patrol may supply only trained and prepared searchers and not incident managers or decision makers. Participation and coordination with your local jurisdiction is important to preparing a SAR preplan.

Ski patrols may be involved in any of the SAR emergencies shown in Table 15-1.

SAR preplans are not "how-to" manuals. Rather, the preplan guides the organization and management of the incident and identifies additional resources. The plan should be re-evaluated on the basis of recent experiences from either training or real responses. In its most simple form the plan should be flexible enough to adapt to the unexpected, though precise about the following:

» How rescuers are notified
» Identifying key leadership positions, including their contact information
» What the leaders' responsibilities are
» Where equipment is cached and how it will be managed
» Contact information regarding supporting agencies and other resources

A more detailed plan typically includes the following:

» Type of emergency (avalanche—in area, lost skier—out of area, mass casualty incident (MCI)—lift accident, etc.)

» Names and information of people and agencies to be contacted immediately
» Incident commander name
» Command staff names
» General staff names
» Other key Incident Command System (ICS)/incident roles
» Radio frequencies
» Possible command posts and staging areas
» Names and contact information for local volunteers
» Types of resources needed and how to contact resources
» Ground transportation for rescuers
» Helicopter support
» Food and lodging sources for rescuers
» Historical results from previous incidents
» Dangerous terrain considerations (cliffs, noxious gas, windsnap/wind-throw trees, etc.)
» Transport for seriously injured people; destination
» Death investigation personnel

FIVE PHASES OF RESCUE

All SAR incidents have five core elements or consecutive phases: alert, locate, access, stabilize, and transport (A-LAST) (Figure 15-1). These elements occur on a continuum with variable timing, based on the conditions and available resources. Time is the critical problem for all wilderness

Figure 15-1. *The five core phases of search and rescue (A-LAST)*

SAR activities, specifically the time frame between being lost (or injured) and found (or delivered) to definitive care. To save time SAR teams rely on a quick and appropriate alert to an emergency. Then SAR teams and ski patrols can save time in the other four phases by being well practiced and skilled in the management, strategies, and tactics of SAR.

ALERT

There can be no SAR operation and no help offered until rescuers are alerted to the problem. Cellular and satellite telephones, satellite emergency notification devices (SENDs) such as SPOT, and personal locator beacons (PLBs) can quickly notify SAR and even provide coordinates of a subject's location. It may take hours for an individual to leave an accident site to get help but only minutes for someone to activate a satellite device or use a cell or satellite phone. The alert phase is sometimes delayed for hours due to a backcountry recreationist fearing the cost of rescue, when in fact in the United States a person needing rescue is generally not held financially liable. When going into the woods, all backcountry recreationists should carry a fully charged cell phone. Check periodically for phone signals during the day.

Backcountry cell phone use tips

Cell phone coverage is often spotty in the mountains, but your ability to make 911 calls may improve with these suggestions:

» Before your trip, activate your phone's automatic location setting. This allows the 911 system to calculate your position. Most new phones do this automatically when placing a 911 call.
» Keep the phone turned off and, in cold weather, warm by carrying it in an inside pocket.
» At least once during the day, turn on the phone for about five minutes. When turned on, phones automatically link to the nearest tower(s). Even if the signal is too weak to make a call, it may be enough to leave an electronic signal.
» Cell phones are line of sight, so the tops of hills and ridges will generally offer the best signal. If you have a signal, hold the phone at arm's length and rotate the phone around you to find the best signal.
» If the signal is too weak for voice, try sending a text message to a friend. Make sure the friend confirms the message.
» If you are lost, stay put after making a call for help. If you move you may lose the ability to make or receive future calls, and you may become more lost.

LOCATE

The injured and/or lost backcountry recreationist must be located before help can be delivered. Just because SAR has been notified does not always mean rescuers can find their subject. This phase, also called the search, may take only minutes, but in other cases the search may take days or even longer. Special techniques and methods have been developed for searching in mountainous terrain.

ACCESS

Once the subject has been located, the search is over and the operation becomes a rescue effort. Reaching the subject may take only minutes on a cell phone, but it might take hours to ski to a lost snowboarder or scramble to an injured climber. Bad weather or challenging terrain may delay the rescue for days.

STABILIZE

Once the victim is reached, rescuers must provide physical, medical, and emotional care before evacuating the patient. Physical care requires protecting the patient from the environment. This might mean protecting the patient from adverse weather, from falling off a cliff, or being hit by rockfall. Medical care should be provided as learned with the Outdoor Emergency Care (OEC) program. Medical care can be as simple as some food and energy drinks, or medical stabilization may require careful

management of an injured person or even aggressive treatment. Emotional support can help settle anxious subjects who may become hazardous to themselves or to rescuers. A thoughtful and calm conversation can soothe a nervous victim.

TRANSPORT

The patient may be evacuated by foot, hoof (as in horse or mule), litter or toboggan, or by machine (snowmobile or helicopter). If the patient is able, transportation may be as simple as SAR using a phone to tell the "lost" recreationist how to return to a trailhead, or SAR may walk back with the subject.

Keep in mind that a horseback or snowmobile ride out of the backcountry may be simple and straightforward for an uninjured recreationist, but for an injured patient even a seemingly simple ride behind a snowmobile can be painful and nauseating. Anytime a patient must be evacuated by sled or litter, he must be stabilized and packaged carefully to ensure comfort and continually assessed by rescuers.

Figure 15-2 provides a timeline for a lost or missing skier reported missing late in the evening. Field teams will have to search into the night or wait until the next

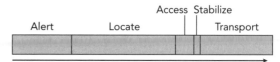

Figure 15-2. *A generalized timeline for a lost or missing skier*

morning to locate the subject. Once the victim is spotted, access will be relatively quick and so, too, will the stabilization or emergency care rendered. If the person must be evacuated by toboggan the transport phase will be lengthy.

CONDUCTING A SAR OPERATION

Within ski resorts missing skier incidents are often resolved simply by notifying lifts and posting the subject's name on message boards, or by making announcements in resort cafeterias and bars. Other than a few radio and telephone calls, no formal response is needed. Quick action by well-trained patrollers gets the job done.

However, when simple actions fail to locate the person, or other information points to potentially bad consequences (deep new snow, a young child, medical condition, worsening weather, etc.) quick action and a formal response are needed. The following two sections address search strategies, search resources, search theory, and overall search management using the Incident Command System.

SEARCH THEORY

Search theory originated during World War II when US Navy military planners searched from planes for the wakes of battleships. From this effort came a mathematical basis for searching. Since then search theory has undergone continuous research and development. The basis of search theory is to quantify the likelihood that the lost subject or object is in a particular area, as well as the likelihood of searchers finding the subject or object. The theory applies to lost people, enemy ships, sunken ships, mineral and petroleum deposits, and even lost archeological treasures.

Using search theory requires probability theory. Fortunately the basic equation is simple as it considers just two variables. First, search leaders must estimate the likelihood of the subject being in a specific area. This is known as the probability of area (POA). The chances that the lost person or clue is in the search area and will be found is called the probability of detection (POD). The product of the two variables results in the probability of success (POS). The challenge to SAR leaders is to deploy the most capable resources, the POD, into sectors where the subject is most likely to be, the POA, to produce the POS in the quickest time. The task is much easier to describe than to do.

In addition to search theory is a second specialty called lost person behavior. Investigations and data about lost individuals were first collected in the 1970s. Specific actions from particular groups of people (e.g., young children, the elderly, hunters, hikers, etc.) were documented. Since then researchers have collected data from more than 50,000 SAR incidents in the

International Search & Rescue Incident Database (ISRID). Of interest to ski patrollers is that the database categories include skier-alpine, skier-Nordic, snowboarders, snowmobilers, and snowshoers. The ISRID contains a lot of useful information, such as the fact that 75 percent of lost skiers and snowboarders tend to be found within three to four miles of the point last seen.

SEARCH STRATEGIES

Quickly locating a missing skier or snowboarder requires not only information about the missing person but also search leaders who are knowledgeable about the local terrain and search strategies. In the alert phase the ski patrol needs to collect and review basic information about the missing person using a lost person questionnaire (see Appendix D).

For most ski-area-related incidents, these forms can be short and concise. The pertinent details include contact information for the reporting person, the point where the person was last seen, and details about the subject's clothing, equipment, route, abilities, and habits. If the search is not resolved quickly, a longer and more detailed questionnaire should be used to gather more information.

While a search is generally considered to be an emergency, a missing skier or hiker does not always require an immediate search action. Sometimes delaying the search action is appropriate when the overdue subjects are likely to turn up under their own effort. To assist leaders in deciding on the speed and scale of the search, a search urgency form may be used. This form can also help leaders recognize allowable risks for searchers.

SEARCH TACTICS

Tactics are the techniques used to locate a person in the shortest possible time. The actions can be indirect, which does not require people in the field searching, or direct, where people are deployed into the field. An example of an indirect method is using a rope line or sign line to direct wayward skiers and snowboarders back into a serviced ski area or out an access road. Other indirect tactics include messages on ski-lift signboards, calls to bars and restaurants, or calls to employers or friends. Usually indirect methods are tried first, but as the search progresses direct tactics are commenced.

Direct tactics involve sending teams into the field to search for clues or the subject. Usually some teams start at the point last seen (PLS) or the last known point (LKP), while other teams may be deployed to likely spots where they might be able to attract the subject or intersect the subject's route. Below are some search methods often used.

Bastard search

The bastard search is a tried and true technique to locate the subject or to determine if the subject is really missing. Sometimes the "missing" person is not really missing, but may be at a friend's house or at work. These incidents remove ski patrollers from their primary responsibility of caring for their mountain and guests. At worst these incidents may put ski patrollers at risk, especially if they must start searching in the field.

The bastard search helps to eliminate these situations by employing some of these steps:

» Calling the person
» Checking with close friends
» Checking with coworkers
» Checking the person's social media websites
» Visiting the person's home or hotel room
» Checking lift pass scans
» Checking parking lots
» Leaving notes at the person's last known location (e.g., on a vehicle, at home, or at a hotel room)

Sometimes the bastard search is an indirect tactic before a full search effort begins. In other cases the bastard search is performed concurrently with other direct tactics.

Hasty search

When high-probability locations must be checked quickly, a small, fast-moving team does a hasty search. These teams are usually the first to go into the field. They check likely routes along creek bottoms, cabins, or nearby trails, or look for clues such as tracks or fresh avalanches.

Hasty search teams usually consist of just two or three individuals who are knowledgeable in search tactics and skilled for the terrain and environment. The teams move quickly and are capable of providing initial emergency care to stabilize a patient until other rescuers arrive.

Grid search

When the subject is presumed or is known to be unresponsive, a more thorough search method is necessary. If an area can be searched quickly with fewer searchers, a loose grid technique is used. Searchers spread out in a line and move across the area. Loose grids allow for relatively quick searching of large areas or for fast searching of open areas.

In the search for a suspected tree well or deep snow immersion incident, the first pass or two may be tried with a loose grid. If the search must be more thorough, a tight grid technique is used. Searchers may need to be close enough to see every bit of ground between the searchers, or even closer in cases when new snow has likely buried the subject. Systematic, tight-grid searching is slow and requires a lot of searchers, so it should only be used when the greatest level of thoroughness is required.

Attraction and confinement search

When the subject is mobile, or presumed to be, searchers should seek highly visible spots and have a means to attract the attention of the lost subject. Depending on the search area and likely location of the subject, a snowcat, snowmobile, ATV, or vehicle with bright overhead lights illuminating the darkness may remain parked all night at a highly visible locale. The occasional blast of a siren can also help guide in a lost person. Be consistent about searchers' whistle use as this may confuse other searchers.

It is also important to confine the subject to a search area with clearly understood boundaries. Searchers may use snowmobiles, ATVs, or personal vehicles to drive trails and roads. Lookouts may scan large or specific areas for clues. If the subject travels into a new area, such as a stream drainage, the search area and complexity of the operation increases significantly.

Clues

When discussing search tactics and methods, it is important to discuss clues. Some searchers advise that clues are the rudder that steer the entire search operation, and this is good advice. Ski patrollers should become "clue aware" and always seek out clues rather than just looking for the subject. There are always many more clues than subjects.

Clues can be visible: footprints or ski tracks, candy wrappers, cigarette butts, or discarded clothing or gear. Some clues are invisible, such as human scent, which is a biological component of dead skin cells and is sloughed off onto the ground or plants. People may also leave electronic clues, such as when they attempt to use cell phones, SENDs, avalanche transceivers, or RECCO reflectors.

Tree well incidents often occur during heavy snowfall or immediately after a storm. When a skier or rider falls into a tree well, they often knock snow off the tree or from its lower branches. Look for a tree with less snow than surrounding trees.

Search resources

Resources include all the people and equipment available to support the SAR effort. An entire ski patrol or just an individual ski patroller can be called a resource. Also referred to as resources are mountain rescuers, dog teams, horse packers, avalanche and swift-water specialists, snowmobiles, snowcats, four-wheel-drive vehicles, helicopters, RECCO detectors, infrared thermal imagers, night vision gear, as well as seers and psychics. Just about any piece of equipment, animal, or person that fills a job receives the moniker "resource." The challenge for SAR leaders is to bring together and manage resources in an effective and efficient way.

Ski patrollers planning to search outside of their ski area boundaries should always plan on an extended stay on the mountain. This means carrying enough gear to stay warm, dry, and fueled with food and water, not only for themselves but also for a lost or injured person. If called to assist in a wilderness SAR operation, searchers should generally be self sufficient for at least 24 hours.

INCIDENT COMMAND SYSTEM

When outside agencies and resources are required to work together, a standardized framework for responding and managing the emergency is critical. Actually, it is mandated.

In 2003 the Department of Homeland Security implemented Presidential Directive 5, which called for a national management system to use the same terminology and incident command procedures for dealing with natural and manmade disasters and emergencies. Called the National Incident Management System (NIMS), all domestic incidents managed by federal, state, local, private, and nongovernmental sectors are mandated to use the Incident Command System. Experienced and wise ski patrollers and rescuers should integrate ICS into their SAR preplans. Ski patrols do not have to implement ICS for its typical on-mountain operation; however, for any incident involving outside organizations and agencies, a working knowledge of ICS is of great benefit.

ICS represents the "best practices" and is the standard for emergency management across the United States. For ski patrols that may respond off-area, ICS is a management system that enables many agencies and disciplines to better work together. ICS may be used for any event, from small to large, from planned occasions to accidental emergencies.

To assure the use of ICS, NIMS requires all agencies that receive federal preparedness funding to be fully compliant at all levels in ICS. Typically a local sheriff has jurisdictional authority in SAR, and federal Homeland Security funding is important to sheriff departments. Therefore the sheriff and all responding resources must be ICS compliant.

Most public safety agencies, such as regional fire departments, can arrange basic ICS trainings for ski patrols and local mountain rescue teams.

ICS FEATURES

ICS benefits SAR because the system

» uses modular organization that is based on the complexity and size of the operation to avoid overloading anyone with too many areas of responsibility.

» provides objectives that determine how the rescue will be managed.

» can be initiated at any time in the operation.

» is capable of growing and contracting with the size of the incident.

» encourages the leaders to delegate responsibility, thereby enabling them to maintain an overall perspective of the operation.

» limits the span of control of any one individual for three to seven subordinates total, reducing the potential for miscommunication.

» provides documentation of activities using a series of forms modified for SAR activities.

» uses common terminology and suggests all radio communications be done in "plain English" (a benefit when working with agencies that have little or no avalanche rescue experience).

» allows for a unified command (permitting more than one agency to provide input into the management of the operation).

» tracks costs incurred during the operation (an important concern for ski areas and law enforcement personnel).

Ski patrollers who organize their SAR operations according to the principles and practices of ICS will be better prepared to work with other rescue teams and agencies. Ski patrollers should remember that ICS provides an umbrella management system that is discipline neutral. ICS qualifications and titles do not correlate with local management titles. For example, someone who holds the title of "chief" or "supervisor" in everyday work may not hold that title in ICS. The purpose of this is to avoid any potential confusion with other position titles, management styles, and organizational structures.

Management functions

The foundation of ICS is based on five major management functions or responsibilities (Figure 15-3). These five functions apply to all incidents, from routine rescues to mass disasters.

Incident Command/Incident Commander (IC). Holds the overall authority and responsibility for the incident and sets the incident objectives, strategies, and priorities. This is the only position always staffed in ICS responses.

Operations. Manages the tactical operations of the incident.

Planning. Supports the incident action planning process by tracking resources, collecting and analyzing information,

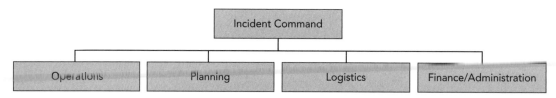

Figure 15-3. *Major management functions of ICS*

TABLE 15-2. ICS SUPERVISORY TITLES

Organizational Level	Title	Subordinate's Title
Incident Command	Incident Commander (IC)	Deputy
Command Staff	Officer	Assistant
General Staff (Section)	Chief	Deputy
Branch	Director	Deputy
Division/Group	Supervisor	N/A
Unit	Leader	Manager
Strike Team/Task Force	Leader	Single Resource Supervisor

demobilizing resources, and managing the incident's documentation.

Logistics. Provides resources and services to support the achievement of the incident objectives.

Finance/Administration. Provides accounting and monitors costs related to the incident.

Supervisory titles in ICS are standardized to help avoid confusion when different agencies are involved (Table 15-2).

ICS ORGANIZATIONAL COMPONENTS

Awareness of the following components is vital for implementing ICS.

Incident Command (IC). The IC has the overall responsibility for the incident.

The IC sets the incident objectives, strategies, and priorities. This is the only position always staffed in ICS responses. On small incidents the IC may be responsible for management functions until he or she delegates the function to others.

Command Staff. Command Staff consists of the Public Information Officer, Safety Officer, and Liaison Officer. Each person is designated as an Officer and may have Assistants as needed.

Public Information Officer. This officer may

» meet with the media.
» establish places and times for press briefings.
» prepare information for media release after approval by the IC.

» coordinate information releases with other agencies or organizations.

Ski resorts and law enforcement agencies usually have individuals trained for this function.

Safety Officer. This officer identifies hazardous situations associated with the incident and mitigates unsafe conditions, operations, or hazards. The Safety Officer can alter, suspend, or terminate activities that pose a danger to rescuers.

Liaison Officer. In a large incident with many rescue teams, this person is the point of contact for coordinating with other agencies and rescue organizations.

General Staff (Sections). These organizational levels have responsibility for a major functional area of the incident response (e.g., Operations, Planning, Logistics, Finance/Administration). The person in charge of each section is designated as a Section Chief. Early in the response or during small incidents, the IC may be responsible for section functions until those functions are delegated to others.

Operations Chief. The Operations Chief is responsible for people. He or she directs operations to attain the incident objectives. The Operations Chief establishes tactics and directs all operational resources.

Planning Chief. The Planning Chief is responsible for paper and records, and for supporting the incident action planning process by tracking resources, collecting and analyzing information, and maintaining documentation.

Logistics Chief. The Logistics Chief is responsible for resources and needed services—rescuers, equipment, food, shelter, etc.—to support the achievement of the incident objectives.

Finance Chief/Administrative. The Finance Chief monitors costs and provides accounting for incident-specific financial management. For most SAR operations this position is not needed and not filled.

The members of the Command Staff and General Staff typically perform their duties at the Incident Command Post with the possible exceptions of the Incident Commander and Operations Chief who both may work at the Incident Site, either early on or in the case of small incidents.

As the size and complexity increases, additional ICS management levels may be implemented to maintain span of control. They may include the following:

Branch. This term is used when the number of Divisions or Groups exceeds the span of control. It is either geographical or functional. The person in charge of each Branch is designated as a Director.

Division. In avalanche response, for example, Divisions are used to divide the site geographically (e.g., dividing a very large or a long debris area, or an avalanche with multiple runout zones). The person in charge of each Division is designated as a Division Supervisor.

Group. Groups describe functional areas of responsibilities. An example of a Group in a backcountry rescue might be the Medical Group. The person in charge of each Group is designated as a Group Supervisor.

Task Force. A Task Force is a combination of resources with different capabilities and with common communications operating under the direct supervision of a Task Force Leader.

Strike Team. A Strike Team consists of a set number of resources with the same capabilities and with common communications operating under the direct supervision of a Strike Team Leader.

Unit. This term is used for a specific incident planning, logistics, or finance/administration activity but not for an operation. For example: Food Unit, Communications Unit, Documentation Unit, etc.

Single Resource. A Single Resource describes an individual, an individual piece of equipment and the personnel required to operate it, or a crew or team of individuals with an identified work supervisor.

Crew. A grouping of Single Resources.

Resources. These are available or potentially available personnel and equipment.

Technical Specialist. An individual with specialized skills or knowledge assigned wherever his skills are required.

Incident Action Plan (IAP). The IAP includes the objectives reflecting the strategy, tactics, and supporting information. The plan may be oral—typical in the initial response phase of incidents—or written, in larger, complex incidents.

Unified Command. Some SAR incidents are multi-jurisdictional. Examples include a county and a national park or two adjoining counties. These situations may be managed using a Unified Command structure, which provides for an IC from each jurisdiction and for the development of a single IAP. In locations where multi-jurisdictional incidents are likely, preplanning meetings and joint training with requisite jurisdictions and rescue teams ensure smoother performance during rescues.

IMPLEMENTING ICS

ICS does not affect the tactical approach of how a SAR operation is performed; ICS only guides how the incident is organized and managed. The functional activities of SAR remain the same.

In ICS the first person receiving the report of a SAR incident becomes the IC until the IC responsibility is transferred to another individual who has more experience. In an incident reported within a ski area, the emergency call is often transferred to a ski patrol dispatcher who alerts the designated IC according to the area's SAR preplan. Two instances most common to ski patrols are an avalanche rescue or a lost skier or snowboarder.

Always remember that small and simple incidents should be managed with a small and simple command structure (Figure 15-4). The IC should only delegate responsibility when needed as the incident's complexity increases.

INCIDENT TYPES

Incidents are "typed" as to their complexity and the capabilities of the leaders to manage the incident. As the complexity in the response increases due to increasing resources or the magnitude of the incident, more highly trained management with more capabilities are needed. Management teams and incidents are categorized in five levels from Type 5 (least complex)

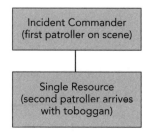

Figure 15-4. *Simple ICS response involving two (and perhaps up to seven) ski patrollers to a routine ski patrol call*

to Type 1 (most complex). Ski patrollers working at ski resorts are most often involved in Type 5 and 4 incidents, though incidents can be expected to become more complex in backcountry rescues.

TYPE 5

Type 5 incidents are the most simple operations managed with a minimum number of resources from a single ski patrol or rescue team. Other than the IC, no other Command and General Staff positions are filled.

There are a limited number of Single Resources composed of single individuals or Crews with a leader. No written ICS Incident Action Plan is needed and the duration is a few hours (a single operational period). The IC is typically located on the Incident Site and provides all tactical direction and incident management. Examples include avalanche rescue in-area or immediately off-area, a lost skier or snowboarder in-area, or a lift evacuation.

In a Type 5 incident, Groups are often used to manage span of control within the

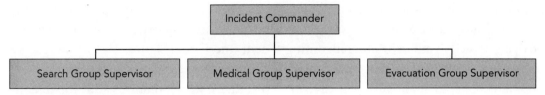

Figure 15-5. *Example of a Type 5 incident response*

Operations Section (Figure 15-5). This leaves the IC to perform the Operations function as well as the Planning, Logistics, and Finance/Administration functions, which are minimal. The IC organizes the Operations functions into Groups and assigns Group Supervisors who manage other rescuers. The IC may also appoint a Safety Officer, particularly when snow or weather conditions are hazardous or changing rapidly. Other organizational schemes for this type of incident are possible using ICS. If span of control limits are reached, the IC may need to delegate the Operations function.

TYPE 4

More complex than the Type 5 incident, a Type 4 incident typically requires several resources and additional management personnel (Figure 15-6). Resources may come from local rescue teams or even nearby ski areas. The IC may or may not be located at the Incident Site. In the case of rescues (e.g., avalanche, technical rock, ice, or river) a dedicated manager (Site Leader) is assigned to manage the operations at the Incident Site. Some Command Staff or General Staff positions may be filled to manage safety issues, media demands, and incoming rescue teams.

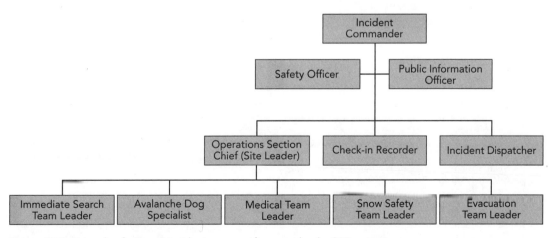

Figure 15-6. *Example of a Type 4 incident response for an avalanche SAR operation*

No written ICS Incident Action Plan is needed, though the operation briefing may be documented to aid in briefing incoming resources. Additional management positions are filled to maintain span of control limits or assist the IC with managing workload demands. This management configuration may be implemented for a single operational period (typically twelve hours) or during multiple operational periods with a limited number of resources assigned.

TYPE 3

When an incident exceeds the capabilities of the initial response and has not been resolved during the first operational period, the complexity and size of the incident increase (Figure 15-7). Increasing complexity means increasing numbers of resources, which requires additional tactical management and supporting personnel. Tactical resources may be organized as Single Resources, Strike Teams, or Task Forces. Some or all Command Staff and General Staff positions are filled as needed to manage span of control and workload. At this level of complexity, a formal incident planning process is implemented, resulting in the production of a written Incident Action Plan. Type 3 incidents

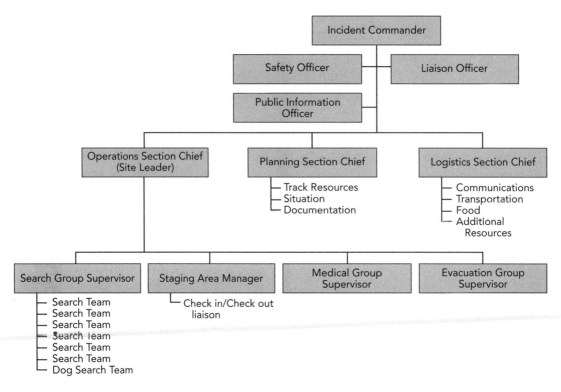

Figure 15-7. *Example of a Type 3 incident response for an avalanche SAR operation*

may use Division/Group Supervisors and/ or Unit Leader level positions. Examples include large or complex avalanche rescues, searches for missing skiers, lost hikers, or any mass casualty incident.

TYPES 2 AND 1

These are very large and complex incidents that are beyond the capabilities of local control. Resources may come from across the country. Type 2 incidents may have upward of two hundred operational people per operational period. Most or all Command Staff and General Staff positions are filled. Type 1 responses are often designated for incidents affecting several states like floods, tornadoes, and hurricanes. Operations personnel often exceed five hundred people per operational period.

ICS TRAINING

The Department of Homeland Security mandates that emergency responders successfully complete basic ICS and National Incident Management System (NIMS) trainings.

Fortunately the Federal Emergency Management Agency (FEMA) makes much of the training and certification available online through the national Emergency Management Institute (EMI). For most rescuers—ski patrollers and mountain rescuers—the following courses should be taken:

» ICS-100, Introduction to Incident Command System
» ICS-200, ICS for Single Resources and Initial Action Incidents
» IS-700.a, NIMS: An Introduction
» IS-800.b, National Response Framework: An Introduction

Each course can be taken in the classroom or by online independent study, in several hours, at www.training.fema .gov/. In addition to the above courses, for middle management positions, rescuers should also take ICS-300; and for top management positions (Command Staff and General Staff), rescuers should take ICS-400. These two courses are state-administered classroom programs. For additional information on these courses rescuers should contact their state emergency management agency.

ENDING A SEARCH

Whether an ICS or a SAR incident, a quick but well-initiated search response will resolve successfully in most searches. However, sometimes the missing person, despite all efforts, is not found. In these cases, SAR managers, in conjunction with the sheriff and others having jurisdictional responsibilities, must decide when to suspend the operation.

A SAR operation is not closed until the person is found. An operation may, however, be suspended when the risks to searchers become too great. Circumstances to suspend a search relatively early in the operation may include darkness, severe weather, or avalanche conditions. Other operations are suspended after a considerable effort has failed to find the subject.

SAR leaders will consider the following factors when deciding to suspend a search:

» Have all search areas been searched, re-searched, and perhaps searched a third time?
» Have all found clues been considered and followed up?
» Was the search operation thorough and well executed?
» Has the question of survivability been thoroughly researched?
» Are the risks to searchers becoming unacceptable?

» Does the current weather or forecasted weather pose serious risks?
» Have appropriate search resources been exhausted?
» Are resources needed for other SAR operations?
» Is there family pressure to continue searching?
» Are further efforts financially practical?

While many search operations may be similar, each operation is unique, so the decision to suspend and to renew the SAR operation must be made on the specific circumstances of the incident. For those searching, especially in the field, the decision to suspend the operation may seem incorrect. However, field searchers need to accept the decision. Field searchers operate with much less information than what is known to and considered by the search managers.

....

SUMMARY:
o The basic strategies for SAR incidents are the same; only the settings differ.
o The acronym A-LAST describes the five core elements or consecutive phases of SAR: alert, locate, access, stabilize, and transport.
o ICS provides a standardized framework to enable emergency management agencies to work together during an incident.

....

CHAPTER 16

EMERGENCY RESCUE TECHNIQUES

Mark Connolly, Genesee Valley Nordic Ski Patrol, Rochester, New York

Matt Fulton, Dartmouth Skiway Ski Patrol, Lyme Center, New Hampshire

Charley Shimanski, Mountain Rescue Association Education Director, Evergreen, Colorado

Matt Speier, Belleayre Ski Patrol, Highmount, New York

OBJECTIVES

o Explain a few of the differences between ski resort and backcountry rescues, including some of the unique challenges backcountry rescuers face.

o Define critical point analysis, white board analysis, and the whistle stop test; and why these assessments are vital to successful rescue planning.

o Describe various types of roped rescue equipment (e.g. ropes, carabiners, harnesses) and proper care and maintenance.

o Describe the basic principles and techniques of high-angle rescue.

o Explain the importance of properly approaching, loading, and unloading patients and equipment from a rescue helicopter.

Excellent training, well-maintained equipment, quality onsite leadership, discipline, teamwork, and creativity are all necessary components of any rescue mission in order to assure the highest possible level of safety for both the rescuers and the victim.

Many differences exist between techniques for recreational climbing and techniques for rescue work. While recreational climbing methods are similar to those used for rescues, the loads placed on equipment and systems during rescue conditions are far greater.

Regarding emergency rescue techniques, nothing can take the place of clear, concise, and safe training from a competent instructor. Skills must be practiced before knowledge is ingrained enough to enable a

STANDARDS IN ROPE RESCUE

The National Fire Protection Association (NFPA) sets minimum standards for rope rescue. These standards cover equipment used for rope rescue, skills required to be a rope rescue technician, and standards on operations and training for technical rescue. These are not law; they are recommendations or guidelines to follow. Refer to these documents for a complete understanding of NFPA standards.

When performing rope rescue, rescuers have an ethical and moral obligation to make each rescue as safe as possible. NFPA has had significant impact on the operations of emergency response agencies worldwide. Its recommendations make up nationally recognized safe practices that can be used as a basis for prosecution in an incident that leads to litigation.

rescuer to make the appropriate judgment during a real rescue. This competence can be achieved only by repetition of rescue skills in a wide variety of applications.

Becoming adept at mountain rescue work requires a long-term commitment. Those interested in becoming rescuers should first begin by developing their competency and knowledge in the art and science of roped travel and climbing.

The National Ski Patrol currently does not provide high-angle rope rescue training, so before attempting to participate in a high-angle rope rescue, patrollers and others should complete specific training by an authorized rescue organization, such as the Mountain Rescue Association (MRA).

SKI RESORT VERSUS BACKCOUNTRY RESCUES

As the popularity of side country and backcountry skiing grows, ski patrols have

continually expanded their reach beyond lift-served ski areas. Clearly, the farther away from established medical care, the more challenging the rescue, and the more additional skills rescuers need to have in order to complete successful missions.

SKI RESORT RESCUES

Ski resort rescues take place within the boundaries of ski resorts. Resort rescuers will usually be supported by mechanized transportation including ski lifts, snowcats, and/or snow machines. Ski resort rescues will have access to complete equipment caches with all the necessary rescue gear, as well as communication systems including radios and phones. Substantial first aid and high-level medical care may be close at hand. Travel time to and from the incident scene will be short and the trip will not be physically demanding. Ground or air transport may be readily available for rapid transport to tertiary medical facilities.

BACKCOUNTRY RESCUES

In recent years backcountry recreationists have been increasingly interested in finding more challenging experiences. This, and the development of more sophisticated backcountry gear, has led them "out of bounds" more frequently. Unfortunately the desire for these experiences has grown faster than proper preparation, so the incidence of emergency situations has increased.

Whether these areas are referred to as front county, side country, slack country, or backcountry, they share a common quality: None of them is within the boundaries of a patrolled, serviced ski area. Additionally, the farther the distance from a ski area, the greater the magnitude of any search-and-rescue SAR endeavor. This has created the need for ski patrol to work more closely and more often with mountain rescue teams and other agencies, and magnifies the need for patrollers to be more familiar with these operations.

Usually recreationists in backcountry incidents have arrived at or plan to leave the area via their own power, which may include hiking, climbing, skiing, snowboarding, or snowshoeing. In some cases travel may be via ski lifts and then through a gated area to the backcountry. Some backcountry access is provided via snow machines or aircraft.

An emergency may stem from a fall, an avalanche, a crash, extreme weather conditions, or a sudden illness. A major backcountry rescue will thoroughly challenge a mountain rescuer's rescue skills, knowledge, flexibility, and creativity. In addition, the physical demands placed on rescuers can be substantial.

CRITICAL THINKING

Individuals trapped or disabled in the high-angle or wilderness environment present rescuers with potentially perilous and challenging situations. Professional and non-professional rescuers can easily become a part of the problem if they do not maintain a clear sense of awareness at all times.

Being involved in the rigging of systems for rescues requires critical thinking. Each system must be continually assessed. Rescuers must always look for the weak link. Systems must be tested for their effectiveness.

This process of critical thinking goes through several stages. The first is the white board analysis. This occurs when the system is drawn and evaluated for weaknesses. One type of evaluation is the critical point test. If any one point of the system were to fail catastrophically the system is modified.

After all components pass the white board analysis, the system is moved to the field for more practical analysis. It is then put through destructive testing. Recent studies show certain systems to be extremely dangerous, even though the instructors of those systems have denied any problems. White board analysis generates safe systems and allows rescuers to make informed decisions to modify a system during a rescue. In the field it is important that everyone performs a safety check on their team members' rigging, rope work, and harnesses. In addition, on Incident Command System (ICS) rescues, an appointed Safety Officer often checks all work and clears all rigging prior to use.

Another mental assessment is the whistle stop test. Not an actual test, the premise is this: If a whistle were blown during a rescue and everyone were to stop and let go of whatever they were doing, would anything catastrophic occur?

During rescues, rope systems should be able to pass the critical point analysis, the white board analysis, and the whistle stop test.

RESCUE PHILOSOPHY

Rescues have many disciplines: mountain rescue, industrial rescue, high-rise rescue, cliff rescue, and dive rescue and recovery. Even searches can be treated as rescue emergencies. None of these disciplines is distinct or stands on its own. While each has certain unique aspects, they all borrow applicable techniques from others.

There is also no one way to do any kind of rescue. Although rescue techniques vary between teams, rescuers should avoid dogmatic, manual approaches. Instructors are obligated to train students by exposing them to as many possibilities as possible. Protocols are acceptable only if they allow rescuers the discretion to use their best judgment at the scene.

Performing rescues is dangerous. All team members need to be capable of performing low-risk methods first, while setting up higher risk methods. All personnel should be prepared to rescue themselves as the first priority, back each other up, and rescue each other as the second priority. Only when these first two priorities are established beyond a reasonable doubt may rescuers undertake the rescue of a victim.

Warning: There is a history of self-sacrifice in rescue services. While this is commendable, it should not be romanticized. This is serious business and the potential is high for loss of human life. Experienced rescuers generally prefer to explain why no action was taken rather than explain why a rescuer was injured or killed.

RESCUE OVERVIEW

A rescue team must look at many variables when organizing a plan of action. The angle of the terrain dictates how a patient will be evacuated after extrication and packaging. Weather, snow conditions, and special hazards to rescuers must be taken into account. Any of these variables can turn a simple, low-angle carry into a technical evacuation, requiring specialized equipment and advanced training.

Most patrollers should have no problem with flat or low-angle terrain, provided they are practiced in carrying or pulling a litter. Although it takes six people to carry a litter, it may take 12 to 15 or more to rotate carrying duties depending on terrain, weather conditions, and the distance of the evacuation.

Rescuers should have a basic understanding of knots used in rescue rigging, and how to effectively operate a belay system, preferably using a tandem prusik belay, when working with rescue loads.

To perform steep or high-angle evacuations safely requires specific equipment and advanced training in technical rigging. When faced with this type of rescue it is important to mobilize additional resources such as the local technical rescue team. An impromptu technical evacuation should never be attempted without proper training.

NON-TECHNICAL RESCUE

One way to determine the difficulty and danger of a rescue is to measure each mission by the steepness of terrain that must be confronted.

Flat (0 to 15 degrees)

Flat terrain should pose no hazard to patients or rescuers. No ropes are required.

The patient is transported in the in-line position by six litter attendants.

Low angle (15 to 30 degrees)

A helmet may be necessary for the patient and rescuers depending on the exposure to hazards. One belay rope may be needed to minimize the risk of the litter sliding down the hill should an attendant slip. The patient is tied into the belay rope or the litter and attendants may be able to carry the litter up a lower angle hill if the terrain allows. When lowering at a higher angle, the six attendants travel facing downhill and mostly support the litter weight, but they also use the belay line for some support as the angle increases. When the victim is on a ski slope, evacuation is easily done by ski toboggan. In the backcountry a flat-bottom stretcher can be used for directly hauling over the snow. Most patrollers should have no problem with flat or low-angle terrain provided they are practiced in carrying a litter or running a toboggan.

TECHNICAL RESCUE

As the angle of a rescue intensifies, so does the degree of danger. Such is the case with technical rescue, which is defined as a mission involving angles of 30 degrees and greater.

Steep angle (30 to 60 degrees)

Severe injury or death can result from an unprotected fall on steep-angle terrain.

Belay and mainline rope systems may be used. The patient is tied into the litter with both internal (directly to the patient) and external (to the litter) tie-downs. The patient may also be secured directly or indirectly to the belay rope via a personal harness. When performing rescues at a steep angle, three to four attendants may be needed to suspend the litter off the ground (if not mostly on snow) to lower or raise the litter in the in-line position. If on steep snow or ice, only one or two attendants may be needed. At these angles (more than 30 to 35 degrees) all attendants are attached to the litter and face uphill during the lowering process, while the litter is carried from an attendant's personal harness via an adjustable tie-in to the litter. The attendants lean back fully against the belay rope bearing the weight from the harness with their legs and have their arms free for maneuvering or other duties. In the case of a two-piece litter, care is taken to secure the attendants to the portion of the litter that is attached directly to the belay or mainline rope. Attendants and patients should wear helmets and eye protection.

High angle (60 degrees plus)

Severe injury or death will result from an unprotected fall from high-angle terrain. Belay and mainline ropes may be used with a single rope lowering system, or a double rope system may be preferred. The litter may be attached to the lowering ropes via a bridle-like or spider system, with one or two attendants dangling from the attachment to the litter via the spider system while lowering on the belay rope. Attachment via adjustable webbing or prusiks allows the attendant to change position and allow maneuvering around the litter in all directions to facilitate lowering around obstacles and for access to the patient for care. The patient is secured as in steep-angle rescue, and patient and attendants should have helmet and eye protection.

RESCUE SAFETY

In reviewing literature about accidents during technical rescue, failure to have adequate control of personnel, equipment, the environment, skills, and systems appears to be the common denominator. Most operations involving evacuations from the backcountry are technical in nature, requiring a sound, well-established ICS. That is why it is imperative to establish ICS protocols as soon as possible during a rescue.

An overview of ICS functions is discussed in Chapter 15, Search and Rescue Basics. The actual roles and responsibilities may vary between rescue teams, controlling or directing agencies, and locations. It is important to become very familiar with the system and the members of local rescue agencies so that when the need arises for a mutually supported rescue it can progress smoothly.

PATIENT SAFETY

The purpose of learning all of the ICS functions and rescue skills is to manage the injured patient in the vertical realm. Rescuers must always be aware of patient needs. When performing a technical rescue the rescuers often must put the patient in potentially exposed positions. Patients should be appropriately protected from the environment at all times, including overall protection from heat, cold, rain, snow, wind, and sun. Helmets and eye protection should be provided. Rescuers should attempt to maintain two points of contact with the patient during lowering and raising operations in steep- and high-angle rescues.

TRAINING

NFPA 1670: Standard on Operations and Training for Technical Search and Rescue helps an organization evaluate itself and determine if it can function at any of three levels of capability—Awareness, Operations, and Technician—in various technical rescue disciplines including rope rescue. In providing the organizational requirements to perform a technical rescue at a given level, the standard also creates guidance for the training they must perform.

All patrollers should be trained to the Awareness level. It should be the patrol's goal to have a majority at Operations level and a core group at Technician level. But if the patrol has only one or two members with a solid understanding of rope systems, how will the team respond to a rescue on a day when those few are not on duty? The patrol must know its limitations and be able to back off and mobilize additional resources such as the local technical rescue team.

The systems and skills discussed in this chapter require detailed, hands-on instruction from qualified rope rescue instructors. Do not attempt any of the techniques in actual rescue conditions until you have completed proper training and certification as required by your state or local government. There are many professional organizations that offer instruction in personal and advanced rigging skills. A 40-hour course is a minimum recommendation.

There is often little continuity in the rescue techniques and procedures used from one patrol to the next. EMTs, paramedics, and physicians are required to stay up-to-date on the latest techniques and developments. Rope rescue technicians have a similar moral obligation to utilize the latest techniques that can minimize risk and improve efficiency.

Since no two rescues are alike, teams should be creative in their training drills. Do not get in the habit of practicing on the same cliff or on the same terrain. Drills should be based on specific rescue objectives and should take place in realistic scenarios representative of mountain conditions. Training should be a mix of classroom instruction and extensive fieldwork.

The skills used in rope rescue are perishable. When not used regularly they quickly decay. Ongoing training and review should take place on a regular basis. Regular training develops competence and confidence. Documentation of all training should include the specific training performed, the date, who attended, the hours, and the trainers.

Although it is necessary to initially learn a particular way to perform a skill, at an advanced level it is important to concentrate on the concepts and to be able to evaluate systems. As the rescuer rigs and analyzes systems, the questions to ask are the following: Is it safe? Will it work? Is it efficient?

RESCUE EQUIPMENT

There is an important distinction between equipment designed for use in rescue operations and recreational climbing equipment: Rescue equipment is designed with much higher potential loads and forces in mind. Recreational climbing equipment used in rescue is usually limited to an individual rescuer's personal gear, such as ice axes, crampons, and harness. Types of rescue equipment and the exact way it is used will vary with teams. The manner in which gear is arranged will vary as well.

ROPE

Rope is commonly used to raise, lower, traverse, provide safety, and construct pulley systems. Under normal circumstances rope is extremely stable and durable, but it must be treated with care. Never allow a rope to be stepped on by crampons, sharp ski edges, or even boots. Ground-in dirt may abrade the core fibers. Periodic washing of rope may be done to decrease the abrasive effects of dirt particles.

Nylon rope is the most common type used in technical rescue. Rescue rope is found with a diameter from $\frac{7}{16}$ inch to $\frac{5}{8}$ inch or larger. Larger rope is too heavy to carry and handle and may require specially sized equipment. Smaller rope may not be able to handle the loads that some rescue work demands.

The strength of rope is determined by the manufacturer. The NFPA rescue guidelines expects half-inch rope to bear the load of two rescuers with a patient, and associated loading of up to 600 pounds of force (lbF). Depending on loads some rescue organizations may be able to use $\frac{7}{16}$-inch rope and still meet the NFPA's guidelines.

Common breaking strengths of nylon low-stretch rescue rope (that may vary with manufacturer):

» 6 mm–1,700 lbF (7.58kN)
» 8 mm–3,100 lbF (13.83kN)
» 11.1 mm ($\frac{7}{16}$ inch)–6,800 lbF (30.24kN)
» 12.5 mm ($\frac{1}{2}$ inch)–9,200 lbF (40.92kN)

Low-stretch, or static, rope has a relatively low-stretch ratio (usually between 10 and 20 percent until failure) due to a non-spiral constructed core bundle. Two to five percent elongation will occur with working loads (200 lbF). Kernmantle low-stretch rope is used by most rescue organizations. Variable rope lengths, often 200- to 600-foot lengths, may be used and are frequently color coded by length.

High-stretch, or dynamic, rope has a relatively high stretch ratio (usually between 20 and 40 percent until failure) due to a spiral constructed core bundle. Five to ten percent elongation will occur with a working load. This type of rope is used in recreational sport and traditional climbing when the possibility of a fall factor of two may be encountered. For rescue scenarios this rope has value when a rescuer must climb above or horizontally beyond the anchor point. The forces generated by a fall are greatly absorbed by the rope, thus decreasing the force on the anchors and the falling climber.

Care, maintenance, and storage

The care of rope used in rescue is of primary importance. Proper care follows the same guidelines as for recreational climbing ropes. Inspect ropes at least monthly, preferably after each use, and document inspection and rope usage. The Penberthy method of rope inspection is considered conservative but has been used for years. It involves close inspection of all the sheath pics, which are the individual squares of the sheath braid. The method also requires close manipulation of the core fibers to look and feel for dents and dimples.

The following is a simple rating system for ropes:

Category I. Rope that is unused, less than five years old, inspected at least quarterly with documentation, and otherwise conforms to rescue rope guidelines.

Category II. Rope that is less than 10 years old, inspected and documented at least quarterly according to the manufacturer's recommendations, has never been shock loaded, never been exposed to heat in excess of 200 degrees F or potentially

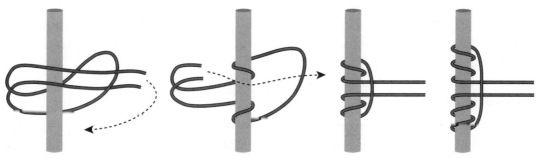

Figure 16-1. *Prusik hitch*

damaging chemicals, and otherwise conforms to rescue rope guidelines.

Category III. Non-life-support rope or any rope greater than 10 years old, regardless of condition or whether it fails any of the provisions of Category II ropes.

A rope is downgraded to Category III if any single pic has 50 percent greater wear (separated fiber), if any core fibers are exposed, if the core manipulation indicates kern damage or separation, or if any other retirement criteria apply. In practice, busy rescue groups examine the ropes each time they are used and replace them at least every five years.

ACCESSORY CORD

Accessory cord is a low-stretch nylon kernmantle rope, commonly used for prusik hitches (Figure 16-1), anchor material, load-releasing hitches, and personal prusiking techniques. It is important to purchase accessory cord for a specific use. The two most common diameters of accessory cord are 6 mm for personal use and 7 mm or 8 mm for rescue loads. The two ends are commonly joined with a double fisherman's knot, set by weighting, and generally not untied. Breaking strength for 7 mm cord is 3,150 lbF.

WEBBING

Nylon webbing is used in rescue work because it is versatile. It is useful for constructing anchor slings, harnesses, and tie-downs. Construction is a nylon, tubular spiral weave; the most common size is one inch, rated at 4,000 lbF (17.79kN). Color coding may vary with teams and may be used to identify different lengths.

CARABINERS

Proper attachment of a carabiner and its orientation is essential for safety and for properly functioning systems. Carabiners are not indestructible and need proper care. Recommended ratings for carabiners should be at least 5,000 lbF (22.24kN) breaking strength and the carabiner should be lockable. If a carabiner has been damaged significantly it should be destroyed. Inspection of carabiners for dents, rust, and gate-locking function should be a mandatory part of the regular equipment check.

PULLEYS

Pulleys are used in rescue work to accomplish several functions:

» To change the direction of travel of a load or the victim
» To provide mechanical advantage so less effort is needed to move greater loads
» To reduce friction so rope work can be done safely and without damage to lifelines

Pulleys are constructed in different ways and in different sizes. In contrast to recreational pulleys, rescue pulleys are larger and have bearings that decrease friction. Those with flat bottoms are constructed to automatically be prusik-minding pulleys (PMP) that reduce the need for a person to manage prusiks that may become entangled in a rigging system.

It is important to use the proper diameter rope for the size of the pulley. Using the four-to-one (4:1) rule, the diameter of the pulley wheel (sheave) should be four times the diameter of the rope. Smaller ratios can potentially decrease the strength of the rope due to the angle of the bend of the rope over the smaller sheave. Rope and webbing need edge protection to prevent rope damage and inefficient hauling.

LOWERING DEVICES

Rescue groups commonly use brake bar racks (Figure 16-2) for rappelling and lowering loads. It allows the rescuer to add or delete bars during use, which adjusts the amount of friction. The brake bar rack is one of the few friction devices that does not cause the twisting of the rescue rope.

A similar device used for lowering is a brake tube that allows a variable number of rope wraps for friction. It can accommodate single or double ropes, and it allows

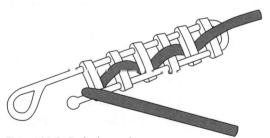

Figure 16-2. *Brake bar rack*

the passage of knots when ropes have been joined together for extra length. It also does not induce rope twisting.

MECHANICAL ASCENDERS

Mechanical ascenders have mostly replaced prusiks as a means of ascending fixed ropes. Multiple manufacturers produce the devices, which have a smooth or toothed camming device that allows easy attachment and detachment from the rope. The cam permits easy sliding in one direction (upward), but when weighted or pulled in the opposite direction (down), it tightly engages the rope. There are different arrangements to attach them to the rescuer's harness to facilitate upward travel on the rope, or to use as an upward hauling device. Be certain the device is correctly chosen to work with the diameter of rope in use. Its design and function is for single loads and should never be used for rescue loads or to catch a load in a dynamic belay situation.

HARNESSES

A harness allows attachment of a climber or rescuer to a rope via a direct tie-in from the rope to the harness. It may also be used on a steep or vertical rescue to tie the rescuer to the litter, usually via a set of two adjustable prusiks. A harness used in mountain rescue is generally a climbing harness that fastens around the waist above the hip bones and incorporates leg loops. It distributes the rescuer's weight over these areas while suspended, or in the event of a fall. Adjustable leg loops facilitate donning the harness with boots, crampons, or skis in place and can accommodate varying amounts of clothing. Care must be taken to ensure that the direct tie-in to the rope and fastening of the harness buckles are done correctly.

LITTERS

A variety of litters will slide over snow, many of them much lighter than the sleds familiar to patrollers. Some may be split into two sections for carrying into the backcountry. Some types are made of foldable material that may be rolled up and carried inside a bag.

RIGGING SYSTEMS

When rigging for rescue there are several common systems, which may differ significantly between rescue teams. Mainline and belay line systems all require anchors. The belay anchor will have the greatest potential for severe loading. Practicing various systems with a rescue unit is essential. Generally, separate anchors are selected for each of these systems to minimize confusion and to avoid relying on only one point of contact.

Riggings should be kept as simple as possible. When a single anchor point is not strong enough for the load, use an equalized load anchor system (see Appendix A).

The webbing should be oriented in the direction of the pull (generally easy and unidirectional on snow since it follows the fall line). This system distributes the load between several anchor points. If one of the anchors fails, a properly constructed set of anchors can smoothly transfer the load to the other anchors without any extension or shock loading.

ANCHORS

Anchors are the foundation for the rigging of the entire rope rescue system. They are what the rope system will be connected to, and they can be manmade as at ski resorts or objects found in nature such as trees, large boulders, and snow and ice. The anchor should be strong enough to withstand the greatest anticipated force on the system. A single "bombproof" anchor may be strong enough to support a rescue system, but it is advisable to use two separate anchor points, one for the main line and one for the belay to keep the equipment and scene better organized.

Anchor systems are made up of the materials used to connect to the anchor. Rope and webbing work well for constructing anchor systems. Sharp or abrasive surfaces should be padded to protect the anchor material. When building anchor systems, there should be a straight line from the anchor to the rope's final destination.

All internal angles created by tensioned anchor materials must be kept below 90 degrees to ensure forces are not multiplied within the system. Exceeding the 90-degree rule puts additional stresses on the anchor. As the mechanical advantage of the system increases, so does the potential force placed on the anchor. Fortunately, in a snow setting the anticipated load is decreased since the sled may rest on the snow and slide with movement. Usually a 2:1 or 3:1 system works for raising (except with the uncommon case of a vertical raise) and thus exerts less force on the anchor. When substantial trees are available, one can quickly and easily utilize a tree wrap for lowering.

Anchor system types

The NSP recommends referring to *On Rope* by Bruce Smith and Allen Padgett and the National Speleological Society's Vertical Section, an internal organization of the society that educates and trains cavers in safe, efficient vertical caving techniques, regarding qualified technical rope rescue instruction for details on the following: (Also see Appendix A.)

» Three-bight anchor, fixed and focused—Used to anchor to a single anchor point.
» Tensionless hitch (aka high strength tie-off)—Provides an easy way to anchor a rope to an object.
» Wrap three, pull two—Used for rescue loads, it has a strength of about 12,000 pounds.

» Load-sharing anchor—This multipoint anchor can be built from two or more anchor points when the strength of one anchor point is questionable.
» Load-distributing anchor—A system that distributes the load amongst anchor points of a load-sharing anchor amongst all anchor points. Failure to rig this anchor properly results in considerable extension, thus failing the non-extending element of ERNEST (see page 228).

A word about girth-hitching anchors: Girth hitches should not be used in the rigging of rescue anchors. The stress of the rope or webbing upon itself can reduce strength by as much as 50 percent, particularly if there is dynamic shifting of the load.

Advanced anchors

In backcountry settings, rescuers need to be particularly knowledgeable about building all types of anchors and using artificial protection.

Snow anchors. Snow anchors should be used as a last resort due to the time required to properly set them up and the variability of their strength. Entire books have been written on the subject and many hours of study, training, and field experience are required to build anchors in snow and ice. Unfortunately, in the backcountry and especially above tree line, snow anchors may be all that are available.

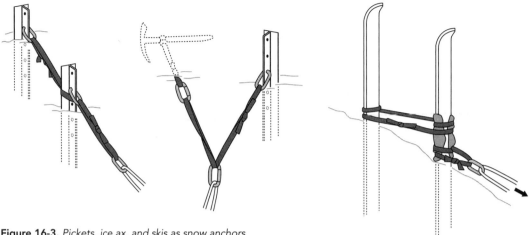

Figure 16-3. *Pickets, ice ax, and skis as snow anchors*

Burying ice axes, pickets, skis (Figure 16-3), or snow flukes (Figure 16-4), to create a deadman anchor is a common method to connect to the anchor system. The strength of these anchors is entirely dependent on the depth and angle of placement and the quality and condition of the snowpack. A bollard—a large knob

Correct
45°
Slope angle

Incorrect

Incorrect

Figure 16-4. *Snow fluke*

of ice or snow—can also be used (Figure 16-5). Tubular ice screws are used to create anchor points in ice.

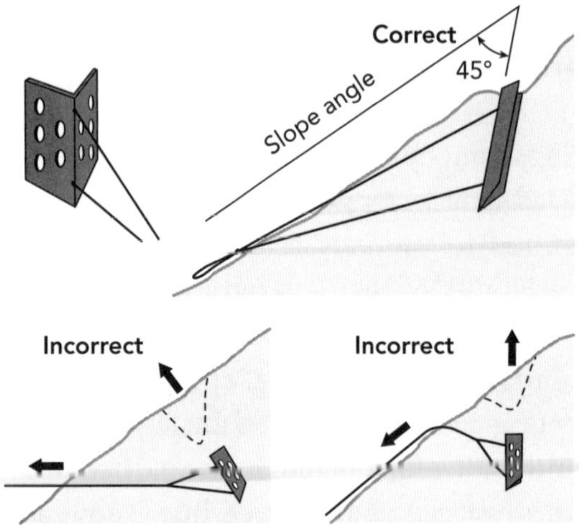

Artificial protection. Many mountain rescue teams make common use of artificial protection where big trees, boulders, or other manmade anchor points cannot be found. Artificial protection such as spring-loaded camming devices or passive chocks, nuts, and hexes are designed to be placed in rock cracks as anchor points.

Proper placement of artificial protection requires training and experience. When artificial protection is used for rescue anchors, use a sufficient number of pieces to achieve a strength rating that will yield a 10:1 static system safety factor (SSSF) (see page 228). Place at least four to five pieces or more, together with a fixed and focused load-sharing anchor.

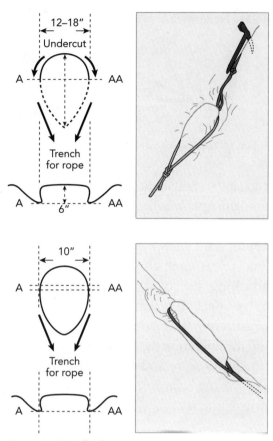

Figure 16-5. *Bollards*

BELAY LINES

Two common belay techniques used by rescue groups are the Muenter hitch and the tandem prusik belay.

Muenter hitch

The Muenter hitch (Figure 16-6) works well for single rescuer loads of up to about 250 pounds, but when the weight is increased to a rescue load of 440 pounds or extreme loads of around 600 pounds, this hitch is unable to consistently catch the load.

The Muenter hitch is a friction hitch that depends on the ability of the operator. The operator must have good hand-eye coordination, grip strength, and the capability to make a correct split-second decision.

Tandem prusik belay

The tandem prusik belay works well with all different loads. It is the only belay technique that can consistently catch the extreme rescue load of 600 pounds. The tandem prusik belay works with two 7 mm or 8 mm prusik loops hitched onto the belay line. When the load is placed on the belay line, the prusik loops grip the rope and avert the fall.

When rigging the tandem prusik belay, the following components are required for proper operation:

» Anchor
» Low-stretch rescue rope
» Tandem prusik loops (one short, one long)
» Load-releasing hitch
» The skills to use this equipment

The prusik loops are made out of 7 mm or 8 mm low stretch nylon kern-mantel accessory cord. This cord should be similar in design to rescue rope (no special coating on the rope, easy-to-tie knots). If using 7/16-inch rescue rope, the cord should be cut to approximately 1.40 meters and 1.70 meters, then tied into loops with a double overhand knot (double fisherman's bend).

Figure 16-6. *Muenter hitch*

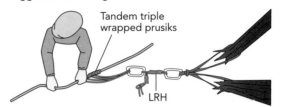

Figure 16-7. *Tandem prusik belay rigging*

Leaving approximately a one-inch tail on the bender, pre-tension the loops between your foot and hand to set the bend. Once the prusik loops have been tied and tensioned, they will generally not be untied. When the prusik loops are hitched onto the rescue rope (the short one on the anchor side and the long one on the load side, usually color coded), there will be about four inches between the long and short loops. This allows for easier gripping of the prusiks during loading and facilitates handling the loops if someone is tending the belay prusiks. Care must be taken to ensure that the belay prusiks are placed correctly in the system on the load side, so that if the load is released they will be oriented toward the rescuer.

Figure 16-7 shows the tandem prusik belay rigged for a lowering and for a raise. The only difference between the two systems is the addition of a prusik-minding pulley (PMP). This controls the prusik rather than a rescuer doing so, freeing up manpower for other tasks.

As with the use of the Muenter hitch for single rescuer loads, the belayer has certain responsibilities when using the tandem prusik belay. These include gathering the correct equipment, rigging an appropriate anchor system, attaching the load-releasing hitch (LRH) to the anchor, attaching the two prusik loops to the belay line, and placing the short and long prusiks into the load-releasing hitch. During the operation the belayer needs to continually observe and correct any excessive slack in the belay line and looseness in the prusik hitches.

Load-releasing hitch

Many rescue groups use a LRH (Figure 16-8), which allows the prusik hitches to be unloaded and also acts as a force limiter on extreme drops. The basic components are a 30-inch piece of 8 mm or 9 mm accessory cord and two locking "D" carabiners. The following steps detail how to construct the LRH:

1. Double the accessory cord with figure-eight stopper knots tied into the running ends. Tie a Muenter hitch with a bight into the carabiner. Hook the

other carabiner into the open bight of the accessory cord.

2. Flip the Muenter hitch back and forth to confirm function, and pull on the running end until the Muenter locks in place around the carabiner. Invert the Muenter hitch and place three wraps with the standing end.

3. Push two bights through and secure the LRH with an overhand safety.

4. Safety check your LRH and tie a spare.

MAIN LINE

The main line is the workhorse of any rescue system. The rope is rigged either to lower or raise a load. Since gravity makes it much easier to lower than to raise a load, whenever possible you should rig a lowering rather than a raising system. Remember,

Figure 16-8. *Load-releasing hitch*

especially with a rescue load, to be careful with edge protection.

Lowering

A rescue-eight device (a figure-eight descender with protuberances for locking off the load) may be used singly, or in tandem for heavier loads, as a lowering device. It cannot be adjusted for friction once it is loaded and is not ideal for heavier loads.

A tree wrap may be quickly set up for a lower, and wraps may be added or removed even when weighted. Its simplicity and rapid set-up make it appealing for lower angle and lighter load evacuations.

Two devices mentioned earlier—the brake bar rack and brake tube—can also be used as lowering devices. Gloved hand placement on a brake rack should be such that the rescuer can push the bars closer to add friction or pull the bars apart to decrease friction. When lowering the victim more vertically or with a heavier load, all the bars may be used. Once the load is fully on the brake rack the operator can remove one or two bars as needed. When managing rescue loads the rescuer should not go below four bars with the fifth and sixth bars ready to be used.

The brake tube device changes friction by varying the number of wraps on the tube, usually three to four depending on the load. Wraps can be added or removed while under a load. This device also permits the use of double ropes, as well as knot passing for ropes that have been joined.

Lowering systems require a person to manage the lowering rope, and often a person to back up the belayer.

Raising

Opposing gravity and the friction generated by the rope running over the snow, ice, or rock edges can increase the load several times, and it is crucial to engineer an adequate pulley system. Multiple options exist. For mountain rescue work in winter, the snow itself assists with anything other than an absolutely vertical rescue. Consequently most systems will be a 2:1 or 3:1 set-up that can easily be changed to a compound system of 4:1 or 6:1, and these will manage a vertical rescue. Be familiar with your local mountain rescue team's preferences.

Simple pulley system. The first basic rule for a simple pulley system is this: If the rope is tied off to the load and then goes through a pulley at the anchor first, then the mechanical advantage is odd, for example, 1:1, 3:1. If the rope is tied off to the anchor and runs through a pulley on the load side first, then the advantage is even, for example, 2:1, 4:1.

The second rule is as follows: If the last pulley in the system is on the anchor side, it only changes the direction of pull and does not add any mechanical advantage.

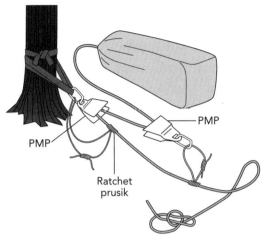

Figure 16-9. *Simple 3:1 system*

This change of direction is used for additional pulling room or to be able to pull downhill instead of uphill.

The last rule for simple pulley systems (to identify the theoretical mechanical advantage) is to count the number of strands between the anchor and the load. This only works if you follow the first two rules. The most common simple pulley system is probably the 3:1, or Z-pulley, system (Figure 16-9).

Compound pulley system. A compound pulley system is a simple pulley system pulling on another simple pulley system (Figure 16-10). With a compound pulley system the results are multiplied. A simple 2:1 pulling on a 3:1 results in a compound 6:1. Generally a compound pulley system is more efficient because it uses less equipment to achieve a given advantage.

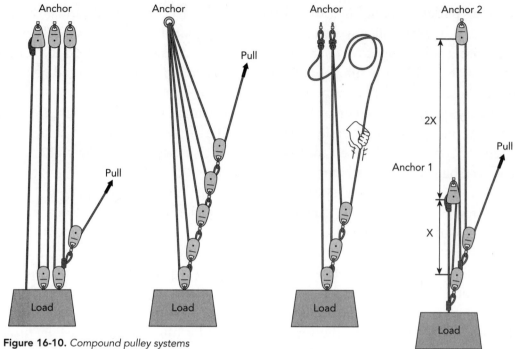

Figure 16-10. *Compound pulley systems*

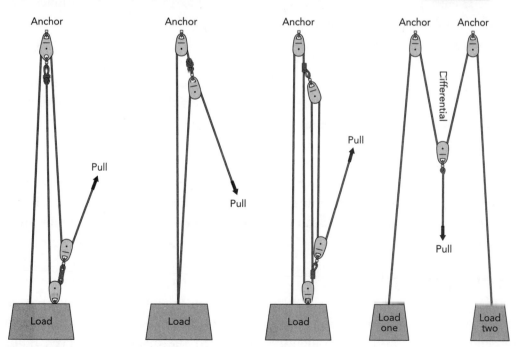

Figure 16-11. *Complex pulley systems*

Complex pulley system. The last pulley system is a complex pulley system (Figure 16-11). It is easily recognized when it does not meet the rules of a simple or compound pulley system. A common complex pulley system is the complex 5:1. The simple 3:1 pulley system can easily be converted to a complex 5:1 with an additional pulley carabiner and prusik loop.

Again, the most common systems for winter rescue are the 1:1, 2:1, and 3:1, which may be readily upgraded to a 4:1 or a 6:1 system. A variable number of prusik-minding pulleys, carabiners, and tandem prusik belays is needed, as well as anchor material. All of this needs to be addressed by the rigger and those working directly with the rigger. The number of people involved with the lowering system increases with its complexity.

TRANSPORTATION

The terrain and conditions in mountain travel add complicated layers to a SAR mission. Besides caring for injured people, rescuers must factor in how to safely move patients and patrollers as quickly and as efficiently as possible, often in difficult circumstances.

PATIENT PACKAGING

One of the most time-consuming aspects of a rescue is immobilizing a patient into a rescue litter. It is important to identify the patient packagers as soon as possible so the correct equipment can be gathered and the patient accessed as quickly as possible. All considerations need to be made for patient comfort, safety, and appropriate medical care.

Mountain rescue teams have sleds that are constructed to slide over the snow. The patient is ready to be packaged after a thorough medical exam and appropriate treatment of injuries. Remember to address proper clothing, insulation, and padding for the patient (especially under the knees of the patient's slightly bent legs), as well as a final tarp covering the head. The main line, or belay line, may be attached to the litter by a figure eight on a bight snapped into a locking carabiner that in turn is clipped into a litter bridle fashioned from a sling. Remember to always secure the top, or uphill end, of a two-part litter to the rescue rope.

In some cases a full complement of gear is not available, and more creative methods must be used. Usually, enough group gear and clothing is available to accomplish the task of insulating, splinting, immobilizing, and packaging. If a sled is not available, one of the last challenges for rescuers is to fabricate some means of transportation for the injured person. Considerations include the nature of the injury, the terrain, snow conditions, equipment available, the number of people available to pull and control the load, and the distance to travel. Equipment used to fabricate a toboggan will

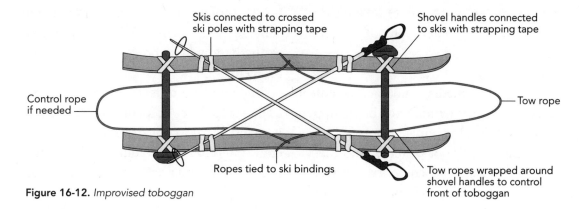

Skis connected to crossed ski poles with strapping tape

Shovel handles connected to skis with strapping tape

Control rope if needed

Tow rope

Ropes tied to ski bindings

Tow ropes wrapped around shovel handles to control front of toboggan

Figure 16-12. *Improvised toboggan*

come from items that a typical group of backcountry skiers have (Figure 16-12). Consequently the construction may vary from one rescue to another. Some designs work reasonably well for longer travel distances. Although some concepts are quite basic, they might be unacceptable for persons with serious injuries such as back or internal injuries.

HELICOPTERS

Helicopters are a vital function in many SAR operations. Because more local areas are gaining access to helicopters for use in search, rescue, and emergency response, it is essential that everyone who may have to work around these aircraft have a thorough orientation to helicopter safety. As a search and reconnaissance platform coupled with rescue and extrication capabilities, the helicopter is unparalleled in its versatility for emergency and disaster response.

Despite the fact that helicopters are uniquely valuable, they can be extremely dangerous. With rotors turning at over 150 miles per hour, the hazard to searchers is real. The threat of a helicopter crash poses another danger.

Use of helicopters

SAR agencies that use helicopters can

» search for or attract a search subject.
» evacuate injured people and/or rescue personnel.
» transport or extricate field members.
» heli-rappel to the site of a subject.
» provide an aerial survey of topography.

The key to the safe utilization of helicopter resources in any SAR operation is for ICS leadership to perform a thorough risk-benefit analysis. Is it worth the risk, for example, to have a helicopter called to evacuate a healthy search subject, simply to avoid the need for a two- or three-mile hike out? Conversely, who can question the need for an air ambulance when a patient is lying unconscious and bleeding profusely in the backcountry? Somewhere between these two examples lies the more difficult decision with regard to helicopter utilization.

Radio traffic

TV, private, media and aero-medical helicopters may or may not be equipped with the MRA 1 channel (155.160). Army helicopters (Chinooks, Hueys, and Blackhawks) may not be equipped with programmable radios and may be required to use specialized aviation frequencies or other common emergency frequencies such as National Law Enforcement Channel (NLEC) at 155.475 Mhz or Fire Emergency Radio Network (FERN) at 154.280 Mhz.

Field teams should avoid ground-to-air radio communication unless they have something very important to communicate. Even though field teams will likely hear air-to-ground radio traffic, including inquiries from the helicopter crew, they will likely have a harder time receiving the traffic from the ground.

On non-military helicopters, either the pilot or the spotter can communicate over specific radio channels, as dictated by the pilot. Generally the pilot will give the spotter specific instructions on how to communicate with the Incident Command Post or ground personnel using the ship's radio.

If a helicopter is used for searching and does not have the MRA 1 frequency, the spotter can use a handheld radio on board, though such communications are generally poor. Using a headset connected to the handheld radio can alleviate some problems.

In the aircraft itself, rescuers should understand the concept of a sterile cockpit. It mandates no conversation on the aircraft intercom radio during departures and arrivals until a safe altitude is reached.

Helicopter management and safety precautions

Prior to each day's operation a briefing should be conducted to establish the plan of operations for the pilots and the ground personnel. Pertinent safety plans and flight hazard maps should be reviewed before the flight is scheduled.

Operation of the helicopter should be during daylight hours whenever possible (defined as a half-hour before sunrise to a half-hour after sunset). Passengers should request a briefing from the pilot prior to the flight to ascertain the location of emergency exits, fire extinguishers, emergency electrical and fuel shut-offs, emergency locator transmitter (ELT) manual switch, first-aid kits, and survival gear. No unauthorized personnel should be allowed to fly on any mission.

Helicopter hand signals should be used whenever possible, but only by trained personnel. Finally, all personnel should stay at least 100 feet away from helicopters, except when loading.

Helispots

Helicopters generally do not take off or land vertically. They need a landing zone (often called an "LZ," or helispot) that may be hundreds of feet long. The ideal helispot is a flat strip 100 feet wide and 300 feet long (roughly the size of a football field). If a helicopter has engine failure—more common upon takeoff due to high engine stress—it needs extra room to land safely.

Helispots should be located so that the helicopter can land and take off into the wind to increase lift. Only as a last resort should a "hover hole" helispot be chosen. A hover hole is a LZ where the pilot must slow to a hover and then descend to the ground. When taking off, the pilot must use all available engine power, which makes a hover hole the least desirable option.

The helispot should be free of light-weight objects that will blow away. A snow-field can make a good helispot, but markers such as backpacks must be placed near the helispot to give the pilot depth perception.

SAR team leaders must consider the risks versus benefits of performing night operations. If this is absolutely necessary the pilot must be advised of optimal flight paths to avoid hazards. At night the helispot may be marked by rescuers' headlamps held on and aimed steady without wavering.

Landings and takeoffs. Landings and takeoffs are generally made easier in the presence of a light, steady breeze. During a landing, all personnel outside the helispot must hold down any loose gear, and look away to avoid injury by flying debris. During final approach, only one ground person, known as the parking tender, should be in the helispot. If no experienced parking tender is available it is important that one rescue member establish communication with any incoming helicopter.

During landings on snow, no rescuers should be in the landing zone at any time. There is always the chance that the helicopter's weight will cause it to settle in the snow, which could be dangerous for any rescuer in the helispot.

Helispot communication. Radio communication from rescuers on the ground to the helicopter pilot and/or crew is essential to safely land a helicopter. The helispot location should be clearly specified and defined using nearby landmarks since pilots generally do not carry quadrangle maps. Its elevation should be stated, as well as any obstructions, including distance and bearing (e.g., "100 foot tower 300 feet SSE of helispot"). Weather conditions must be described, as well as aerial, as these are often unmarked and very difficult for a pilot to see. Pilots may require longitudinal/latitudinal coordinates when attempting to find a helispot. (CAUTION: Do not confuse longitude/latitude coordinates with UTMs or the helicopter may end up in Bolivia!) Once the parking tender has the helicopter in sight, it should be easy to direct the pilot to the helispot using the clock method (e.g. "The helispot is at your two o' clock.")

Safety precautions on the ground
It is important that rescue teams train their personnel in these basic safety operations:

» Ground personnel should never run when approaching or leaving a helicopter. They should always approach and leave the helicopter with head and equipment low.
» A helicopter should never be approached from the side where the ground is higher than where the chopper is standing or hovering.
» Any rescue passenger should wear a helmet, fire-resistant clothing, and leather boots at all times when near or on board the helicopter.
» Rescue members should carry a portable two-way radio capable of transmission on air-to-ground and ground-to-ground frequencies at a minimum.
» All gear should be stored securely.
» Explosive, flammable, or otherwise dangerous materials carried on board need to be reported to the pilot.

Approaching the helicopter. Working around helicopters requires extra awareness. The mere actions of approaching, loading and unloading the helicopter can have fatal consequences if not done properly (Figure 16-13):

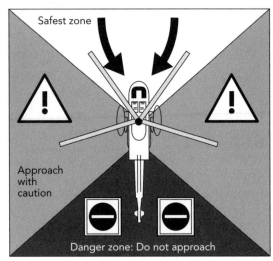

Figure 16-13. *Approaching a helicopter*

» Make sure the pilot has the helicopter down all the way. The universal "thumbs up" sign might be given by the pilot.
» Only one person should approach the ship. When approaching, all equipment such as packs, skis, snowshoes, and ice axes must be carried horizontally below waist level.
» Approach the helicopter only at an angle visible to the pilot.
» No rescuer should approach the ship until the rotors have come to a full stop.

Loading and unloading safety procedures. When rotors are operating keep the following points in mind:

» All loading or unloading must take place on the downhill side of the ship.
» The tail rotor must be avoided.

» Wear personal protective equipment (PPE), which includes a helmet with a chinstrap, eye and ear protection, leather boots, and fire-resistant clothing.
» Packs should be carried, not worn.

Loading and extricating subjects. When using a helicopter, rescuers need to not only pay attention to their own actions, but they need to be aware of the patient's safety, too:

» If the subject is in good physical condition, consider guiding ground teams to the subject, then walking or driving the subject out of the field.
» When loading a patient on the helicopter, SAR personnel should take the lead from the flight nurse or pilot. Once the patient is securely loaded, rescuers should immediately exit the area by walking directly to the front of the helicopter and beyond it.
» Subjects should not offload the helicopter on their own; if possible, allow the engine to come to a complete rotor stop before offloading.

In-flight precautions

While helicopters are in flight, rescue personnel on board the chopper must be aware of the following:

» The pilot's word is final as to whether or not the flight can be made.
» Before takeoff all passengers must fasten and adjust the safety belt and shoulder harness, and keep this equipment fastened until otherwise instructed.
» Passengers must locate the emergency exits and review instructions. There is no smoking during takeoffs, landings, or during the flight.
» Rescuers must keep clear of all controls and keep geographically oriented at all times.
» Do not throw objects out of the helicopter at any time, except when instructed by the pilot to do so.

Additionally, rescuers aboard helicopters should do the following:

» Board the helicopter fully prepared to hike out. A helicopter may be able to safely land but be unable to take off later.
» Study the appropriate topographic map carefully before takeoff; look for prominent landmarks as soon as the ship is airborne.
» Be prepared physically by having a stomach strong enough for helicopter flying. Unlike fixed wing flights, helicopter flights may often be akin to a roller coaster ride without the tracks.

HIGH-ANGLE ROPE RESCUE

The Hollywood image that comes to mind in a "typical" mountain rescue is of a skier or climber who has taken a dramatic fall off a ledge or into a crevasse. In reality there is no such thing as a typical rescue operation.

Although the National Ski Patrol does not provide training in high-angle rope rescue, it is important to know that specific training by a qualified technical rope rescue organization and many hours of training in a variety of scenarios must be completed prior to a patrol or rescue organization attempting a high-angle rescue. The following, therefore, serves only as an overview of high-angle rope rescue and is not a substitute for formal instruction. Some of the material that follows may be repeat information from earlier in the chapter; the intention here is to provide more detailed information for the rescuer seeking further education than previously provided in the more general discussion.

High angle refers to an environment in which the load is predominantly supported by the rope rescue system. A two-rope system protects the rescuers and patient from a fall that would likely result in serious injury or death. The only exception to a two-rope system for a high-angle rescue would be the need to perform an immediate rescue of a patient who is critically injured or in imminent danger of a fall causing further injury or death. In this case a risk/benefit analysis must be done.

Low-angle rescue methods described earlier in this chapter provide an initial foundation for rope rescue work. However, they may not be suitable for high-angle work where the potential forces placed on the equipment are much greater. High-angle terrain may require the patrol to use a higher level of protection. Failure to assess terrain and the risks and consequences of falling could prove fatal.

TERRAIN ASSESSMENT

High-angle terrain is generally defined by slope angles greater than 45 degrees. However, to rig a rope system based purely on slope angle would overlook other criteria necessary. No team should formulate a rescue plan based on slope angle alone.

Instead, use the Mountain Terrain Assessment System, which addresses many of the shortcomings of classifying terrain as simply high or low angle:

» Class 1—Easiest with fewest hazards
» Class 2
» Class 3
» Class 4
» Class 5—Most difficult with the most hazards

Several factors determine the use and type of rope systems. In deciding whether or not to use a rope system, or what type of system to use, the rescuer must ask the following questions:

» What is the exposure to hazards?
» How secure is the footing and the footwear being worn?

» What is the likelihood of the rescuers or patient taking a fall?

» What would be the consequence of the fall?

» Is it possible to accurately judge the likelihood of a fall and the consequences?

To make these determinations, rescuers need to be honest regarding ability and experience. When in doubt it is best to choose a higher level of protection.

SYSTEMS

A high-angle rope system is made up of many components, such as anchors, rope, carabiners, etc. Each of these components is just a link in the chain. The system can only be as strong as the weakest link.

When rigging for high-angle rope rescue it is necessary to build redundancy into the system. The use of a two-rope system (main and belay line) provides the safest means for rescuers operating in Class 4 and 5 terrain. The main line bears the weight of the load created by the rescuers, the patient, and all equipment used. The belay line provides a back-up safety line to the main line. It is not loaded unless there is a main line failure.

The anchors to which the main and belay lines are attached should meet ERNEST standards, which is a set of guidelines used to assess the anchor system:

Equalized. Various parts of the anchor system should carry equal parts of the load.

Redundant. Failure of one system component must not lead to complete failure of the anchor.

Non-extending. Shifting of one part of the anchor system should not cause significant movement of the load.

Solid. The anchors themselves must be the strongest available.

Timely. Consideration must be given to the amount of time it will take to construct the anchor.

Not all anchors meet all of the criteria, which may be acceptable. For example, if two anchor systems are needed, two small trees may be used for the first anchor system and a boulder for the second. The first anchor may warrant a self-equalizing system that would fail the non-extending element of ERNEST. The experienced rigger may feel that this is acceptable for the main line if the belay system is rigged correctly to prevent the load from shifting in case of a main line failure.

Static system safety factor

The rope systems built for rescue loads must be strong enough to safely accommodate the additional forces placed on

COMMUNICATIONS/COMMANDS

A uniform set of commands is necessary to avoid dangerous miscommunication. Below is a set of standard commands that are commonly used in the rescue community.

In addition to the use of commands, it is of utmost importance that one team member is assigned to perform a safety check of the entire system prior to its operation.

LOWERING SYSTEMS OPERATIONS

Ready on main?	Leader asks if main line operator is ready.
Ready on main!	Main line operator confirms.
Ready on belay?	Leader asks if belayer is ready.
Ready on belay!	Belayer confirms.
Down slow!	Main line operator told to lower slowly.
Down fast!	Main line operator told to lower quickly.
Slack on main!	Leader requests that main line be loosened.
Slack on belay!	Leader requests that belay line be loosened.
Tension on main!	Leader requests that main line be tensioned.
Tension on belay!	Leader requests that belay line be tensioned.
STOP!	Everything stops.
ROCK!	Called if anything is dropped or falling.

HAUL SYSTEMS OPERATIONS

Ready on belay?	Leader asks if belayer is ready.
Ready on belay!	Belayer confirms.
Haul team ready?	Haul team confirms.
Haul team haul!	Leader requests haul team to pull.
STOP!	Everything stops.
SET!	Leader tells team to set the progress capture prusik.
SLACK!	Leader tells team to slack the haul line.
ROCK!	Called if anything is dropped or falling.

the equipment. In most Class 4 and 5 rescue operations, the rescue load is in the range of two to three kilo Newton (kN), or 440 to 660 pounds. This includes the patient, litter, equipment, and at least one rescuer.

So how does one determine what is safe? When evaluating systems, rescuers should aim for a static system safety factor (SSSF) of 10 to one (10:1). The SSSF refers to the ratio between the weight—and more accurately the force—of a static load and the load capacity of the system. In other words, if there is a single person going over the edge and that person weighs 1kN, roughly 220 pounds, then the load-bearing capacity of the weakest link in the system must be no less than 10kN or 2,200 pounds (10 times the weight of the load).

Rope system analysis should include a hands-off or whistle-stop test to help determine what the rope system will do if all rescuers were to let go of the rope simultaneously. The load should not drop or end up at the bottom of the slope.

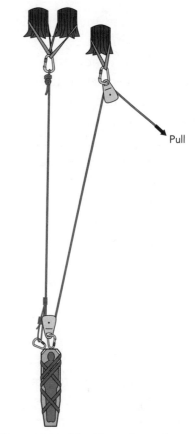

Figure 16-14. *2:1 raising system with change of direction at top*

Mechanical advantage haul systems

Haul systems are used to raise a load in order to overcome the effects of gravity. Mechanical advantage (MA) systems are rigged to ease the work of hauling by the use of pulleys. It can be calculated by comparing the amount of input force, expressed as the amount of output force. When discussing theoretical mechanical advantage, the friction inherent in the system—rope drag on rough surfaces, inefficient pulleys, excessive angles, etc.—is not taken into account.

Pulleys used in a haul system can function either as change of direction (COD) pulleys or MA pulleys. The COD pulley is a non-moving or anchored pulley that simply redirects the haul rope (Figure 16-14). It can make it easier to move a load by allowing the team to pull down rather than up, but it adds no mechanical advantage.

MA pulleys are moving pulleys. They travel in the same direction as the load, toward the anchor. They provide a mechanical advantage by sharing the load among the ropes in the pulley system.

The decision about which MA system to rig for a rescue load should be based on a number of factors including:

» The number of haulers
» The amount of friction on the main line
» The weight of the load

Haul systems have more inherent risk than lowering systems due to the increased forces at work on the system. Rescuers must be aware of the potential to overpower the system by building too much MA or by having too many people hauling on the system. In general it is best to use the fewest number of haulers on the lowest ratio MA system that will work to complete the task safely.

The simple 3:1 and complex 5:1 MA systems are commonly used in high-angle rescue haul systems. The 5:1 is essentially a simple 2:1 pulling on a simple 3:1.

Knot passing and load transfers. When operating a lowering or haul system it is important to be able to safely pass a knot (Figure 16-15). This may occur when two ropes have been tied together or, due to poor rope management, a knot appears in the rope. A LRH (see Figure 16-8 and Appendix A) can be used to transfer the load from one point in the system to another. The LRH is just one tool that makes up a load transfer system. A load transfer system can be used to facilitate a changeover from a lower to a haul and back again. It organizes the equipment and gives the

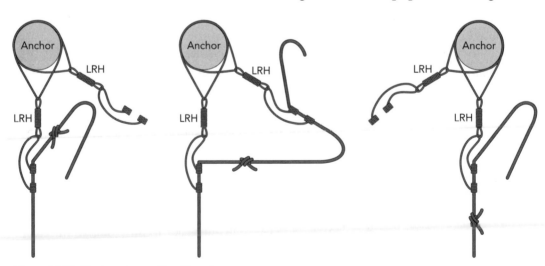

Figure 16-15. *Knot passing and load transfers*

rescuers the ability to efficiently transfer the load from one tool to another.

PERSONAL SKILLS

Just as a rope rescue system is only as strong as the weakest link, the same is true of the rescue team. For the team to perform safely and efficiently each rescuer must have a baseline set of skills.

NFPA 1006: Standards for Technical Rescuer Qualifications, 2008 edition, details the minimum requirements necessary for emergency response personnel who perform technical rescue, including rope rescue. It makes good sense for all patrollers and rescuers to be trained in the following, as these techniques are the building blocks of a strong team. Proficiency in these skills should be second nature.

Rappeling

Rappeling is simply the act of sliding down a rope in a controlled manner. In the rescue world it is common to use a descent-control device such as a figure eight, brake bar rack (see Figure 16-2), and self-braking devices.

These devices put friction on the rope and allow the rescuer to control the descent. Unlike the figure eight, the brake bar rack allows the user to significantly vary the friction while in use. Self-braking devices use a rotating cam that locks down on the rope when the device receives a forceful tug, such as from a fall. The benefit of a self-braking device is that in

the event the rappeler lets go of the rope, the device automatically stops the descent. The downside is that care must be taken when using icy or muddy rope.

Prior to rappeling,

» safety check the system.
» verify that the rappel rope reaches the ground.
» tie a stopper knot, which helps prevent the rescuer from rappeling off the end of the rope.

It is wise to consider a belay line for rappeling. Single rope techniques should be carefully considered and unless the patient is extremely ill or injured, a belay line should be used.

The guide's rappel backup. A guide's rappel backup (GRB), or autoblock friction hitch (Figure 16-16), should be used when rappeling without a belay. The GRB has been used for years by the American Mountain Guides Association to increase the safety margin when rappeling. It's necessary to

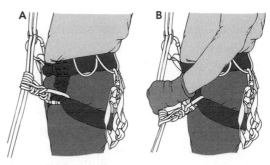

Figure 16-16. *Guide's rappel backup*

rig the rappel device with an extension attached to the harness D-ring to insure that the GRB does not come in contact with the rappel device. A GRB is not needed if using an auto-locking descent-control device (DCD).

Lock and tie-off. Another skill associated with rappeling includes being able to lock and tie off the DCD securely and operate hands-free of the rope and device. Techniques for tying-off vary with each device. A good rescuer should be comfortable using various rappel devices.

Self-rescue. It does not happen often, but it is possible for the device to become jammed or entangled with clothing or hair. If this occurs the rescuer must have a way of transferring weight off of the device in order to free it. After locking off the DCD, attach a nine-foot prusik to the rope above the jammed DCD. Slip one foot into the bight of the prusik loop and stand up. Use your dominant hand to clear the jammed device.

Knot pass. A proficient rescuer should be able to safely pass a knot while rappeling. This may occur when two ropes have been tied together or, due to poor rope management, a knot appears in the rope. Rappel to just above the knot, lock off the DCD, and place two prusik loops on the rope coming from the harness. Remove the DCD and rerig below the knot.

Ascending

Ascending is the opposite of rappeling and is a way to move up a rope using friction hitches or mechanical devices. Ascending a fixed line can be used to clear a jammed DCD or to access an incapacitated victim during lift evacuation. A skilled rescuer should be able to perform a changeover: a safe transfer between rappeling and ascending.

The process of ascending works by alternately weighting and unweighting at least two attachment points to the rope. After weighting one attachment point, the unweighted attachment is then moved up the rope and the weight is transferred to that point. The process then repeats.

There are many types of ascending systems, including mechanical ascenders that use cams and are more efficient than prusik hitches.

The lightest and most economical system is a set of three personal prusiks that can be easily assembled using three prusik loops. Correct sizing of the prusik loops to the rescuer's height is critical. Make each loop by joining the ends together with a double fisherman's knot and then use a two- or three-wrap prusik hitch to secure them to the rope.

Belaying

Belaying is a critical skill in the high-angle environment. To belay is to protect against a fall by managing an unloaded rope in a way that secures a load from falling in the event of failure of the main line rope. The belayer has the well-being of the person at the other end of the rope in his hands. A direct tie-in to the load is used to prevent off-axis loading of a carabiner in the event that the belay line becomes tensioned. Proper rope management is vital. The end of the belay rope must be secured to the anchor, and the middle of the rope should be flaked out in a pile or fed directly out of the rope bag to eliminate tangles and knots.

Belaying single person loads. A Muenter hitch (see Figure 16-6) is a simple and efficient means of belaying a single body weight. Additionally, recent technology in self-braking devices offer multipurpose functionality, which allows belaying and lowering rescue loads, rappeling, and ascending to be incorporated into a haul system. Changeovers from a lower to a raise can easily be accomplished while under load.

Team belaying rescue loads. The tandem prusik belay (see Figure 16-7) is widely recognized and accepted as a reliable method for belaying a rescue load. It has been extensively tested and found to be a safe technique, but it requires significant training. Two triple-wrapped prusiks—one long and one short—are placed in line on the belay rope and connected to the anchor by a single locking carabiner. In the event of a main line failure, the prusiks grab the rope.

The effectiveness of the tandem prusik belay depends on the interaction of the material in the prusik hitch with the rope material. The prusik cord must be of proper diameter in relation to the host rope and the sheaths must be well matched. Tests for compatibility of the prusik cord with the host rope should be performed prior to use.

Proper operation of the tandem prusiks is dependent on making certain the prusiks have been tied correctly, dressed properly, and are the proper distance apart (about four inches). The belayer must use correct hand positioning. The goal of the belayer is to minimize slack without allowing the prusiks to lock off unintentionally.

There are numerous load-release hitches. The radium load-release hitch (Figure 16-17) has become a favorite in the rescue community. It is easy to make using two carabiners and 33 feet of 8 mm cord.

Figure 16-17. *Radium-release hitch*

Pre-tensioning device. The use of a pre-tensioning device in conjunction with a tandem prusik belay further increases the safety margin during lowering operations. It does this in two ways: It eases the work of the belayer by carrying some of the weight of the belay line; and it minimizes slack in the belay line, which reduces the impact force on the system in the event of a main line failure. Apply a friction device (micro rack, Air Traffic Controller [ATC], or similar tubular device) to the belay line and attach it to the anchor with an extension. It should be rigged within reach of the belayer.

Lowering

Rescues involving lowering allow gravity to assist in efforts to get injured parties off the mountain and to care as soon as possible. It is usually best not to fight gravity, so lowering a rescue load is preferred over raising it. Lowering puts less

Figure 16-18. *Pre-tensioning device*

stress on the system and there are fewer components to rig.

Pick-off rescue. A pick-off is a quick and easy way to access, secure, and lower a subject to the ground. It can be the method of choice unless the subject's condition warrants a mid-face litter package. This skill can be performed by a single rescuer or by a team, which requires additional personnel, equipment, and good communication. The advantages are that the rescuer has both hands free, and both rescuer and subject can be lowered and raised.

The pick-off may be appropriate where

» there is a shortage of personnel or equipment.
» the benefits outweigh the risks involved.
» a climber or skier has fallen and is only slightly injured but needs help in getting off the face.

In the pick-off, a rescuer rappels or is lowered to the subject. The subject is then attached directly to the rescuer's rappel system with a pick-off strap. If the patient is not wearing a harness one must be provided. The rescuer then proceeds to rappel or be lowered to control the weights of both rescuer and subject.

Single rope technique pick-off. The single rope technique is an advanced technique that employs the rescuer's own equipment, including the anchor and rope, to build a lowering system.

The rescuer rappels down to the side of the patient and ties off the rappel device. A pick-off strap is attached to the patient's harness. If the patient is not wearing a harness, one must be provided. The rescuer builds a lowering system by attaching a prusik on the rope above the rappel device and then clipping a carabiner into the prusik loop. This technique is especially helpful if there are multiple subjects to be removed from the same area.

Team lowering operations. Many rescue teams use four-bar micro racks with double hyper bars as the lowering device of choice (see Figure 16-2). The hyper bars increase the rack's load-handling abilities. These racks save weight and are rated to 62kN.

Litter rigging

Different scenarios require different types of litter rigging to transport the patient safely and efficiently. Many of these decisions are determined by the class of terrain in which rescuers are negotiating.

Class 4 litter rigging. There are a number of ways to rig a litter for movement over Class 3 or 4 terrain. Only one method is described here because it is quick and efficient. Typically in Class 1–4 terrain, the litter will be oriented vertically to the fall

line. A widely accepted method is to create a litter bridle attachment point at the head of the litter. Wind a 10- to 15-foot length of 8 mm or 9 mm rope or one-inch tubular webbing around the head rails of the litter. Tie the two ends of the rope or webbing together with an appropriate knot. Attach the main line with a carabiner to the two strands of the bridle. When using

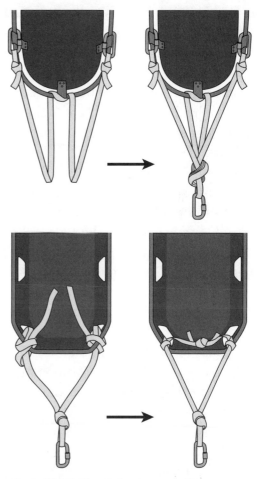

Figure 16-19. *Class 1–4 or low-angle litter harness rigging*

a separate belay line, it should be tied directly to the head of the litter.

Attendants should be rigged with two points of attachment to the litter. They lean back against the tie-ins allowing their weight to be taken by the litter and the rope. One hand holds the litter while the other is used for balance.

The tie-in points can be either a piece of 8 mm or 9 mm rope or one-inch tubular webbing girth hitched to the litter and connected to the attendant via a carabiner. For adjustability the second point of attachment can be a 6 mm or 7 mm prusik loop hitched to another piece of cord that has been girth hitched to the litter and connected to the attendant via a carabiner (Figure 16-19).

Class 5 litter rigging. There are a number of ways to rig a litter for movement over vertical terrain. The method described here is but one option. Generally the litter is rigged with a litter bridle (aka litter spider) that provides a means of connecting the litter to the rope system. It consists of a group of lines that are attached at separate points to the litter and then together at the master point. The master point can be a steel O-ring. There are many litter spiders available commercially or they can be easily made from rope. Some spiders have fixed legs and others have adjustable legs that allow the litter attendant to vary the position of the litter. The main and belay

lines are attached to the litter attachment point via long-tail bowlines.

In addition to caring for the patient, the attendant's job is to hang next to the litter and keep it clear of any obstructions during movement. The attendant should be rigged to allow for movement around the litter.

Connection to the litter happens via two points of attachment:

» The first point of attachment is to the tail of the main line. An ascender connected from the attendant's harness to the tail of the main line is used as

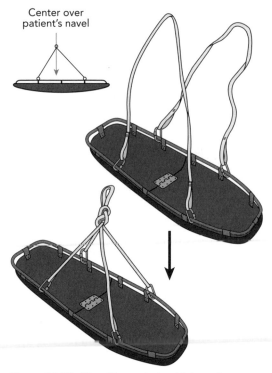

Center over patient's navel

Figure 16-20. *Class 5 or vertical or high-angle litter rigging*

a working or traveling line for repositioning higher or lower on the litter.

» The second point of attachment is to the tail of the belay line. This should be a direct tie-in to the attendant's chest harness. A Purcell prusik attached to the attendant's chest harness is placed on the tail of the belay below the master point and above the direct tie-in (Figure 16-20).

An etrier attached to the master point allows the attendant to step up to help reposition. Edge tenders assist the litter attendant in getting the litter over the edge, as well as with communication.

....

SUMMARY

o No other rescue work will as thoroughly challenge a mountain rescuer's total rescue skills, knowledge, flexibility, and creativity as a major backcountry incident.

o Backcountry rescues are mentally and physically challenging; therefore the people who make up rescue teams must be highly motivated and resourceful.

o When you are part of a rescue involving a helicopter, remember that the pilot in command of any aircraft is directly responsible for, and is the final authority as to the operation of, that aircraft.

o The time commitment required for ongoing training is substantial; however, the satisfaction of successfully completing these difficult but humanitarian missions in a professional and competent manner is what keeps rescue members returning to the mountains.

....

APPENDIX A: KNOTS AND ANCHORS

The knots and anchors diagrammed here represent many of the industry standards for emergency rescue scenarios. These are knots all patrollers should know. As incidents occur, more efficient methods of rescue are being discovered, and both rescuers and patients are consequently safer during the rescue process.

Some of these knots have evolved with time. The bowline knot, for example, has for the most part been replaced by the rewoven figure eight. As the name infers, it's easy to see if the knot is tied correctly by tracing over the original figure eight pattern, which is not as easy to determine with a bowline.

By incorporating rope systems knowledge into patrol training, rescuers are able to leverage patients and equipment. This keeps patrollers from muscling through rescues, expending valuable energy that's better spent on safe and efficient outcomes.

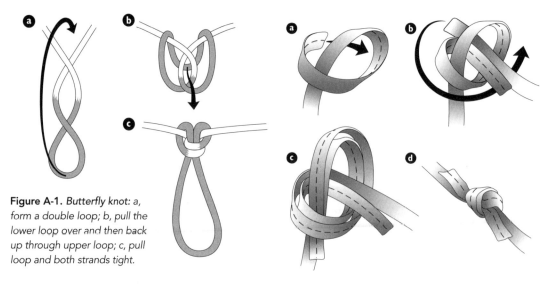

Figure A-1. *Butterfly knot: a, form a double loop; b, pull the lower loop over and then back up through upper loop; c, pull loop and both strands tight.*

Figure A-2. *Water knot (ring bend): a, draw a loose end through a bight of webbing; b, bring other loose end through the bight, around the first end, and under itself; c, draw ends well through knot so 2- to 3-inch tails extend; d, pull all four strands tight.*

Figure A-3. *Fisherman's bend: a, overlap a loose end of each rope, and tie each end in an overhand knot around the other rope's standing end; b, pull all four strands tight.*

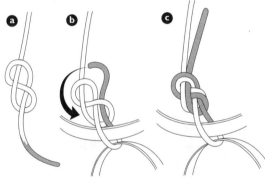

Figure A-5. *Rewoven figure eight: a, tie a figure eight; b, double the loose end back and retrace the 8 so the loose end is parallel to the standing end; c, pull both the ends and the end loop tight.*

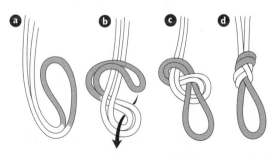

Figure A-7. *Figure eight on a bight: a, bring a bight back parallel to the standing ends; b, bring bight under and then over the ends, forming an 8, then bring the bight down through the bottom loop of the 8; c, dress the strands; d, pull all four strands tight.*

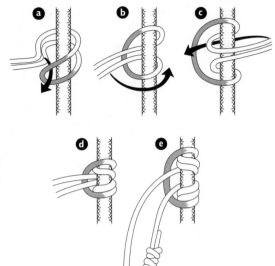

Figure A-4. *Prusik hitch: a, girth-hitch cord around rope; b, bring loose ends of cord around the rope and under cord; c, wrap loose ends around rope again; d, two-wrap prusik hitch; e, three-wrap prusik hitch.*

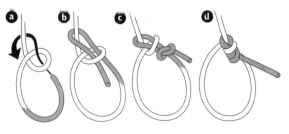

Figure A-6. *Single bowline: a, make a loop and pass the loose end of the rope under and through it, then around the back of the standing end; b, bring the loose end back through the loop; c, pull ends tight and tie an overhand knot; d, dressed and backed-up knot.*

(Figures A-1 through A-7 are from *Mountaineering: The Freedom of the Hills,* 8th Edition and used by permission from The Mountaineers.)

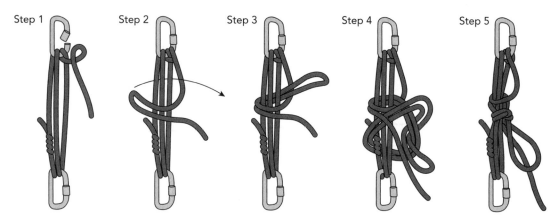

Figure A-8. *Radium-release hitch: a, clip carabiner on tied loop of rope and clip rope up and over both carabiners, as if doing a 3:1 and then lock down with a Muenter hitch; b, wrap a bight of rope around middle of rope between carabiners; c, thread bight of rope through loop; d, pull the bight of rope back around the rope as if creating an overhand knot; e, complete overhand knot.*

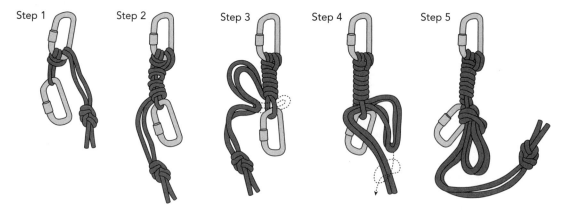

Figure A-9. *Load-releasing hitch: a, clip carabiner in loop and Muenter hitch second carabiner; b, wrap tail around middle of cord between carabiners; c, thread a bight of cord through bottom loop; d, tie an overhand knot with bight of cord and remaining tail of cord.*

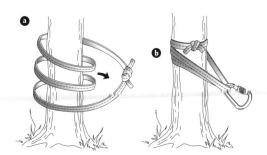

Figure A-10. *Wrap-three–pull-two anchor around a tree: a, wrap webbing three times around a natural feature like a tree and join ends with water knot on load side of tree; b, attach a locking carabiner to two strands of the webbing.*

Version 1

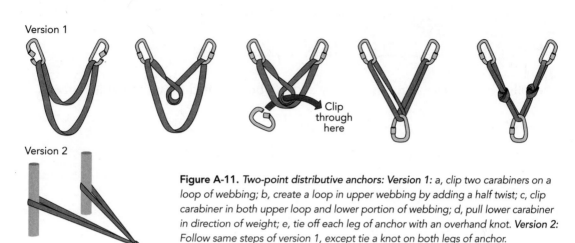

Version 2

Figure A-11. *Two-point distributive anchors: Version 1: a, clip two carabiners on a loop of webbing; b, create a loop in upper webbing by adding a half twist; c, clip carabiner in both upper loop and lower portion of webbing; d, pull lower carabiner in direction of weight; e, tie off each leg of anchor with an overhand knot.* **Version 2:** *Follow same steps of version 1, except tie a knot on both legs of anchor.*

Figure A-12. *Three-point distributive (equalized multi-point) anchor: a, clip three carabiners onto loop of cordelette; b, pull all legs of anchor down in direction of weight equally; c, tie all legs of anchor and clip with a carabiner.*

Figure A-13. *Tensionless hitch: a, clip carabiner onto figure eight on a bight or bowline and evenly wrap around anchor until rope no longer slips on anchor; b, clip the carabiner to the mainline of the rope.*

APPENDIX B: EQUIPMENT LIST

The following lists are suggestions only and can be modified to suit individual needs.

GROUP GEAR

SHELTER
- » Expedition-quality tent
- » Snow stakes and/or tent flukes
- » Sponge and whisk broom
- » Snow shelter construction tools: large snow shovel (for moving a lot of snow), small snow shovel (for delicate trimming), snow saw (for cutting blocks)

RESCUE GEAR
- » Ropes
- » Hardware: snow and ice gear (pickets, flukes, ice screws); rock gear (pitons, spring-loaded camming devices, chocks); carabiners; runners; fixed line; extra climbing equipment (spare ice ax or tool, spare crampons)

KITCHEN
- » Stove gear: stove; wind screen and stove pad; fuel containers and fuel filter; matches and/or butane lighters
- » Cook gear: pots, pot gripper, sponge/scrubber, dip cup and cooking spoon; snow sack
- » Food

REPAIR KIT
- » Tent repair kit (pole splices, spare pole)
- » Stove repair kit
- » Crampon repair kit (extra screw, connecting bars, straps)
- » Tape (duct, filament, ripstop fabric repair tape)
- » Tools (standard, Phillips, and Allen screwdrivers; small pliers; small wire cutter/shear)

» Sewing kit: assorted needles and thread; assorted buttons, snaps, buckles, and "D" rings; Velcro (hook and rug); fabric (cordura, ripstop); flat webbing
» Miscellaneous: extra ski pole basket; wire and cord

PERSONAL GEAR

CLOTHING
» Synthetic fabric underwear
» Insulating layers
» Down clothing
» Wind protection garments (top and bottom)
» Extremities: hands (liner gloves, insulating gloves, and mittens); feet (liner socks, insulating socks, vapor-barrier socks); head (balaclava, sun hat, face mask)
» Miscellaneous: bandanna; sun shirt; plastic double boots; supergaiters and/or over-boots

SLEEPING
» Sleeping bag
» Bivouac sack
» Vapor-barrier liner
» Inflatable foam pad
» Closed-cell foam pad

TRAVEL
» Ice ax
» Second ice tool
» Ski poles
» Seat harness with ice tool holsters
» Chest harness
» Crampons
» Personal carabiners
» Personal runners
» Ascenders and/or prusiks

- » Helmet
- » Large-volume pack
- » Snowshoes or skis
- » Sled with associated hardware (haul lines, carabiners, prusiks)
- » Skins
- » Waxes
- » Skis

MISCELLANEOUS GEAR

- » Avalanche beacon
- » Sunglasses and goggles
- » Spare prescription glasses
- » Personal hygiene: toilet paper, pee bottle; toothbrush; comb; chemical wash/wipes; sunscreen; lip balm; foot powder; ear plugs
- » Personal recreation: camera and film; books; journal (waterproof paper); personal steno
- » Shovel
- » Map of area
- » Compass
- » Water bottle
- » Trail food
- » Cordage
- » Headlamp
- » Whistle
- » Matches
- » Pocket knife
- » Repair kit (spare parts, tools)
- » Sewing kit

APPENDIX C: EMERGENCY CARE AND MEDICAL EQUIPMENT LISTS

Prescription medications are marked with an asterisk (*) and controlled substances are marked with two asterisks (**) except where listed as part of a physician's kit.

CONTENTS OF A BASIC MEDICAL KIT

Suitable for a day trip or to be carried by each member of a party on a multiday trip:

- » 2 cravats
- » 1 or 2 rolls of 3- or 4-inch self-adhering roller bandage (e.g., Kling)
- » 1 roll of 2-inch adhesive tape
- » 4 sterile gauze compresses, 3-inch x 4-inch or 4-inch x 4-inch (non-adhesive—Telfa or equivalent)
- » 6 or more prepackaged bandage strips (Band-Aids, Curads)
- » 20 325 mg aspirin or acetaminophen (Tylenol) and/or 200 mg ibuprofen tablets
- » Sunscreen or sunblock
- » Lip salve
- » Multiple-use knife with scissors and tweezers (Swiss Army knife)
- » Safety pins
- » Plastic sandwich bags
- » Personal medications, if any
- » Water purification equipment
- » Small flashlight or headlamp with spare batteries
- » 1 pair of disposable rubber gloves

OPTIONAL
- » 1 sheet of moleskin
- » Antacid (Digel, Tums, etc.) or antacid/anti-gas preparation
- » Small, foil-packaged, disposable, moist towelettes

OPTIONAL FOR MULTIDAY TRIP
- » Sleeping pills of choice, if desired, with directions for use (consult physician)
- » Pee bottle

CONTENTS OF A MASTER KIT

Designed for multiday recreational tours; each party should have one master kit:

» Additional cravats to provide at least 6 per party
» 12 additional sterile, non-adhering gauze compresses
» 4 ABD pads or Surgipads, 2 medium, 2 large
» 3-inch-wide rubberized bandage (Ace, etc.)
» 4 extra self-adhering roller bandages, 2 2-inch, 2 3-inch
» 6 tongue blades
» 30 inches of ⅛- to ¼-inch diameter nylon cord (or several tongue blades taped together)
» Spreader for ski pole splint
» Seam ripper
» Sewing needle
» Small bottle of antiseptic cleanser (10 percent povidone-iodine, Phisohex)
» Thermometer
» Single-edge razor blade or packaged sterile #15 scalpel blade
» 30 cc syringe and #18 gauge needle
» Turkey-baster syringe or 60 cc syringe and Foley catheter
» 2 extra pairs of disposable rubber gloves (consider sterile ones)
» Pocket mask with one-way valve, or mouth shield
» Notebook and pencil
» Oropharyngeal airways (at least 2 sizes such as large and small adult)

MEDICATIONS
» 5 g tube *Neosporin or *Garamycin ophthalmic ointment
» 24 25 mg or 12 *50 mg diphenhydramine hydrochloride (Benadryl) capsules
   Alternatives: (Consult physician for doses of alternatives.)
   » * Tripelennamine (Pyribenzamine)
   » * Dexchlorpheniramine (Polaramine)
   » * Terfenadine (Seldane), etc.
» 12 30 mg **Acetaminophen with 30 mg Codeine (Tylenol #3) tablets
   Alternative:
   » ** Propoxyphene napsylate 100 mg and acetaminophen (Darvocet N 100)

OPTIONAL
» SAM splint
» Kendrick traction device
» 12 2.5 mg **Diphenoxylate with atropine sulfate (Lomotil) tablets
  Alternative:
  » 2 mg capsules of Loperamide
    (Imodium A-D)
  » 6 10 mg *Thiethylperazine (Torecan) rectal suppositories
  Alternative:
  » 25 mg *Prochlorperazine (Compazine) suppositories

OPTIONAL FOR THOSE WITH SPECIAL TRAINING AND LICENSING
» 16-gauge over-needle catheter (Angiocath, etc.)
» Foley catheter with lubricating jelly
» Cricothyroidotomy set
Additional considerations
» 12 100 mg **Meperidine (Demerol) tablets
  Alternative:
  » *Oxycodone and acetaminophen (Tylox, etc.) capsules
  » Injectable *Epinephrine (Ana kit, EpiPen)

FOR EXTENDED TRIPS INTO REMOTE COUNTRY, ADD:
» Several packets of powdered sport drink (Gatorade, etc.) or Oralyte
» 20 *Trimethoprim/sulfamethoxazole (Septra DS, Bactrim DS) tablets, or 20 *Ciprofloxacin 500 mg tablets (Cipro), or 1 from each of the following two groups of antibiotics:
Group one:
» 20 *Cephalexin (Keflex) capsules, 250 mg, 1 capsule four times daily
  Alternatives:
  » *Cefaclor (Ceclor) 250 mg three times daily
  » *Cefuroxime (Ceftin) 250 mg twice daily
  » *Amoxicillin/clavulanate (Augmentin) 250 mg three times daily
  » *Erythromycin ethyl succinate (EES 400), 400 mg four times daily
Group two:
» 14 *Doxycycline 100 mg tablets, 1 tablet twice daily

Alternative:
» *Tetracycline 250 mg tablets, 1 tablet four times daily

RECOMMENDED FOR HIGH ALTITUDE
» 12 or more 250 mg *Acetazolamide (Diamox) tablets
» 30 4 mg *Dexamethasone (Decadron or Hexadrol) tablets
» 6 10 mg and 20 long-acting (20 to 30 mg) *Nifedipine (Procardia, Adalat)

RECOMMENDED FOR UNDEVELOPED COUNTRIES
» 20 *Trimethoprim/sulfamethoxazole (Septra, Bactrim) DS tablets or 20 *Ciprofloxacin (Cipro) 500 mg tablets
» Pills for malaria prophylaxis if needed

OPTIONAL FOR WOMEN
» 7 Miconazole nitrate (Monistat 7) vaginal suppositories
» 21 250 mg *Metronidazole (Flagyl) tablets

RECOMMENDED FOR SNAKE COUNTRY
» Sawyer extractor
» Occlusive band

WILDERNESS SEARCH AND RESCUE (SAR) EMERGENCY CARE KIT

DRESSINGS, BANDAGES, AND WOUND CARE
» 10 3-inch x 4-inch non-adhesive gauze compresses
» 4 ABD pads or Surgipads, 2 medium, 2 large
» 4 self-adhering roller bandages, 2 2-inch, 2 3-inch
» 2 packs of povidone-iodine or bottle of 10 percent povidone-iodine
» 1 500 ml bag (with IV tubing) of sterile physiological saline, sterile 30 cc syringe with sterile 18-gauge needle for wound irrigation
» 2 packets Vaseline gauze

- » 1 roll each, ½-inch, 1-inch, and 2-inch adhesive tape
- » 4 feet of plastic wrap such as Saran, folded or rolled
- » 24 prepackaged bandage strips (Band-Aids)
- » Steristrips, ⅛-inch and ¼-inch
- » 1 3-inch rubberized bandage
- » 1 2-inch rubberized bandage
- » 12 plastic storage bags, 6 small, 6 medium
- » 4 pairs disposable rubber gloves, non-sterile
- » 2 pairs disposable rubber gloves, sterile
- » 2 disposable face shields

SPLINTS AND LITTERS
- » Rigid collars (Stifneck set, medium Stifneck, or improvised from SAM splint)
- » Sager splint or Kendrick traction device with 55-gallon clear plastic garbage bag
- » Pneumatic splint for lower extremity, long size
- » Kendrick extrication device or Oregon spine splint II
- » 8 cravats
- » 2 SAM splints
- » 1 litter (SKED, Ferno-Washington, etc.) preferably lightweight or break in half for backpacking

CARDIORESPIRATORY
- » 6 oropharyngeal airways, 2 each of 3 sizes
- » Nasopharyngeal airways, 2 each of 3 sizes
- » Pocket mask with one-way valve and oxygen intake nipple
- » Suction apparatus (V-Vac, Res-Q-Vac, or portable battery-operated)
- » Bag-valve-mask

DRUGS
- » Same as drugs suggested above in the master kit. Add epinephrine injection kit (*EpiPen, *Ana-kit, etc.) for anaphylactic reactions, sublingual nitroglycerine tablets (Nitrostat 0.4 mg), and instant glucose (Glutose, etc.) for hypoglycemia.

OTHER

- » Lightweight stethoscope
- » Blood pressure cuff
- » Hypothermia thermometer
- » Clinical thermometer
- » Blood glucose test strips
- » Bandage scissors
- » Paramedic shears
- » Tags
- » Urinal or pee bottle
- » Penlight
- » Razor blade, single-edge
- » Seam ripper
- » Steel sewing needle
- » Lubricant jelly
- » Safety pins
- » Tweezers
- » Notebook and pencil
- » Headlamp

ADDITIONAL ITEMS FOR HYPOTHERMIA

- » Rewarming equipment such as chemical heating pads, Heatpac, hydraulic sarong, device for heating inspired air
- » Extra sleeping bag or casualty bag
- » Tent

OPTIONAL

- » Pneumatic antishock garment
- » Oxygen backpack (2 tanks, regulator, masks, nasal cannulae, and tubing)

WILDERNESS SAR PHYSICIAN/PARAMEDIC KIT

» Stethoscope
» Blood pressure cuff
» Small otoscope/ophthalmoscope with tongue blades
» Cricothyroidotomy set
» Endotracheal intubation kit
» 14-gauge Intracath for needle thoracotomy
» Flutter valve (Heimlich or improvised from finger of rubber glove)

Intravenous fluids:
» Liter bags of lactated Ringers 5 percent glucose solution
» Liter bags of 10 percent glucose/ half-normal saline solution
» IV administration sets
» 18-gauge Intracath needles
» 1-inch adhesive tape
» ½-inch adhesive tape
» Alcohol swabs
» Tourniquets

Parenteral drugs, general (include sterile syringes and needles for injection):
» Meperidine
» Thiethylperazine or prochlorperazine
» Morphine
» Epinephrine 1:1000
» Naloxone
» Aminophylline (requires 50 cc syringe)
» Diphenhydramine
» Digoxin
» Furosemide
» 50 percent glucose (requires 50 cc syringe)
» Dexamethasone
» Diazepam

OPTIONAL
» Chest tube set and insertion pack
» Water seal apparatus and bag of sterile water
» Nasogastric tubes
» Foley catheter (18 French) with collection bag and clamp
» Lubricant
» Povidone-iodine swabs
» Monitor/defibrillator or automatic external defibrillator
Parenteral drugs, ACLS: (monitor/ defibrillator desirable)
» Atropine
» Lidocaine
» Epinephrine 1:10,000
» Bretylium
» Verapamil
» Morphine
» Procainamide
» Adenosine
» Dopamine
» Additional sterile syringes and needles.

APPENDIX D: SEARCH AND RESCUE SAMPLE FORMS AND CHARTS

COLLECTING INFORMATION ABOUT LOST/MISSING PERSON(S)

Follow these steps when collecting information:

1. Interview persons with first-hand knowledge as quickly as possible.
    a. Keep the witness(es) available.
    b. Continue to ask questions.
2. Conduct separate interviews of each witness in an informal, relaxed, comfortable setting.
3. Control your own biases and record the witnesses' responses.
4. Vital information for adequate search planning strategy:
    a. Category of subject(s) (age, outdoors abilities).
    b. Last seen or last known point (as small an area as possible) and when.
    c. Events leading up to victim(s) becoming lost.
    d. Physical condition and preparation of victim(s) (equipment, experience, medical complications).
    e. Mental condition and personality traits that may influence behavior of subject(s).
    f. Weather.
    g. Terrain analysis.
5. Vital information for adequate searching:
    a. Name and physical description of victim(s).
    b. Color and description of clothing, including shoe size and pattern.
    c. Description of equipment.

SAMPLE LOST/MISSING PERSON QUESTIONNAIRE

Fill out a separate form for each lost/missing individual.

Personal Information

Missing person's name _____ _____

    Aliases _____

    Nicknames _____

    Age _____ Sex: Male _____ Female _____

Where last seen _____

When last seen (date and time) _____

Local address _____

      Local phone _____

Home address _____

      Home phone _____

Business address _____

      Business phone _____

....

Rescue leader _____

Person filling out form _____

Date _____ Time _____

Information taken by: phone _____ in person _____ other (explain) _____

Witnesses

      Name _____

      Address _____

      Phone #(s) _____

      Relationship to missing person _____

      Name _____

      Address _____

      Phone #(s) _____

      Relationship to missing person _____

....

Physical description of victim

Height _____ Weight _____ Build _____ Hair color _____

Hair length _____ Facial hair _____ Eye color _____

Glasses or contacts _____ Complexion _____ Race _____

Facial features, shapes _____

Distinguishing marks, tattoos, scars, features _____

General appearance _____

Mental condition _____

Clothing

Shirt Style _____ Color _____

Sweater Style _____ Color _____

Pants Style _____ Color _____

Jacket Style _____ Color _____

Raingear Style _____ Color _____

Footgear Style _____ Color _____

Sole type _____ Is a sample available? _____ If so, where? _____

Gloves/mittens Style _____ Color _____

Hat Style _____ Color _____

Glasses? . Contacts? _____ Regular (Rx) Sun _____ Style _____

Extra clothing? _____

Are scent articles available? Yes _____ No _____

....

Personal articles and habits

Smoker?   Yes _____ No _____

If yes, cigarettes _____ cigar _____ pipe _____ brand _____

Matches?   Yes _____ No _____ Type _____

Lighter?   Yes _____ No _____ Brand, style _____

Gum?   Yes _____ No _____ Brand, style _____

Candy?   Yes _____ No _____ Brand, style _____

Other food?   Yes _____ No _____ Describe _____

Other misc?   Yes _____ No _____ Describe _____

Drink alcohol?   Yes _____ No _____ Describe _____

Drugs?   Yes _____ No _____ Describe _____

Hobbies/interests? _____

Outgoing? _____ Quiet? _____ Social person? _____ Loner? _____ Leader? _____ Follower? _____

Any criminal record? Yes _____ No _____

Hitchhike? Never _____ Sometimes _____ Often _____

Any current family/significant other problems? _____

Any history of depression or running away? Never _____ Sometimes _____ Often _____

Give up easily or keep going? _____

Will person hole up or keep moving? _____

Who is the person closest to? _____ Is this person available? _____

Where was person born? _____ Raised? _____

Is family nearby? Yes _____ No _____ Location _____

....

Equipment

Pack   Style _____ Color _____

Tent   Style _____ Color _____

Sleeping bag Style _____ Color _____

Water   Size and color of container _____

Flashlight   Style _____ Color _____

Knife _____

Map _____

Compass _____

Ice ax _____

Snowshoes _____

Crampons _____

Skis _____

Type of binding _____

Poles _____

Ropes/climbing gear _____

Fishing equipment _____

Camera _____

Money _____

Firearms _____

Other _____

_____

....

Trip plans

Objective _____

Route (use a map if possible) _____

Intended length of trip _____

Number in group _____ Affiliation with group _____

Starting point _____Transportation _____

Car? Yes No If a car, location _____ Type _____ License number _____

Any alternate plans/routes/objectives discussed? _____

Last seen point

Date _____ Time _____

Exact location (use map if possible) _____

_____

Witness name _____

      Address _____

      Home phone _____ Business phone _____ Local phone _____

      Is this person available? _____

Weather conditions at the time _____

Direction of travel _____

Specific stated reason for leaving _____

Unusual comments upon leaving _____

....

Experience

Familiar with proposed area of travel? _____ Surrounding area? _____

Experience level with this mode of travel: Advanced _____ Intermediate _____ Beginner _____

Has the victim camped out? Often _____ Sometimes _____ Never _____

Other relevant areas of experience _____ _____

Has the victim had training in: First aid _____ Outdoor survival _____ Avalanche awareness _____

      Other (describe) _____

....

Health

Any physical handicaps? _____

Any known medical problems? _____

Name of family doctor _____

    Phone _____

Any known psychological problems? _____

Name of psychiatrist _____ _____

    Phone _____ _____

Medication? _____

Requirement of medication for normal function? Low Intermediate High

Amount of medication probably in possession _____ Good for (time) _____

Action taken so far

Who has been notified? _____

Who notified them? _____

What action has been taken? _____

....

Questions for lost children

Afraid of dogs?   Yes _____ No _____

Afraid of horses?   Yes _____ No _____

Afraid of dark?   Yes _____ No _____

Afraid of strangers?   Yes _____ No _____

Any training on what to do if lost?   Yes _____ No _____

Likely behavior if scared: Lethargic Active Other (describe) _____

....

Family

Spouse's occupation _____

        Spouse's address _____

Father's occupation _____

        Father's address _____

Mother's occupation _____

        Mother's address _____

Family desire to employ assistance? Strongly favor _____ Don't care _____ Strongly disfavor _____

Most appropriate kin to contact when found okay

    Relationship _____

    Name _____

    Address _____

    Phone _____

Person to notify if found in poor condition or dead (should be next-of-kin, close relative, close friend, or minister)

    Relationship _____

    Name _____

    Address _____

    Phone _____

EXAMPLE OF A PROBABILITY ZONE CHART

Reference: Sarda-Syrotuck 1977

This chart reflects the distances that other subjects of the same category have traveled, plus patterns of lost subject behavior. (DN= downward; UP=upward; Numerals represent distance in miles from point last seen)

Probability Zones (for determining distance traveled)

	Hilly or Mountainous Terrain					Flat Terrain				
	Median	25%	50%	75%	Max. Zone	Median	25%	50%	75%	Max. Zone
Children 1–6 years	0.3 DN	0.5 DN– 0.1 UP	0.5 DN– 0.5 UP	1.4 DN– 1.5 UP	89% 2.6 DN– 1.6 UP	1.1	1.0–1.6	0.6–1.7	0.5–2.1	92% 0–2.2
Children 6–12 years	1.6 DN	1.0– 2.0 DN	2.1 DN– 0.5 UP	4.0 DN– 2.0 UP	92% 4.1 DN– 2.6 UP	1.2	0.8–1.2	0.7–2.0	0.2–2.2	92% 0–3.0
Elderly	1.2 DN	0.5– 1.8 DN	0– 2.4 DN	2.6 DN– 0.4 UP	90% 3.0 DN– 1.0 UP	1.0	0.8–1.0	0.7–1.2	0.1–1.3	93% 0–3.0
Hikers	2.5 DN	2.0– 3.0 DN	0.6– 3.6 DN	6.1 DN– 0.4 UP	83% 6.0 DN– 4.0 UP	2.0	1.4–2.4	1.0–3.2	0.2–3.3	94% 0–4.0
Hunters	2.0 DN	1.8– 2.8 DN	0.7– 3.1 DN	4.0 DN– 0.8 UP	93% 6.0 DN– 3.0 UP	1.6	1.0–1.6	0.9–2.2	0.1–2.3	89% 0–3.0
Misc. Persons	1.6 DN	0.6– 1.6 DN	0– 3.0 DN	3.1 DN– 1.4 UP	84% 3.2 DN– 2.5 UP	1.6	1.1–1.6	0.5–1.8	0.1–2.8	89% 0–4.0

MODEL SEARCH AND RESCUE RESPONSIBILITIES

Note: Adjust the questions to fit the needs of a particular location or environment.

Rescue Leader
(Incident Commander)

1. Hold the witness. Give into custody of scribe after determining the last point seen and when last seen.
2. Notify patrol director, hill captain, etc.
3. Notify area management and call authorities.
4. Notify patrollers.
5. Assign scribe and give applicable sheets as well as responsibility of witness.

> In out-of-area boundary, wait to proceed until area management orders search and sheriff or other regulatory agency is notified.

6. Assign communications officer.
7. Assign bastard search team leader and give applicable sheets. Initiate a perimeter search and/or sweep of the area.
8. Deploy bastard search, reevaluate after their findings and either terminate or,
9. Assign hasty search team leader and give applicable sheets.
10. Deploy hasty search team.
11. Assign equipment officer and have officer bring all rescue equipment and personnel to staging area.
12. Assign search team leaders and give applicable sheets.
13. Reevaluate after hasty search team findings and either terminate search or deploy additional search teams.
14. Assign logistics officer who should begin to acquire additional personnel, equipment, food, and other appropriate supplies.
15. Assign liaison officer who should contact other applicable organizations and agencies.
16. Arrange appropriate transport of search teams to and/or from search area(s).
17. Assure returning personnel and equipment are checked in.
18. Reevaluate.

Scribe

1. Record all pertinent information on lost person questionnaire.
2. If applicable, perform the position of dispatch with radio communications, monitoring, and guiding position of columns.
3. Record when and where all personnel are dispatched and with what equipment.
4. Record events chronologically.

   a. Area management notified? _____ When? _____

   b. Parol alerted? _____ When? _____

   c. Governing agency notified? _____ When? _____

   d. Bastard search team leader _____

   e. Bastard search team _____

   _____

   _____

   _____

   f. When dispatched? _____ Where? _____

   _____

   _____

   _____

   g. Scratch search team leader _____

   h. Scratch search team _____

   _____

   _____

   _____

   i. When dispatched? _____ Where? _____

   _____

   _____

   _____

   j. Team I team leader _____

   k. Team I team _____

   _____

   _____

   l. Team II team leader _____

   m. Team II team _____

   etc.

Bastard Search Team Leader

1. Select three to six team members. List names.

_____

_____

_____

2. Get radio(s).

    (Radio number) _____ checked out.

3. Time bastard search initiated. _____ Terminated _____

    Reason for termination _____

    _____

4. Check all rooms in all buildings in area.

    _____ Bottom lodge

    _____ Top lodge

    _____ Rental shop

    _____ Patrol room

    _____ Ticket office

    _____ Bar

    _____ Other, explain _____

5. Check all parking lots in area.

    _____ Lower lot

    _____ Upper lot

    _____ Other, explain _____

6. Check likely nearby areas.

    _____ Pool

    _____ Gas station

    _____ Other, explain _____

7. Report findings to rescue leader and then re-search, expand perimeter, or return to base for further assignments as per instructions.

8. Additional information, events, or possible clues.

9. Make sure each member of the team checks out when leaving or when rescue effort is complete.

10. Make sure all equipment is returned to its respective location.

Bastard Search Team Member

1. Know the identity of the victim and then carefully search each room of each assigned building. If the victim reported is not present, be sure you are in agreement with that report. This may require that observers who can also identify the victim are posted at entrances as you search.
2. Notify the team leader of any additional information that may assist the search. This means asking a few key personnel if and when they have seen a person matching the description of the person you are looking for.
3. Follow the directions of the team leader and report back to the team leader when the specific task assignment to you is completed. Wait for the team leader to assign you a specific task before beginning your search.
4. Be sure to sign out and return any issued equipment when you leave the search.

....

Hasty Search Team Leader

1. Select three to six team members.

   _____

   _____

   _____

2. Get radio(s).

   (Radio number) _____ checked out.

3. Time hasty search initiated _____ Terminated _____

   Reason for termination _____

   _____

4. Get directions from rescue leader for well-defined area to search resulting from:

   Tracks _____ Location discussed by victim _____

   Geological features forcing limited route selection _____

   Other,_____ Explain _____

5. Make sure that everyone in team is clearly aware they must not disturb any possible clues (including tracks).
6. Thoroughly search most likely areas and then report findings to rescue leader.
7. Were rescue leader's instructions to re-search _____, terminate hasty search _____, expand search ___, other _____

   Explain _____

8. Make sure each member of the party checks out when leaving or when rescue effort is complete.

9. Make sure all equipment is returned to its respective place.

10. Additional information, events, or possible clues

_____

_____

_____

Hasty Search Team Member

1. Identify the victim and know how to get to the areas assigned to search.

2. Search the assigned locations until you are sure the victim is not present in those areas.

3. Look for any possible clues and report them immediately to the team leader without disturbing the clues.

4. Search only the assigned areas and report the findings to the team leader upon completion. Wait for further assignments or an order to return to base.

5. Be sure to return any equipment that has been issued at the end of the search or when you leave the search.

Team Leader

1. Select three to six team members.

_____

_____

_____

2. Get radio(s).

   (Radio number) _____ checked out.

3. Other equipment (list).

   Item   Number

_____

_____

_____

_____

4. Time team initiated search _____ Terminated search _____

   Reason for termination _____

5. Review with rescue leader the area to search. Use a map.

6. Communicate with search team the area to search and how to search. Use a map.

7. Thoroughly search assigned area until you are sure the victim is not there.

8. Report findings to the rescue leader.

   Were rescue leader's instructions to re-search _____, search new area _____, expand old search area _____, terminate search _____, other, _____

   Explain _____

9. Be sure that all team members sign out when leaving the search or when the search is terminated.

10. Return all equipment to appropriate location.

11. Additional events, information, or possible clues.

   _____

   _____

   _____

Search Team Member

1. Be able to identify the victim and know how to get to the areas assigned to search.

2. Search the assigned locations until you are sure the victim is not present in those areas.

3. Look for any possible clues and report them immediately to your team leader without disturbing the clues.

4. Search only the assigned areas and report your findings to the team leader upon completion. Wait for further assignments or an order to return to base.

5. Be sure to return any equipment that has been issued at the end of the search or when you leave the search.

GROUND TO AIR SIGNALS

Body Signals—Stand in open, be sure background is not confusing, motion slowly, and repeat until pilot understands.

Message	Body Signal
Need medical help	Lie prone
All okay; don't wait	Standing, wave one arm overhead
Our receiver operating	Standing, cup hands over ears
NO	Standing, one hand waves white cloth horizontally
YES	Standing, one hand waves white cloth vertically
Can proceed soon; wait if practical	Standing, one arm horizontal to side
Don't attempt to land	Standing, both arms wave from side-to-side overhead
Pick us up; plan abandoned	Standing, both arms vertical
Need mechanical parts or help	Standing, both arms horizontal to sides
Land here	Squatting, both arms horizontal pointing in direction of landing
Use drop message	Standing, make throwing motion

Signals Made on the Ground—Stamp in snow or use pine boughs or cloth panels; should be over 8 feet long.

Message	Signal	Message	Signal
Require doctor, serious injury	I	Help	SOS
Require medical supplies	II	Aircraft seriously damaged	⌐⌐
Require food and water	F	Require fuel and oil	L
Require map and compass	□	Require mechanic	W
Require signal lamp with battery, radio	I I	Require firearms, ammunition	Ⅴ̌
		Require engineer	\/\/
Unable to proceed	X	Operation completed	LLL
Indicated direction to proceed	K	Found all personnel	LL
Am proceeding in this direction	↑	Found some personnel	++
Probably safe to land	△	Unable to continue; returning to base	XX
Will attempt take-off	▷	Have divided into two groups; each proceeding in direction indicated	⚡
All well	LL		
NO	N	Information received that aircraft in this direction	➔➔
YES	Y		
Not understood	⌐L	Nothing found; will continue search	NN

RESOURCES

Allen, Dan. *Don't Die on the Mountain.* 2nd ed. New London, NH: Dispense Press, 1998.

American Mountain Guides Association. *Technical Handbook for Professional Mountain Guides: Alpine, Rock, and Ski Guiding Techniques.* Boulder, CO: AMGA, 1999.

Armstrong, Betsy R., and Knox Williams. *The Avalanche Book.* Golden, CO: Fulcrum Publishing, 1992.

Atkins, Dale, and Lin Ballard. *Avalanche Rescue Fundamentals.* 2nd ed. Lakewood, CO: National Ski Patrol, 2010.

Auerbach, Paul S. *Medicine for the Outdoors: The Essential Guide to First Aid and Medical Emergencies.* 5th ed. Philadelphia: Mosby, 2009.

Barnes, Scottie, Cliff Jacobson, and James Churchill. *The Ultimate Guide to Wilderness Navigation.* New York: Lyons Press, 2002.

Barry, Roger G. *Mountain Weather and Climate.* 3rd ed. Cambridge: Cambridge University Press, 2008.

Bein, Vic. *Mountain Skiing.* Seattle: The Mountaineers Books, 1982.

Bezruchka, Stephen. *Altitude Illness: Prevention & Treatment.* 2nd ed. Seattle: The Mountaineers Books, 2005.

Blandford, Percy W. *Maps and Compasses: A User's Handbook.* 2nd ed. Blue Ridge Summit, PA: TAB Books, 1991.

Bowman, Warren D., Lawrence S. Leff, National Ski Patrol, and American Academy of Orthopaedic Surgeons. *Outdoor Emergency Care: Comprehensive Prehospital Care for Nonurban Settings.* 4th ed. Sudbury, MA: Jones and Bartlett, 2003.

British Mountaineering Council. *Winter Essentials: Skills and Techniques for the Winter Mountain,* DVD. Manchester, UK: British Mountaineering Council, 2006.

Broeder, C. E., K. A. Burrhus, L. S. Svanekvik, and J. H. Wilmore. "The Effects of Aerobic Fitness on Resting Metabolic Rate." *American Journal of Clinical Nutrition 55, no. 4* (April 1992): 795-801.

Brower, David. *Manual of Ski Mountaineering.* 4th ed. San Francisco: Sierra Club Books, 1969.

Brown, Michael G. *Engineering Practical Rope Rescue Systems.* Albany, NY: Delmar Cengage Learning, 2000.

Budworth, Geoffrey. *Everyday Knots: For Fishermen, Boaters, Climbers, Crafters, and Household Use.* New York: Skyhorse Publishing, 2007.

Burns, Bob, and Mike Burns. *Wilderness Navigation: Finding Your Way Using Map, Compass, Altimeter, and GPS.* 2nd ed. Seattle: The Mountaineers Books, 2004.

Chouinard, Yvon. *Climbing Ice.* 2nd ed.New York: Random House, 1982.

Cliff, Peter. *Mountain Navigation.* 6th ed. Birmingham, AL: Menasha Ridge Press, 2006.

Conover, Garrett, and Alexandra Conover. *Snow Walker's Companion: Winter Camping Skills for the North.* Wrenshall, MN: Stone Ridge Press, 2005.

Crouch, Gregory. *Route Finding: Navigating with Map and Compass.* Guilford, CT: FalconGuides, 1999.

Cunningham, Andy, and Allen Fyffe. *Winter Skills: Essential Walking and Climbing Techniques.* Manchester, UK: Mountain Leader Training UK, 2007.

Dabberdt, Walter F. *The Whole Air Weather Guide.* rev. ed. Los Altos, CA: Solstice Publications, 1985.

Daffern, Tony. *Avalanche Safety for Skiers, Climbers, and Snowboarders.* 2nd ed. Calgary, AB: Rocky Mountain Books, 1999.

Danielsen, John A. *Winter Hiking and Camping.* 3rd ed. Albany, NY: Adirondack Mountain Club, 1986.

Dawson, Lou; www.wildsnow.com; (*The Backcountry Skiing Blog*).

Egbert, Robert I., and Joseph E. King. *The GPS Handbook: A Guide for the Outdoors.* 2nded.. Springfield, NJ: Burford Books, 2008.

Eng, Ronald C., ed. *Mountaineering: The Freedom of the Hills.* 8th ed. Seattle: The Mountaineers Books, 2010.

Federal Emergency Management Agency. *An Introduction to the National Incident Management System (NIMS), IS-700.* (Course available online, www.fema.gov/.) Hyattsville, MD: FEMA, 2010.

Federal Emergency Management Agency. *Incident Command Systems (ICS) for Single Resources and Initial Action Incidents, IS-200.b.* (Course available online, www.fema.gov/.) Hyattsville, MD: FEMA, 2010.

Federal Emergency Management Agency. *Introduction to Incident Command Systems, ICS-100.* (Course available online, training.fema.gov.emiweb/is/is100b.asp.) Hyattsville, MD: FEMA, 2010.

Feeney, Robert. *Polar Journeys: The Role of Food and Nutrition in Early Exploration.* Fairbanks, AK: University of Alaska Press, 1997.

Frank, James A., and Donald E. Patterson. *CMC Rappel Manual.* 2nd ed. Goleta, CA: CMC Rescue, 1997.

Giesbrecht, Gordon G. "Cold Weather Clothing." Presentation, Winter Wilderness Medicine Conference, Jackson Hole, WY, Feb 13-18, 2003. http://umanitoba.ca/faculties/kinrec/research/media/Cold_Weather_Clothing.pdf.

Giesbrecht, Gordon G. "It's a Dry Cold! Hypothermia and the Athlete." Health Leisure and Human Performance Research Institute. University of Manitoba, Winnipeg, MB. http://umanitoba.ca/faculties/kinrec/research/media/Cold_and_Athlete.pdf.

Gonzales, Laurence. *Deep Survival: Who Lives, Who Dies, and Why.* New York: Norton, 2003.

Hampton, Bruce and David Cole. *Soft Paths: How to Enjoy the Wilderness Without Harming It.* 3rd ed. Mechanicsburg, PA: Stackpole Books, 2003.

Hardy, James D., and Eugene F. DuBois. "Regulation of Heat Loss from the Human Body." *Proceedings of the National Academy of Sciences of the United States of America 23, no. 12* (December 1937): 624-631.

Heap, Rich, and Ben Bevan-Pritchard. *Off Piste Essentials,* DVD. Slackjaw Film, 2008. www.slackjaw.co.uk.

Hinch, Stephen W. *Outdoor Navigation with GPS.* 3rd ed. Birmingham, AL: Wilderness Press, 2010.

Houston, Charles S. *Going Higher: The Story of Man and Altitude.* New York: Little, Brown, 1987.

James, W. P. T., and E. C. Schofield. *Human Energy Requirements: A Manual for Planners and Nutritionists.* New York: Oxford University Press, 1990.

Jones, Jeff. *NIMS Incident Command System Field Guide.* 2nd ed. Tigard, OR: Informed Publishing, 2008.

Kals, W.S. *Land Navigation Handbook: The Sierra Club Guide to Map, Compass, and GPS.* 2nd ed. San Francisco: Sierra Club Books, 2005.

Kirkconnell, Sarah Svien. *Freezer Bag Cooking: Trail Food Made Simple.* Self-published, 2007.

Koester, Robert J. *Fatigue: Sleep Management During Disasters and Sustained Operations.* Charlottesville, VA: dbS Productions LLC. 1997.

Koester, Robert J. *Lost Person Behavior: A Search and Rescue Guide on Where to Look—for Land, Air, and Water.* Charlottesville, VA: dbS Productions LLC. 2008.

Kosseff, Alex. *AMC Guide to Outdoor Leadership: Trip Planning, Group Dynamics, Decision Making, Leading Youth, Risk Management.* 2nd ed. Boston: Appalachian Mountain Club Books, 2010.

Ladigin, Don, and Mike Clelland. *Lighten Up!: A Complete Handbook for Light and Ultralight Backpacking.* Guilford, CT: FalconGuide, 2005.

Laidlaw, Kenneth N. "Considerations for Rope Rescue in 2009." Last modified 2012. www.scribd.com/doc/38859515/Considerations-of-Rope-Rescue-2009.

Lansing, Alfred. *Endurance: Shackleton's Incredible Voyage.* 2nd ed. New York: Basic Books, 1999.

Larson, Arnor. "Belay Competence Drop Test Method." British Colombia Council of Technical Rescue. Presentation, August 2, 1990

Letham, Lawrence. *GPS Made Easy: Using Global Positioning Systems in the Outdoors* 5th ed. Seattle: The Mountaineers Books, 2008.

Lipke, Rick. *Technical Rescue Riggers Guide.* 2nd ed. Bellingham, WA: Conterra, 2009.

Lois, Jennifer. *Heroic Efforts: The Emotional Culture of Search and Rescue Volunteers.* New York: NYU Press, 2003.

Long, John, and Bob Gaines. *Climbing Anchors.* 2nd ed. Guilford, CT: FalconGuides, 2006.

Luebben, Craig. *Knots for Climbers.* Guilford, CT: FalconGuides, 2001.

Mason, Elizabeth, ed. *Mountain Travel and Rescue: A Manual for Basic and Advanced Mountaineering Courses.* Lakewood, CO: National Ski Patrol, 1995.

Matthews, Jeff. *Technical Rescue: Rope Rescue Levels I & II.* Clifton Park, NY: Delmar Cengage Learning, 2009.

McArdle, William D., Frank I. Katch, and Victor L. Katch. *Exercise Physiology: Nutrition, Energy, and Human Performance.* 7th ed. Philadelphia: Lippincott Williams & Wilkins, 2009.

McCammon, Ian. "Evidence of Heuristic Traps in Recreational Avalanche Accidents." *Avalanche News, no. 68* (Spring 2004). http://avtrainingadmin.org/pubs/McCammonHTraps.pdf.

McClean, Andrew; www.straightchuter.com; *Backcountry Skiing & Beyond* .

McClung, David, and Peter Schaerer. *The Avalanche Handbook* 3rd ed. Seattle: The Mountaineers Books, 2006.

McNamera, Edward C., David H. Johe, Deborah A. Endly., and National Ski Patrol, eds. *Outdoor Emergency Care.* 5th ed. Boston: Brady Books, 2011.

McNamara, Joel. *GPS for Dummies.* 2nd ed. Hoboken, NJ: Wiley, 2008.

National Association for Search and Rescue. *Fundamentals of Search and Recue.* Sudbury, MA: Jones & Bartlett , 2005.

National Fire Protection Association. "NFPA 1006: Standards for Technical Rescuer Professional Qualifications." www.NFPA.org, 2008.

National Fire Protection Association. "NFPA 1670: Standard on Operations and Training for Technical Search and Rescue." 2009 ed. Quincy, MA: NFPA, 2009.

National Geodetic Survey; *North American Datum Conversion Chart;* www.ngs.noaa.gov/cgi-bin/nad-con.prl.

National Weather Service; *National Weather Service Wind Chill Chart;* http://www.nws.noaa.gov/om/windchill/.

National Wildfire Coordinating Group. *Basic Land Navigation.* Boise, ID: National Wildfire Coordinating Group, 2007. www.Nwcg.gov.

O'Bannon, Allen and Mike Clelland. *Allen & Mike's Really Cool Backcountry Ski Book: Traveling & Camping Skills for a Winter Environment.* 2nd ed. Guilford, CT: FalconGuides, 2007.

O'Bannon, Allen and Mike Clelland. *Allen & Mike's Really Cool Backpackin' Book: Traveling & Camping Skills for a Wilderness Environment.* Guilford, CT: FalconGuides, 2001.

O'Bannon, Allen and Mike Clelland. *Allen & Mike's Really Cool Telemark Tips: 123 Amazing Tips to Improve Your Tele-Skiing.* 2nd ed. Guilford, CT: FalconGuides, 2008.

Oden, Jimmy. *Free Skiing: How to Adapt to the Mountain.*Sweden: Choucas Production AB, 2007.

Parker, Paul. *Free-Heel Skiing: Telemark and Parallel Techniques for All Conditions.* 3rd ed. Seattle: The Mountaineers Books, 2001.

Petzoldt, Paul. *The New Wilderness Handbook.* New York: W.W. Norton, 1984.

Raleigh, Duane. *Knots & Ropes for Climbers.* Mechanicsburg, PA: Stackpole Books, 1998.

Renner, Jeff. *Lightning Strikes: Staying Safe Under Stormy Skies.* Seattle: The Mountaineers Books, 2002.

Renner, Jeff. *Mountain Weather: Backcountry Forecasting and Weather Safety for Hikers, Campers, Climbers, Skiers, and Snowboarders.* Seattle: The Mountaineers Books, 2005.

Richardson, Alun. *Rucksack Guide—Ski Mountaineering and Snowshoeing.* London: A&C Black, 2009.

Richardson, Alun. *Rucksack Guide—Winter Mountaineering.* London: A&C Black, 2009.

Ryan, Monique. *Performance Nutrition for Winter Sports.* Boulder, CO: Peak Sports Press, 2005.

Setnicka, Tim J. *Wilderness Search and Rescue.* Boston: Appalachian Mountain Club Books, 1981.

Sierra Club, San Diego Chapter.. *Wilderness Basics.* ed. Kristi Anderson and Arleen Tavernier. 3rd ed. Seattle: The Mountaineers Books, 2004.

Singh, Anita, Tamara L. Bennett, Patricia A. Deuster, Department of Military and Emergency Medicine, Uniformed Services University of the Health Sciences, F. Edward Herbert School of Medicine, eds.

US Navy—Peak Performance Through Nutrition and Exercise. Portsmouth, VA: Navy and Marine Corps Public Health Center, 1999. www.nehc.med.navy.mil/Healthy_Living/Nutrition/peak.aspx.

Shillington, Ben. *Winter Backpacking: Your Guide to Safe and Warm Winter Camping and Day Trips.* Beachburg, ON: Heliconia Press, 2009.

Smith, Bruce and Allen Padgett. *On Rope: North American Vertical Rope Techniques.* 2nd ed. Huntsville, AL: National Speleological Society, 1997.

Snowshoe Magazine. "Snowshoe Magazine's Guide to Snowshoeing: Knowing What to Buy, Where to Go, How to Get Started and Learn What's Important." http://www.snowshoemag.com/first-timers/.

Soles, Clyde. *The Outdoor Knots Book.* Seattle: The Mountaineers Books, 2004.

Splitboard.com. "Choosing a Splitboard and Initial Set-up." Last modified 2012. www.splitboard.com/index.php/splitboard101/choosing-a-splitboard-and-initial-set-up.

St. Clair, Lucas, and Yemaya Maurer. *AMC Guide to Winter Hiking and Camping: Everything You Need to Plan Your Next Cold-Weather Adventure.* Boston: Appalachian Mountain Club Books, 2009.

Tilton, Buck. *Don't Get Sunburned: 50 Ways to Save Your Skin.* Seattle: The Mountaineers Books, 2009.

Tilton, Buck, and Rick Bennett. *Don't Get Sick: The Hidden Dangers of Camping and Hiking.* 2nd ed. Seattle: The Mountaineers Books, 2002.

Townsend, Chris. *The Backpacker's Handbook.* 2nd ed. New York: International Marine / Ragged Mountain Press, 1997.

Tremper, Bruce. *Staying Alive in Avalanche Terrain.* 2nd ed. Seattle: The Mountaineers Books, 2008.

Tyson, Andy, and Mike Clelland. *Glacier Mountaineering: An Illustrated Guide to Glacier Travel and Crevasse Rescue.* rev. ed. Guilford, CT: FalconGuides, 2009.

United States Army. *Army Field Manual FM 31-70 (Basic Cold Weather Manual).* Washington, DC: Department of the Army, 2007.

Vines, Tom, and Steve Hudson. *High-Angle Rescue Techniques.* 2nd ed. St. Louis: Mosby, 1998.

Vives, Jean. *Ski Randonnée: Backcountry Skiing for the Alpine Skier.* Self-published, 2006.

Volken, Martin, Scott Schell, and Margaret Wheeler. *Backcountry Skiing: Skills for Ski Touring and Ski Mountaineering.* Seattle: The Mountaineers Books, 2007.

Whiting, Nicole. *Knots to Know–20 Fundamental Knots for the Outdoors,* DVD. East Petersburg, PA: Fox Chapel Publishing, 2011.

Williams, Knox, and Betsy Armstrong. *The Snowy Torrents: Avalanche Accidents in the United States 1972–1979.* Jackson, WY: Teton Bookshop Publishing, 1984.

Williamson, Jed. *Accidents in North American Mountaineering 2010.* Golden, CO: American Alpine Club, 2010.

Wood, T. D. "How to Load a Backpack." REI.com, last modified December 2011. www.rei.com/expert advice/articles/loading+backpack.html.

GLOSSARY

acute mountain sickness (AMS). The most common form of high altitude illness; a condition caused by prolonged exposure to high altitude.

adiabatic rate. The speed at which the temperature of rising air falls with altitude.

A-LAST. The five phases of rescue: alert, locate, access, stabilize, and transport.

alpine start. Starting before daybreak.

altimeter. An instrument for determining elevation.

ataxia. Loss of muscle coordination.

AvaLung. A breathing device carried by a winter recreationist that can be used to aid in breathing while dissipating carbon dioxide in the event of potential suffocation in an avalanche.

azimuth. The horizontal direction from one point on Earth to another, measured clockwise in degrees (0–360) from a north or south reference line; also called a bearing.

baffle. In a sleeping bag, the chambers created between the outer shell and the inner lining.

bergschrund. German for "mountain crevice," a bergschrund marks the zone near the top of a glacier where flowing ice separates from the stationary ice or rock above.

bivouac, or bivy, sack. French for "temporary encampment."

brake bar rack. A descending device that directs the rope straight through the device and allows the amount of friction to be adjusted when under tension.

brake tube. A device that allows a variable number of rope wraps for friction.

camber. The upward curvature built into the ski's body; essential in a ski's ability to float in powder.

Cheyne-Stokes respirations. Periodic breathing during sleep.

Chinook. Warm, dry air rushing down the leeward slope of a mountain range.

cold sink. A pit dug into the floor of a snow shelter where cold air settles, leaving the floor level somewhat warmer.

conduction. The transfer of heat by direct contact of one object to another, when the two objects have different temperatures.

convection. The transfer of heat when a different temperature liquid or gas is passed over another material.

couloir. A steep, narrow gully on a mountainside.

critical point test. An examination that determines if any one component of a white board analysis (see below) were to fail, that rescue would catastrophically fail.

cyanosis. Bluish skin coloration due to poor circulation.

cyclonic flow. The counterclockwise pattern air moves around low pressure systems in the Northern Hemisphere; in the Southern Hemisphere this flow is clockwise.

daisy chain. A loop system on some packs to clip on equipment and gear.

dew point. The temperature at which it is cool enough for water to condense out of the air as dew, fog, or frost.

edema. Excess fluid in the body's cavities and tissues.

electrolyte. A chemical compound that separates into charged particles in a solution.

elephant foot bag. A highly compactable, lightweight sleeping bag that comes up to the armpits and can be combined with a jacket to keep an occupant warm in an emergency bivouac.

erythema. Superficial reddening of the skin.

evaporation. The loss of heat when liquids are converted to vapors.

dehydration The loss of body water and electrolytes in excess of the amount needed for normal body function.

golden hour. The first 60 minutes following a serious traumatic event.

graupel. Soft hail.

hang fire. Snow adjacent to an existing fracture line that remains after an avalanche release.

hasty shelter. A temporary shelter made with available materials, such as a tarp, snow, tree limbs, or other types of natural cover.

heat exhaustion. A form of hyperthermia, or elevated body core temperature, characterized by sweating, exhaustion, and dizziness. While not life-threatening, it can lead to heat stroke, a deadly condition.

heat stroke. A life-threatening condition identified by a decreased level of consciousness, a body temperature more than 104 degrees F, and decreased sweating.

high-altitude cerebral edema (HACE). A potentially deadly condition in which the brain swells in individuals at high altitude.

high-altitude illness. The collective term for acute mountain sickness (AMS), high-altitude cerebral edema (HACE), and high-altitude pulmonary edema (HAPE), usually occurring in elevations above 7,000 feet.

high-altitude pulmonary edema (HAPE). A potentially life-threatening condition in which fluid accumulates in the lungs of individuals at high altitude.

hyperthermia. Elevated core body temperature.

hyponatremia. A metabolic condition in which the amount of sodium in fluids outside the cells drops, causing the cells to swell with too much water.

hypothermia. An abnormally low body temperature, below 95 degrees F.

hypoxia. A deficiency of oxygen in the lungs and brain causing increases in circulatory pressure that leads to blood vessel damage, swelling, and edema.

Incident Commander (IC). The lead person in an ICS operation.

Incident Command System (ICS). The standard of emergency management mandated by the Department of Homeland Security to be used domestically when a variety of agencies work together.

inclinometer. A device for measuring the angles of a slope.

lost person behavior. Data collected by the International Search & Rescue Database that indicates the actions of subjects when lost.

magnetic declination. The difference between true north and magnetic north.

magnetic north. The direction a compass points; the direction of the magnetic north pole from the observer's position.

moat. The point where ice meets rock on a glacier along its flanks; heat from the rock may melt the ice at the edge of the glacier, leaving a wide, deep gap.

moraines. Piles of rock fragments pushed together by the snowplow-like effects of flowing ice. Terminal moraines form at the lower end of a glacier; lateral moraines, along the margins; and medial moraines, in the middle.

moulins. French for "mills," these features often take the form of vertical shafts that drain deep into glaciers.

Muenter hitch. A friction hitch used for belaying and rappeling.

National Digital Cartographic Data Base (NDCDB). A collection of digital data maintained by the US Geologic Survey and organized by cartographic units.

New Nordic Norm (NNN). Developed by Rottefella in 1985, this binding system consists of a horizontal rod mounted just underneath the tip of the boot toe and two ridges running parallel down the binding plate.

objective hazards. Hazards independent of backcountry group decisions such as rockfall, avalanches, slick footing, bad weather, etc.

parking tender. A ground person designated to guide a helicopter to and from a helispot.

planimetric map. A map showing horizontal general features such as roads, creeks, trails, and ridge tops; does not show elevations.

primary hypothermia. Hypothermia due to environmental exposure.

probability of area (POA). The likelihood of a subject being in a specific area.

probability of detection (POD). The chances that a lost subject is in the search area and will be found.

probability of success (POS). The result of POA and POD.

Profil (SNS) step-in bindings. A ski binding that connects the toe of the boot to the ski through a three-pin attachment system.

prusik. A sliding knot that locks under pressure.

radiation. The loss of heat when infrared waves emanate from the body outward.

RECCO. System used by rescue organizations to assist in the location of people buried under avalanches.

rock glaciers. Slowly flowing mixtures of rock and ice.

Rutschblock ("Rootch-block") test. A snowpack compression test for assessing avalanche danger by simulating the pressure a winter outdoor recreationist applies, helping to predict whether an area of snow will slide.

Salomon Nordic System (SNS) Profil binding. Similar to the NNN binding system, but the toe rod from which the boot pivots is in front of the toes instead of just beneath them.

scene size-up. The first step of the assessment process, consisting of four components: scene safety, mechanism of injury, total number of patients involved, and the need for additional resources.

secondary hypothermia. Hypothermia caused primarily by injury or illness.

sidecut. The difference between the width of the shovel, the middle, and the tail of a ski.

signaling devices. Flashlights, signal mirrors, strobe lights, and brightly colored tarps used to alert rescuers of backcountry recreationists' location when injured and/or lost.

snow immersion suffocation (SIS) hazard. A result of an individual falling, usually headfirst, into a tree well or deep snow, becoming immobilized and suffocating.

snow trench. A simple hasty shelter constructed by digging a trench large enough to lie in and a roof made from snow blocks or a tarp.

span of control. An ICS principle wherein any one individual has a limit of three to seven subordinates total.

spindrift collar. An extendable collar near the top of some packs that helps minimize the chances of snow entering the pack.

splitboard. A snowboard that can be divided down the middle and used like skis for climbing uphill, then reattached into a standard snowboard for descent.

stationary front. A boundary between two different air masses.

sterile cockpit. A mandate that no conversation take place on an aircraft (such as an emergency helicopter) intercom radio during departures and arrivals until a safe altitude is reached.

subjective hazards. Hazards over which a backcountry group has direct control, such as not wearing helmets, starting a trip when a storm is brewing, etc.

three-pin binding. Largely replaced by New Nordic Norm (NNN) and Salomon SNS.

topographic map. A map that uses contour lines to show the shape and elevation of manmade and natural features.

tree well. A void or depression that forms around the base of a tree, which can lead to snow immersion suffocation.

true north. The direction of the North Pole from your current position; magnetic compasses indicate north differently due to the variation between true north and magnetic north.

Universal Transverse Mercator grid system. A common mapping system that establishes zero longitude at the Greenwich Meridian and uses longitude and latitude as a grid to divide Earth into segments.

whistle stop test. A mental assessment that asks rescuers to consider the following: If a whistle were blown at any time during a rescue and all team members were to stop and drop whatever they were doing, would anything catastrophic occur?

white board analysis. The first stage of critical thinking when a rescue is drawn out and evaluated for weaknesses.

whiteout. A weather condition that causes the features of snow-covered landscapes to be undistinguishable due to uniform light diffusion.

ABBREVIATIONS AND ACRONYMS

ABCs. Airway, breathing, circulation

ACLS. Advanced cardiac life support

AED. Automated external defibrillator

AHJ. Agency having jurisdiction

AIARE. American Institute for Avalanche Research and Education

A-LAST. Alert, locate, access, stabilize, transport

AMS. Acute mountain sickness

AT. Alpine touring

ATC. Air traffic controller

cm. Centimeter

COD. Change of direction

CPR. Cardiopulmonary resuscitation

DCD. Descent control device

DIN. "Deutsche Industrie Norm" German industrial standards

DWR. Durable water repellent finish

ELT. Emergency locator transmitter

ERNEST. Equalized, redundant, non-extending, solid, timely

FERN. Fire Emergency Radio Network

ft. Foot

GPS. Global positioning satellite

GRB. Guide's rappel backup

HACE. High-altitude cerebral edema

HAPE. High-altitude pulmonary edema

IAP. Incident Action Plan (in ICS)

IC. Incident Commander

ICS. Incident Command System

in. Inch

ISRID. International Search & Rescue Incident Database

km. Kilometer

kN. Kilo Newton

lbF. Pounds of force

LKP. Last known point

LRH. Load-releasing hitch

LOR. Level of responsiveness

LZ. Landing zone

m. Meter

MA. Mechanical advantage

MCI. Mass casualty incident

mi. Mile

mm. Millimeters

MOI. Mechanism of injury

MRA. Mountain Rescue Association

NDCDB. National Digital Cartographic Data Base

NFPA. National Fire Protection Association

NIMS. National Incident Management System

NLEC. National Law Enforcement Channel

NNN. New Nordic Norm binding system

NOAA. National Oceanographic and Atmospheric Administration

NTN. New Telemark Norm system

OEC. Outdoor Emergency Care

PAUL. Positive Azimuth Uniform Layout

PLB. Personal locater beacon

PLS. Point last seen

PMP. Prusik-minding pulley

POA. Probability of area

POD. Probability of detection

POS. Probability of success

PPE. Personal protective equipment

SAR. Search and rescue

SIS. Snow immersion suffocation

SEND. Satellite emergency notification device

SNS. Salomon Nordic System Profil binding system

SSSF. Static System Safety Factor

SPF. Sun protection factor

TIA. Transient ischemic attack

UPF. Ultraviolet Protection Factor

USGS. United States Geological Survey

UTM. Universal Transverse Mercator grid system

INDEX

ABOUT THE NATIONAL SKI PATROL

The National Ski Patrol is a member-driven professional organization of registered ski patrols striving to be recognized as the premier provider of training and education programs for emergency rescuers serving the outdoor recreation community. To meet that goal, and promote the safe enjoyment of snow sport enthusiasts, NSP supports its members through accredited education and training in leadership, outdoor emergency care, safety programs, and transportation services.

ABOUT THE MOUNTAINEERS

THE MOUNTAINEERS, founded in 1906, is a nonprofit outdoor activity and conservation organization whose mission is "to explore, study, preserve, and enjoy the natural beauty of the outdoors . . . . " Based in Seattle, Washington, it is now one of the largest such organizations in the United States, with seven branches throughout Washington State.

The Mountaineers sponsors both classes and year-round outdoor activities in the Pacific Northwest, which include hiking, mountain climbing, ski-touring, snowshoeing, bicycling, camping, canoeing and kayaking, nature study, sailing, and adventure travel. The Mountaineers' conservation division supports environmental causes through educational activities, sponsoring legislation, and presenting informational programs.

All activities are led by skilled, experienced volunteers, who are dedicated to promoting safe and responsible enjoyment and preservation of the outdoors.

If you would like to participate in these organized outdoor activities or programs, consider a membership in The Mountaineers. For information and an application, write or call The Mountaineers Program Center, 7700 Sand Point Way NE, Seattle, WA 98115-3996; phone (206) 521-6001; visit www.mountaineers .org; or email info @mountaineers.org.

The Mountaineers Books, an active, nonprofit publishing program of The Mountaineers, produces guidebooks, instructional texts, historical works, natural history guides, and works on environmental conservation. All books produced by The Mountaineers Books fulfill the mission of The Mountaineers. Visit www.mountaineersbooks.org to find details about all our titles and the latest author events, as well as videos, web clips, links, and more!

The Mountaineers Books
1001 SW Klickitat Way, Suite 201
Seattle, WA 98134
800-553-4453
mbooks@mountaineersbooks.org